The Heirs of Plato

The Heirs of Plato

A Study of the Old Academy
(347–274 BC)

John Dillon

CLARENDON PRESS · OXFORD

OXFORD
UNIVERSITY PRESS

Great Clarendon Street, Oxford OX2 6DP

Oxford University Press is a department of the University of Oxford.
It furthers the University's objective of excellence in research, scholarship,
and education by publishing worldwide in

Oxford New York

Auckland Bangkok Buenos Aires Cape Town Chennai
Dar es Salaam Delhi Hong Kong Istanbul Karachi Kolkata
Kuala Lumpur Madrid Melbourne Mexico City Mumbai Nairobi
São Paulo Shanghai Taipei Tokyo Toronto

Oxford is a registered trade mark of Oxford University Press
in the UK and in certain other countries

Published in the United States
by Oxford University Press Inc., New York

British Library Cataloguing in Publication Data
Data available

Library of Congress Cataloging in Publication Data
Dillon, John M.
The heirs of Plato : a study of the Old Academy (347–274 B.C.)/
by John Dillon.
p. cm.
Includes bibliographical references (p.) and index.
1. Platonists—History. 2. Philosophy, Ancient. I. Title
B517.D536 2003   184—dc21   2002035577

ISBN 0-19-823766-9

3 5 7 9 10 8 6 4 2

Typeset in Calisto MT by
Cambrian Typesetters, Frimley, Surrey
Printed in Great Britain
on acid-free paper by
Biddles Ltd., King's Lynn, Norfolk

Preface

When Plato died, full of years, in 347 BC, he left behind him, not only a body of philosophical writings the like of which had never been seen before (or indeed, in respect of their peculiar quality, since), but also a remarkable organization, the 'Academy' (though just how much of an organized institution it was is something that will have to be discussed in our first chapter), and a devoted, though independent-minded, body of disciples. This book is an attempt to recreate something of the atmosphere of the seventy years or so following on the Master's death, and the intellectual paths taken by his chief disciples. It is a period which, though formative in the history of Platonism, has suffered from a remarkable degree of neglect down the centuries.

This, though regrettable, is not entirely surprising. Many a prudent scholar would say, with much justification, that, desirable as it would be to unravel the obscurities of what has been known conventionally, since at least the later Hellenistic era, as the Old Academy, the evidence is just not there. The more controversial claim would also be made in many quarters that, even if it were, these figures, Speusippus, Xenocrates, Polemo, and their associates, are not of a distinction that merits much attention. The real philosophical action in this period was taking place across town, in the Lyceum of Aristotle, Theophrastus, and their associates.

Both these claims I am concerned to controvert. It will be the thesis of this book that, between them, Speusippus and Xenocrates set the agenda for what was to become, over the succeeding centuries, the intellectual tradition which we call Platonism (Xenocrates initiating the mainstream of 'Middle Platonism', Speusippus, with some of his more daring speculations, stimulating certain developments in 'Neopythagoreanism', which proved fruitful for the 'Neoplatonism' of Plotinus and his successors[1]), while even that practical man Polemo would seem to have anticipated the Stoics in a number of their chief doctrines. Other, more minor figures, such as Heraclides of Pontus, Philippus of Opus, and Crantor, made significant contributions as well to the rich tapestry of later Greek thought.

The plan of this book is designed to combine continuity of doctrinal exposition with a biographical approach. There is certainly a complex of themes characteristic of the Old Academy as a whole, but it is also undeniable that the three chief successors of Plato had each very distinctive approaches to many of those themes, and this creative diversity would be obscured by an exclusively thematic treatment. I propose, then, to begin with a chapter discussing the structure of the Academy, as regards both its physical establishment and its methods of operation, a conspectus of the personalities involved, and a survey of the chief themes characteristic of the Platonism of the period. This will be followed by three chapters, devoted respectively to each of the three heads, Speusippus, Xenocrates, and Polemo, focusing on both the continuities and the distinctive features exhibited in their doctrinal positions; and that in turn will be followed by a chapter devoted to the minor figures connected with the Academy. The book will conclude with a short epilogue, examining the relations of the Academy with both Peripatos and Stoa, and the reasons for the move to scepticism associated with Arcesilaus.

What I hope will be revealed is a series of innovations in, and consolidations of, Plato's teaching which, taken together, form the foundation of all later Platonism, and to some extent of Stoicism as well. What will also become apparent is how much of Aristotelianism becomes absorbed (or absorbed back?) into the bloodstream of Platonism during this period, leaving the successors of Aristotle, to all appearances, somewhat at a loss, leading to some centuries of comparative obscurity for the Peripatos. The Athens of the early

---

[1] The quotation marks employed here, which will not be repeated, serve to indicate that none of these terms were such as would have been adopted by the thinkers concerned, who would have seen themselves simply as either *Platonikoi* or *Pythagoreioi*.

Hellenistic era was, after all, a relatively small town by modern standards, in which everybody knew everybody else, and where little in the way of intellectual innovation could escape the notice, malevolent or otherwise, of rival thinkers.

As I suggest above, this is perforce a rather speculative book, and no doubt it will be criticized for that. What I have tried to do, at every stage, making the assumption that the various figures with whom I am dealing were not philosophical imbeciles, is to put the most favourable construction on the evidence available to us that that evidence will allow of—miserable and tendentious though it often is—in order to construct something like a coherent philosophical theory for the individuals concerned. I have also tried to relate the doctrines of the various Academics that emerge both to what we can discern of Plato's teaching, both written and oral, and to those of each other—bearing in mind that there was no requirement of, or concern for, strict 'orthodoxy' within the school; simply a tendency to likemindedness on a set of basic principles.

I am most grateful to various colleagues and friends for reading sections of this work, and making constructive comments, Richard Sorabji, David Sedley, Luc Brisson, and John Cleary, though they must not be held responsible for what appears here. More remotely, I am much indebted to the work of Harold Cherniss, both in *The Riddle of the Early Academy,* and in that monument of learning, *Aristotle's Criticism of Plato and the Academy*, i (sadly, a project never completed), and to that of his disciple Leonardo Tarán, both in his magisterial collection of the fragments of Speusippus (*Speusippus of Athens*) and in his excellent monograph on Philippus of Opus, including an edition of the *Epinomis.* I say this despite venturing to disagree with both of them in my approach to the evidence. Their great virtue is to present so comprehensively the evidence on which such disagreement may be based. I am much indebted, too, to the manifold works of Margherita Isnardi Parente, who has for so long been a major authority in the field, and whose collection of the fragments of Xenocrates—and Hermodorus!—(*Senocrate–Ermodoro: frammenti*) is the definitive one, while her edition of the fragments of Speusippus remains most useful. I have also benefited greatly from

Preface

the work of Hans-Joachim Krämer (*Arete bei Platon und Aristoteles; Der Ursprung der Geistmetaphysik; Platonismus und Hellenistische Philosophie*), though without going along with the full range of his speculations on Plato's own 'unwritten doctrines'—preferable though I find them to the scepticism of Cherniss. Mainly, I do not feel it necessary to postulate, as do the scholars of the 'Tübingen School', a fixed esoteric set of doctrines which Plato will have held from the time when he began to compose the dialogues. I would envisage something much more fluid and developmental—though without wishing to deny that Plato always has much more in his head than he is putting down on papyrus.

In conclusion, I wish to express my gratitude to Trinity College, Dublin, and to my colleagues in the School of Classics, for providing a most congenial atmosphere in which to work, and to the Oxford University Press, and to Peter Momtchiloff in particular, for encouraging me in this enterprise, and for their patience in seeing it through. Lastly, I am much indebted to the friendly and constructive criticisms of the two anonymous readers for the Press.

Table of Contents

Contents

The Riddle of the Academy   1

For the title of this first chapter, I make a bow in the direction of the
influential work of Harold Cherniss, *The Riddle of the Early
Academy*[1], with which, however, while recognizing its many important contributions, I find myself in radical disagreement. As I have
suggested in the Preface, any approach to Plato which absolutely
declines to go beyond the evidence of the dialogues—or rather, what
is deemed to be the evidence they provide—and which therefore
treats Aristotle, in his various reports of or allusions to Plato's doctrines, as simply misinterpreting such evidence, seems effectively to
preclude our penetrating very far into the true dynamics of the
Academy as an institution, and into the relation of the doctrines of
Plato's disciples and successors to what they conceived to be his
teachings. On the basis of such premisses, a book such as this could
not be written at all.

There is, however, a riddle, or rather a number of riddles, involved
in the nature and structure of the Academy which Plato founded and
bequeathed to his successors, as well as in the nature of the basic doctrines that he arrived at before his death, and that is what I wish to
explore in this introductory chapter.

---

[1] (1945; repr. 1962), and, in French trans., with an introduction by Luc Brisson, as
L'Énigme de l'ancienne Académie (Paris, 1993).

The Physical Structure of the Academy

There is, first of all, the question of the nature of the physical plant. The tradition of 'academies', both private and public, is so deeply ingrained in European (and now world) culture that it is not easy for us, when considering the Platonic Academy, to divest ourselves of all the connotations which have grown up round the name. But that is precisely what we must do, if we are to arrive at a reasonably accurate understanding of the nature of Plato's school.[2]

What, after all, was the Academy? On this question, there is much opportunity for confusion. The Academy was, properly speaking— to quote the formulation of Diogenes Laertius[3]—'a *gymnasion* [or place of exercise], outside the walls [of Athens], in a grove, named after a certain hero, Hekademos': that is to say, a public park, accessible to all who wished to walk, or exercise, or converse in it. In this grove, or *gymnasion,* it had been the practice for sophists and philosophers[4] to meet with their disciples for a generation or so before Plato thought of establishing himself there at some time in the early 380s, after his return from his first visit to Italy and Sicily. What Plato himself seems to have done was to purchase a property, possibly with the financial help of his Syracusan friend Dion,[5] where he lived, and where his disciples were no doubt welcome to visit and dine, while the main philosophical business of the school was conducted within the Academy grove, which was a public park. Within this grove, we are told that a shrine of the Muses, or *mouseion,* was at some stage

---

[2] On this see Dillon (1983), of which what follows is largely an expansion, and Baltes (1993). Also most useful are the discussions of Glucker (1978: 226–46), where he examines the evidence for the physical plant of the Academy, and of Lynch (1972), where he discusses, among other things, the problem of the legal status of the institution.

[3] *Lives of the Philosophers* III 7.

[4] Including, for instance, Cratylus, the 'neo-Heraclitean', to whom Plato attached himself for a while, DL II 5–6.

[5] The circumstances of this transaction, if it is historical, are exceedingly murky, involving as they do the extraordinary story (preserved by DL III 19–21) of Plato's being sold as slave on Aegina and then being ransomed, either by 'his friends' in general, or by Dion in particular, or both, from one Anniceris of Cyrene, who then gallantly sent back the money. It was this sum, we are asked to believe, to the amount of thirty minae, with which the property which became the base for Plato's school was bought.

erected by Plato (to which later, we are also told, his nephew Speusippus, presumably on his accession to the headship of the school, added statues of the Graces[6]), and this may have in some way marked out the area in which the school habitually met,[7] but it is hard to see what other territorial rights could be established.

How the business of the school was divided between the public park and the private estate is less than clear. There is considerable evidence, at least, that much of the philosophical disputation went on in the park, either in the open air or in some corner of the gymnasium building. For one thing, we have the famous passage from a play of the Middle Comedy playwright Epicrates (Fr. 11 Kock), portraying Plato and Speusippus and Menedemus taking 'a troop of lads' through the diaeretic analysis of a pumpkin. Quite apart from any light this delightful satire may throw on the interests of Speusippus in particular, the chief message we may derive from it is that the proceedings of the school were conducted in the public domain, where, in principle at least, they might be observed by passers-by.

Another anecdote, of which I see no reason to disbelieve at least the essential accuracy,[8] is one told by Aelian,[9] which casts some light on the relationship between the public park and Plato's private estate. This story relates to a time not long before 347 BC, the date of Plato's death:

---

[6] DL IV 1. There is actually some confusion about this shrine, as later, in his life of Polemo (IV 19), Diogenes speaks of a shrine to the Muses as being situated 'in the garden' (*en tōi kēpōi*), which should refer to Plato's own property. There may possibly have been two shrines, or Diogenes may be speaking loosely in the first passage.

[7] It did not, as John Lynch has convincingly argued (*Aristotle's School*, chs. 2 and 3), signify that Plato had incorporated his school as a *thiasos*. Might it, however, have been something more than a mere ornament? Pierre Boyancé [1937], 261–2, has made a persuasive connection with Plato's identification of philosophy at *Phd.* 61A as the 'greatest of the arts' (*megistē mousikē*). This would then constitute something of a programmatic statement of Plato's view of the dominant role of philosophy.

[8] Strangely, Tarán (1981: 221), wishes to dismiss it as spurious, as being 'unworthy of the little we know about Plato and Aristotle'. On the contrary, it seems to me to fit that little extremely well.

[9] *Varia Historia* 3. 19—probably gleaned from some such Hellenistic relayer of philosophical gossip as Antigonus of Carystus.

Once, when Xenocrates went off on a visit to his homeland [i.e. Chalcedon], Aristotle set upon Plato, surrounding himself with a gang of his own partisans, including Mnason of Phocis and people like that. Speusippus at that time was ill,[10] and for this reason was unable to stand by Plato. Plato was by now eighty years of age and at the same time, because of his age, was to some extent losing his memory. So Aristotle devised a plot and set an ambush for him, and began to put questions to him very aggressively and in a way 'elenctically', and was plainly behaving unjustly and unfeelingly. For this reason, Plato left the concourse outside (*tou exō peripatou*), and walked about inside with his companions (*endon ebadize sun tois hetairois*).

After an interval of three months, Xenocrates arrived back from abroad and, checking in to the School, found Aristotle perambulating where he expected to find Plato. When he observed that Aristotle with his cronies did not go back to Plato's house (*ou pros Platōna anachōrounta*) at the end of the day, but seemed to be heading off to his own place in the city, he asked one of those who had been participating in the *peripatos* where Plato was, for he suspected that he was not well. The other replied, 'He is not ill, but Aristotle has been giving him a bad time, and has forced him to retire from the *peripatos,* so he has retired and is philosophizing in his own garden (*en tōi kēpōi tōi heautou*).'

The rest of the story concerns us less. Xenocrates scolds Speusippus, gathers the loyal forces, and reinstates Plato in his usual haunts (*apodounai to sunēthes khōrion tōi Platōni*). This story is no doubt biased, gossipy, and tendentious, but it is unreasonable, I think, to dismiss it on that account as having no foundation in fact. In any case, in respect of what is of concern to us at present, it seems to me to present a valuable picture of the relationship between the public *peripatos* and Plato's private estate, in each of which philosophizing could take place.

We may note first that the only two pieces of real estate concerned in the story are the *peripatos* and Plato's own *kēpos.* I have refrained from translating *peripatos,* as I am wary of giving it the wrong connotation. It could be a formal 'walk', even with colonnades (such as seems to have been the case later, at least, in respect of the

---

[10] Perhaps with an attack of the arthritis which is said to have afflicted him in his later years. See Ch. 2, p. 32 below.

Aristotelian *peripatos* in the Lyceum park), or it could be just that part of the Academy where the group walked and deliberated. Either way, that is plainly where Plato's normal activity is centred. When discomfited there, he leaves the Academy altogether, and returns to his *kēpos*. Then, in the story, Xenocrates comes first to the *peripatos*, not to Plato's house, and Aristotle, at the end of the day, is heading back into town to go home, instead of calling in on Plato on the way and perhaps staying for dinner. Xenocrates is surprised, not that he should be going home, but that he should do so without first calling in at the *kēpos*. So Aristotle, though a foreigner and a long-time pupil of Plato, does not live with him, but keeps, at this stage at least, an establishment of his own. It is not quite clear in this story where Xenocrates (who is also, of course, a non-citizen) lives, but later, as we shall see, he is presented in anecdote as having his own little establishment. All in all, then, this anecdote seems to reveal, artlessly and incidentally, the true state of affairs prevailing in Plato's 'Academy', and, properly evaluated, should serve to dissipate much windy speculation as to its physical aspect.

What, then, are we to imagine Plato's *kēpos* to have consisted of? Is it to be thought of as what later ages spoke of as Plato's Academy? This is a question I find to be systematically ignored by the authorities who describe to us the workings of the Academy. A *kēpos* is not necessarily just a garden. Epicurus' *kēpos*, after all, included a suburban villa of considerable dimensions as well as a garden, enough to hold a community. We could, therefore, imagine living-quarters for Plato himself and at least a few companions, with room, also, for an ever-growing library; but we cannot be sure that there was even as much as that.

I am not concerned at the moment with the system of study and other activities pursued in the Academy (we will turn to that presently), but simply with the nature of the physical plant. I want, however, to give an example—a reasonably sober and well-informed one, indeed—of the sort of systematic ambiguity that tends to surround the topic of both the physical plant and what went on in it. Here is W. K. C. Guthrie:[11]

---

[11] In Guthrie (1975: 19–20).

The Academy of Plato does not correspond entirely to any modern institution, certainly not to a university of modern foundation. The nearest parallels are probably our ancient universities, or rather their colleges, with the characteristics that they have inherited from the mediaeval world, particularly their religious connexions and the ideal of the common life, especially a common table . . . The institution takes its name from its site, nearly a mile outside the walls of Athens, supposedly sacred to a hero Academus or Hecademus, and including a grove of trees, gardens, a gymnasium and other buildings. The sanctity of the place was great, and other cults, including that of Athena herself, were carried on there.

Already, I think, we are getting into trouble. Guthrie knows perfectly well the story of the purchase of the garden, but in speaking of the 'site', he carries on here as if the garden and the Academy were the same thing. He goes on:

To form a society owning its own land and premises, as Plato did, it appears to have been a legal requirement that it be registered as a *thiasos,* that is, a cult-association dedicated to the service of some divinity, who would be the nominal owner of the property. Plato's choice was the Muses, patrons of education, not so much, perhaps, because he believed that 'philosophy was the highest "music" ' (*Phaedo* 61A), as because a Mouseion or chapel of the Muses was a regular feature of the schools of his day.

He goes on to mention the attested common meals or *syssitia,* renowned for their moderation and philosophic quality. Things now, however, seem to become thoroughly mixed up. John Lynch has effectively disposed of what was simply Wilamowitz's assumption that the Academy must have been a *thiasos* dedicated to the Muses.[12] The evidence does not support this at all. What we know is that Plato, as mentioned earlier, dedicated a shrine to the Muses in the Academy grove, and that his successor Speusippus added to it statues of the Graces.[13] This shrine may indeed have provided a focal point for the group's perambulations in the Academy, but the fact of its existence does not require the postulation of a *thiasos;* it need not

---

[12] Lynch (1972: 108–27). Wilamowitz derived this idea from Foucart (1873), and propounded it in his *Antigonos von Karystos* (1881: 263–91). Nowhere in the ancient sources is either the Academy or the Peripatos referred to as a *thiasos,* but always as a *skholē* or *diatribē.*

[13] Cf. n. 5 above.

be interpreted as any more than the staking of a claim, in so far as that is possible on public ground. As for the *syssitia*, they would have been held in the *kēpos* or in some other suburban villa nearby, as no doubt was a good deal of the activity of the group.

It is plain, however, that a certain proportion of the day was spent in the park, either in an alcove in the gymnasium, or walking about among the trees (the *peripatos*), in full view of the public. We have contemporary evidence from comic poets, Epicrates and Alexis, for example, to attest this. The fragment of Epicrates (Fr. 10 Kassel–Austin) is perhaps worth quoting in full, as affording a unique glimpse, albeit through comic spectacles, of how the activities of the school might have appeared to a member of the general public. Two characters are conversing:

A: What are Plato and Speusippus and Menedemus up to? On what subjects are they discoursing (*diatribousin*) today? What weighty idea, what line of argument (*logos*) is currently being investigated by them? Tell me this accurately, in Earth's name, if you've come with any knowledge of it.

B: Why yes, I can tell you about these fellows with certainty. For at the Panathenaea I saw a troop of lads in the exercise-grounds of the Academy (*en gymnasiois Akadēmias*), and heard utterances indescribable, astonishing! For they were propounding definitions about nature (*peri physeōs aphorizomenoi*), and separating into categories the ways of life of animals, the nature of trees, and the classes of vegetables. And in this connection they were investigating to what genus one should assign the pumpkin.

A: And what definition (*horos*) did they arrive at, and of what genus is the plant?'

B: Well now, first of all they all took up their places, and with heads bowed they reflected a long time. Then suddenly, while they were still bent low in study, one of the lads said it was a round vegetable, another that it was a grass, another that it was a tree. When a doctor from Sicily heard this, he dismissed them contemptuously, as talking rubbish.

B: No doubt they got very angry at that, and protested against such insults? For it is unseemly to behave thus in such public gatherings (*en leskhais taisde*).

A: No, in fact the lads didn't seem to mind at all. And Plato, who was present, very mildly, and without irritation, told them to try again to define the genus to which the pumpkin belongs. And they started once again to attempt a division (*diairesis*).

Comedy this may be, but it can also be seen as a valuable glimpse of real life by an eye-witness. Epicrates testifies to the conduct of the school's business in public, in the park (the phrases *en gymnasiois Akadēmeias, en leskhais taisde* make this plain enough); he is also acquainted with the technical terminology (*aphorizein, genos, diairein*). What he portrays the students as doing is trying to fix on a starting-point for a 'division', or *diairesis*, which would lead to a properly scientific definition, identifying all the differentiae of the particular species within a given genus to which the pumpkin belongs—and thus the suggestions 'grass', 'tree', while comical enough, are not entirely crazy, despite the strictures of the Sicilian doctor. In short, it is not unreasonable to credit Epicrates with knowing something of what he is portraying, and expecting his audience to have similar knowledge.

We have, then, two separate entities, both important to the life of the school, the *kēpos* and the public park, with its gymnasium and walks. The problem that now arises is, what ultimately happened to this *kēpos,* and what entity is it that in later times came to be known as 'Plato's Academy'?

If this 'garden' was in effect presented to Plato by Dion or Anniceris, then, one would think, it should appear in some form in Plato's will, of which Diogenes Laertius preserves what seems to be the complete text (III 41–2). There are two estates mentioned in this will, the estate at Iphistiadae and the estate at Eiresidae, and neither of them sounds unequivocally like the 'garden near Colonus', though the latter is at least a possible candidate. They are both given a careful legal description, and neither of them is described as bordering either upon the Academy or upon Colonus. Nor is there any mention, as there is in the wills of the scholarchs of the Lyceum later, of any school property or books. The estate at Iphistiadae is left to Adeimantus, who is either a nephew or a grand-nephew—perhaps a son of Plato's half-brother Glaucon, or a grandson of his half-brother

Adeimantus—with the provision that it should not be sold or alienated. Presumably this is the, or an, ancestral family property, which would explain its inalienability, and its inheritance by a member of the family (which Speusippus, strictly speaking, is not).

What is to happen to the other estate is not said, but this one at least is bounded on the west by the river Cephisus, which puts it in the approximate vicinity of Colonus and the Academy. Plato declares that he bought this estate from a certain Callimachus. If this is the property bought for him by either Anniceris or Dion, he makes no acknowledgement of this, but then it was hardly incumbent on him to do so in the context of a will.[14] On the whole, despite the curious lack of any mention of the existence of the school, this seems the best candidate for the 'garden near Colonus'.[15] If the school were not strictly a legal entity, as John Lynch has cogently argued,[16] then there would be no call to mention it in a legal document.

The property is described in various ancient sources, with a diminutive, as a 'little garden',[17] but this description must be seen, I think, as reflecting the more spacious perspective of the Roman imperial period. The evidence indicates that it must have comprised a couple of acres at least, since, in Polemo's day, according to Diogenes Laertius (IV 19), the students of the Academy were able to live in huts or cabins (*kalybia*) of their own construction 'near the shrine of the Muses and the lecture-hall (*exedra*)'. In my earlier treatment of this question,[18] I assumed that Diogenes meant that the pupils established themselves in the Academy grove, and I wondered

---

[14] It is an interesting circumstance that this property is described as being bounded on both the north and the east by that of Eurymedon of Myrrhinus, who is presumably (since the Eurymedon who was Plato's brother-in-law, husband of his sister Potone, and father of his nephew Speusippus, must himself have been long dead by 347 BC) a younger brother—or possibly cousin—of Speusippus, and who is mentioned, along with Speusippus, as an executor of the will.

[15] This was not my view when I composed the article mentioned in n. 2 above (Dillon 1983), but reconsideration has persuaded me that my reservations there were not cogent, and that John Glucker is nearer the truth (1978: 231–3).

[16] Lynch (1972: 106 ff).

[17] *Kēpidion*, DL III 20; *khōridion*, Plutarch, *De Exilio* 10; *illi hortuli*, Cicero, *De Finibus* V 2.

[18] Dillon (1983: 57–8).

how that was possible within the grounds of a public park, but in fact Diogenes says, not 'in the Academy', but 'in the *garden*', so that I now think we must assume, not only room for a group of simple cabins as well as the main building, but space for a *mouseion* and *exedra* as well.

As regards the dimensions of the main building, there is really not much to go on. Extrapolating from the circumstances of an anecdote about Xenocrates, some authorities[19] wish to maintain that Plato's house comprised just one room, which served as living and dining quarters, as well as lecture hall. This is the amusing story[20] of the famous courtesan Phryne, who tried to seduce Xenocrates by pretending to take refuge with him from people who were pursuing her, and, when he let her in, it was into his 'little house' (*oikidion*), and then into his 'little bed' (*klinidion*)—where, however, he resisted her advances. But this *oikidion* of Xenocrates, if it relates to any reality, may refer to a personal cabin which he had in the grounds (the evidence is that, like Polemo, but unlike Speusippus, he *did* live in the Platonic Garden), rather than to the main house, which in his day may only have been used for communal purposes, as a library, science and natural history museum, and for communal dinners and symposia (all or most lecturing or deliberating may have taken place rather in the *exedra* that is mentioned at DL IV 19, or in the public park). At any rate, it does not seem to me credible that the main building should have consisted of a single room.

This, however, is not perhaps a matter of primary importance. What would be of more interest would be to work out the precise nature of the relations between master and pupil, or between associates, in Plato's school, and of the educational and research procedures followed. Of these, however, there is disappointingly little evidence. The famous fragment of Epicrates referred to above (p. 7) may give some indication of what a 'lesson' was like, and the anecdote about Aristotle's harassment of Plato some hint as to the format of disputations, but what form lectures took, who felt qualified to give them, and how sessions of dialectic were arranged, are questions that

---

[19] e.g. Baltes (1993: 7–8).
[20] Relayed by DL IV 7. See also Ch. 3, p. 90 below.

remain quite obscure. In particular, there is unfortunately no evidence to back up suggestions that the course of preliminary studies adumbrated in *Republic* VII, comprising arithmetic, geometry, stereometry, astronomy, and harmonics, was ever pursued in the Academy in any organized way, though we do have anecdotes of Plato setting problems to his mathematical companions, Eudoxus, Menaechmus, and others, such as that of the Delians about the doubling of the cube,[21] and an interest in mathematics, or at least arithmology, is very much a feature of the philosophy of his immediate successors, as we shall see. Certainly, a good deal of mathematical and astronomical research seems to have gone on in and around the Academy, but as to how it fitted into the regular programme we have no clues.

As regards the practice of dialectic, a certain amount may perhaps be learned from a study of Aristotle's *Topics*. It is generally agreed that this is a relatively early work, and reflects the procedures of at least the later Academy under Plato. Aristotle, in the eight books of the *Topics*, and in the appendix to the work entitled *Sophistical Refutations*, takes us through all the rules of procedure, not to mention the underhand tricks, relative to what must have been the primary activity of his comrades and himself. Though he claims in the epilogue to the whole work, at the end of the *Sophistikoi Elenchoi* (*Sophistical Refutations*) (183^{b}34 ff.), to have invented the whole *tekhnē* from scratch, we may nevertheless reasonably assume, I think, that he has taken much of his raw material from his experiences in the Academy.

To take one example, Books 6 and 7 of the work are devoted to the question of definitions (*horoi*), a basic aim of the dialectical process. Here is how Aristotle introduces the topic at the beginning of Book 6 (139^{a}24 ff.):

Of the treatment of definitions there are five parts. You must show either (1) that it is absolutely not correct to use the description (*logos*) also about the subject to which the name is given (for the definition of 'man' must be true of every man); or (2) that, though the subject belongs to a genus, your opponent

---

[21] Cf. Riginos (1976: 141–5).

has not put it into the relevant genus, or has not put it into its proper (*oikeion*) genus . . .; (3) or that the description is not peculiar (*idios*) to the subject . . .; or (4) that, although he has satisfied all the above requirements, he has not given a definition, that is, he has not stated the essence (*to ti ēn einai*) of the subject which he is defining. Apart from the above conditions, (5) it still remains to see whether, although he has given a definition, he has failed to give a correct definition.   (trans. E. S. Forster. *Loeb,* slightly altered)

Aristotle then goes on warn against common errors in giving definitions (139^b12 ff.). One is obscurity, the other is redundancy. I select two examples of redundancy, since they involve pot-shots at Xenocrates, such as Aristotle may actually have fired at him in person, before their ways parted. The first involves Xenocrates' definition of the soul (140^a33 ff.):[22]

Or, again, you must see whether, though the addition is proper (*idios*) to the subject, yet, on its removal, the account is left still proper (to the subject) and demonstrative of the essence. For example, in the description of 'man', the addition of 'receptive of knowledge' is superfluous; for, if it is removed, the rest of the description is still proper and demonstrates the essence. In a word, anything is superfluous the removal of which leaves a clear statement of the subject of the definition. The definition of the soul, if stated as a 'number moving itself', is a case in point; for the soul is 'that which moves itself', according to Plato's definition.[23]

The other example is directed at Xenocrates' definition of *phronēsis,* or 'wisdom'[24] (141^a5 ff.):

The absurdity here consists not in uttering the same word twice, but in predicating the same thing more than once of anything; for example, when Xenocrates says that *phronēsis* is 'definitive and contemplative of true being (*ta onta*)'; for what is 'definitive' (*horistikē*) is in a way 'contemplative'

---

[22] Cf. below, Ch. 3, pp. 121–3.

[23] That is, at *Phdr.* 245E. The point of the objection is that the definition comes out as 'that which moves itself is a number moving itself', which is redundant. Xenocrates would be confined to defining the soul as simply 'number', which, as we shall see, he does not want to do.

[24] Xenocrates, as we shall see (below, pp. 150–1), although distinguishing between *sophia* and *phronēsis,* makes a division between practical and theoretical *phronēsis,* such as Aristotle would not approve of.

(*theorētikē*), so that when he adds 'and contemplative' he is saying the same thing twice.

Such examples can only give a taste of the sort of dialectical battles that may have occupied the days of Plato's pupils, and of his successors. Aristotle was certainly a master of the art, but he cannot have been completely out on his own. Dialectic is a game which it takes at least two to play, and played it undoubtedly was, with vigour. It is profoundly regrettable that no proper example of a dialectical joust survives to us, but from the *Topics* we can derive some idea of the rules of engagement.

To conclude our study of the physical circumstances of the school, it may be convenient to give as complete a list as we can muster of the known members at the time of Plato's death. What we will observe, I think, is the relatively small size of the establishment, compared to any modern centre of learning. Of course, we may assume a few more members and hangers-on than we have any record of, but it is reasonable to assume that we have to do here with a total of not much more than a couple of dozen members at the outside. The most comprehensive list is given by Diogenes Laertius in his *Life of Plato* (III 46). I give it here, omitting those known to be dead by 347 BC:

His disciples were the following: Speusippus of Athens, Xenocrates of Chalcedon, Aristotle of Stagira, Philippus of Opus, Hestiaeus of Perinthus, Amyclus of Heraclea, Erastus and Coriscus of Scepsis, Timolaus of Cyzicus, Euaeon of Lampsacus, Python and Heraclides of Aenus, Demetrius of Amphipolis, Heraclides of Pontus, and many others, among them two women, Lastheneia of Mantinea and Axiothea of Phlius, who is reported by Dicaearchus to have worn male clothing.

This list, with its tantalizing suggestion of 'many others', and including the two enterprising ladies, amounts only to sixteen, but we can add a few more. The list given in Philodemus' *History of the Academy* (VI) adds a name or two:[25] Menedemus of

---

[25] The 'Heraclides and Amyntas of Heracleia' listed here may in fact refer simply to Heraclides of Pontus and the Amyclus listed by Diogenes.

Pyrrha,[26] Chaeron of Pellene, Hermodorus of Syracuse, Calligenes,[27] Chion. We are also informed that Menedemus of Eretria was a member of the Academy for a period (DL II 125), but this may well be based on a confusion with the other Menedemus, since he is stated to have been captivated by Plato himself, which is quite impossible chronologically (he was born c.345).

On Speusippus, Xenocrates, Philippus, Hestiaeus, Hermodorus, and Heraclides we shall have something to say in subsequent chapters. Of the others, we can only note the interesting fact that a number of them seem to have gone back to their home states and involved themselves in politics. Python and Heraclides of Aenus (an old-established Aeolic colony on the south coast of Thrace) are celebrated as having assassinated King Cotys of Thrace in 359,[28] and as a result gained Athenian citizenship, and crowns of gold (King Cotys being then at odds with Athens); but it is not clear whether they joined the Academy before or after this achievement. Chaeron, after studying with Plato and Xenocrates (and presumably with Speusippus also), and (presumably before this) having achieved high distinction as an Olympic wrestler, returned to his native Pellene (in Achaea) and, with the support of Alexander of Macedon, established a tyranny, probably in 335.[29] However, it does not sound as if he set up anything like a Platonic ideal constitution; he is reported to have driven out many of the citizens, and handed over their possessions and wives to their slaves!

Others, though, it seems, had more benign relationships with their native states. Plutarch, in his *Reply to Colotes* (1126c), contrasting Plato with Epicurus, tells us that 'Plato sent one disciple,

---

[26] This man must be distinct from the more famous Menedemus of Eretria. He stayed around long enough to compete (unsuccessfully) with Xenocrates for the headship of the school in 339 (*Acad. Hist.* VII).

[27] At this point there seems to be some confusion, as there is listed after this an 'Athenian Timolas' (who looks very like a doublet of Timolaus of Cyzicus, listed just previously), and Calligenes and this Timolas are said to figure in the *Funeral Feast of Plato,* a literary composition of some sort, of unknown authorship.

[28] Demosthenes, *Against Aristocrates* 119; *Acad. Hist.* VI.

[29] Ps.—Demosthenes, *On the Treaty with Alexander,* 10; *Acad. Hist.* XI–XII; Pausanias, *Guide to Greece,* VII 27, 7.

Aristonymus, to the Arcadians to reform their constitution, another, Phormio, to the Eleans, and a third, Menedemus, to the Pyrrhaeans. Eudoxus drew up laws for the Cnidians, Aristotle for the Stagirites.' All this activity, however, except possibly that of Aristotle, antedates Plato's death, and so does not strictly concern us. It does, however, serve to remind us that Plato's Academy had a certain public dimension, and this continued under his successors, as we shall see.

A word may be said, finally, about the process, or processes, of selection of Plato's successors as heads of the Academy. As has been observed earlier, it is less clear than used to be assumed just what sort of organization the Academy was, though it is now fairly generally agreed that it was not any sort of formal legal entity, such as a *thiasos,* that we can identify. Certainly the assumption of the headship by Speusippus in 347 is not presented as a formal procedure. No mention of it is made in Plato's surviving will, as we have seen. In the *History of the Academy* of Philodemus (s. VI) it is just stated that Speusippus 'succeeded to' (*diedexato*) the *diatribē.* There is no record of an election; it may simply have been the result of consensus. On his death in 339, by contrast, Philodemus (s. VII) tells of a formal vote by the 'young men' (*neaniskoi*) which elected Xenocrates by a short head, over Heraclides of Pontus and Menedemus of Eretria (who both left in dudgeon, Heraclides to return to his native Heraclea and Menedemus to found his own school in Eretria)— Aristotle, it is noted, was absent in Macedonia, and so not a candidate.

In the case of Polemon, it is once again merely stated that he 'succeeded' Xenocrates (s. IV, and DL IV 16); there is no hint in the sources of an election, though there may have been one. Polemon presided over the school for almost forty years, and when he finally passed on, probably in 276, he is merely stated to have been 'succeeded' by his favourite pupil, Crates—an appointment which he might reasonably be supposed to have had a good deal to do with. Crates, however, only survived for a couple of years, and on his death slightly murky goings-on are reported (DL IV 32). A certain Socratides, a complete nonentity, was elected by the members (*Hist.*

15

Acad. XVIII: once again, the term 'young men', *neaniskoi,* is used) simply on the grounds that he was the oldest, but he stepped down in favour of Arcesilaus. Was this decision then ratified by the *neaniskoi?* We have no idea, but it seems probable.

On the whole, then, we have some indication that in the Academy (contrary to the procedure across town in the Lyceum, where, from Aristotle on, the succession seems to have been formally bequeathed by the previous incumbent), a certain degree of democracy prevailed, whether by formal voting or simply by consensus, in deciding the headship. Later in the Academy's history (in around 216 BC), admittedly, Lacydes, the successor of Arcesilaus, simply 'handed over' (*paredōke*) the school to a pair of successors, Telecles and Evander (DL IV 60), but we need not extrapolate such a procedure back into our period.

Plato's Intellectual Legacy

We now may now turn to consider the content of Plato's spiritual and intellectual legacy. This book is predicated on the assumption that, despite Plato's strong views on many subjects, it was not his purpose to leave to his successors a fixed body of doctrine which they were to defend against all comers. What he hoped that he had taught them was a method of enquiry, inherited by himself from his master Socrates, which, if correctly practised, would lead them to the truth; but, if so, it was a truth which everyone would have to arrive at for himself.

Not, of course, that there was no body of doctrine at all. The problem is, however, that, if one is seeking to do justice to the various ways in which Plato's immediate successors developed his doctrines, one must resolve to look beyond the dialogues. The spiritual heirs of Plato had, not unnaturally, a far more accurate perspective—since at least the older generation of them had witnessed the 'publication' of many of them—on the relation of the dialogues to the serious ongoing work of the school than do we. Because the oral tradition that sustained the Old Academy broke down during the centuries of scepticism that followed the accession of Arcesilaus to the headship in the mid-270s, we are left only with these written remains, which, literary masterpieces though many of them are, were for Plato only 'entertainments'[30]—by no means devoid of substance, but certainly not straightforward presentations of his most serious speculations.

But if not the dialogues, then what?[31] There is in fact considerable secondary evidence as to the views entertained by Plato on certain basic questions. A good deal of this is preserved only in late authorities, such as the commentators on Aristotle, but the greatest single source is Aristotle himself, and Aristotle had been an associate of Plato's for fully twenty years. We must always remember with Aristotle, however, that, although he doubtless knew what he was talking about in each instance (to assume otherwise, as Harold Cherniss and his followers are driven to do, is quite absurd), yet he is nearly always giving a polemical and, furthermore, an allusive, rather than a scholarly and systematic, account of what he knows. It is rather like trying to piece together Conservative Party policy during an election campaign solely on the basis of scattered criticisms from Labour spokesmen. Nevertheless, by looking at Aristotle's evidence with a properly critical eye, one can deduce a body of doctrine which is, in its main lines at least, coherent and reasonable, and fits in well, as we shall see, with the developments attributed (often by the same source) to Speusippus and Xenocrates.

To begin with first principles, it seems clear that Plato, at least in his later years, had become more and more attracted by the philosophical possibilities of Pythagoreanism, that is to say, the postulation of a mathematical model for the universe. Mathematics seems to have been a discipline much worked on in the Academy,[32] and the insights

---

[30] This may seem an extreme characterization of them, but it is meant in the distinctively Platonic sense of *spoudaia paidia*, 'serious play-acting'. For the sense in which I use the term, the reader is referred to the interesting lines put into the mouth of Timaeus by Plato at *Tim.* 59C–D.

[31] I here repeat much of what I wrote in Dillon (1977: 2–11), since that still very much expresses my views on this subject.

[32] See the useful discussions of Mugler (1948), and, more recently, Fowler (1987).

derived from this (amplified by the researches of such colleagues as Eudoxus, Menaechmus, and Theaetetus) drove Plato progressively to certain general conclusions. He arrived at a system which involved a pair of opposed first principles, and a triple division of levels of being, which latter doctrine gave a vital central and mediating role to Soul, both World-Soul and individual souls. Reflections of these basic doctrines can be glimpsed in such dialogues of the middle and later periods as the *Republic, Timaeus, Philebus*, and *Laws,* but they could not be deduced from the dialogues alone.

As first principles Plato postulated the One and the Indefinite Dyad (given by him, it would seem, the distinctive title of 'the Great-and-Small')[33]—in this, as in many other respects, developing the doctrine of the Pythagoreans. The One is an active principle,[34] imposing 'limit' (*peras*) on the indefiniteness (*apeiria*) of the opposite principle. The Dyad is regarded as a kind of duality, as being infinitely extensible or divisible, being simultaneously indefinitely large or small. The influence of the Dyad is to be observed all through the physical world in the phenomena of continuous magnitudes, excess and defect in which has continually to be checked by the imposition of correct measure. This process has an ethical aspect as well, since the virtues are to be seen as correct measures ('means') between extremes of excess and deficiency on a continuum. That such a theory of virtue was not distinctive to Aristotle is shown by such a passage as *Politicus* 284D–285B, where the all-pervasiveness of measure is asserted, with a probable reference to the Pythagoreans as originators of this concept.[35]

---

[33] Aristotle, *Met.* A 6, 987^{a}29 ff. Aristotle here (987^{b}20) speaks, somewhat tendentiously, of 'the Great and the Small' (*to mega kai to mikron*), as if there were somehow two opposing principles involved, but it is plain from other testimonies (and indeed from his own testimony just below, 987^{a}26) that what Plato had in mind was a single 'material' principle.

[34] Aristotle characterizes it (*loc. cit.*, n. 33) as *ousia*, 'essence', as opposed to the Dyad as *hylē*, 'matter'.

[35] That this doctrine is Platonic as well as Aristotelian has been well demonstrated by Krämer (1959).

The Indefinite Dyad is primarily the basic unlimitedness or 'otherness' on which the One acts, but it is also the irrational aspect of the soul, and again the substrate of the physical world, represented by the 'receptacle' of the *Timaeus*.

By acting upon the Dyad, 'limiting' it, the One generates the system of natural numbers.[36] At this point, however, the evidence becomes confused, mainly because Aristotle, in his always tendentious testimony, assumes that his readers, or hearers, know what he is talking about. We, unfortunately, do not have this knowledge. As well as postulating a set of archetypal numbers, the so-called 'Form-Numbers',[37] it seems that Plato came finally to view the Forms in general as numerical entities. A special importance is attached by him, as it was by the Pythagoreans, to the 'primal numbers', one, two, three, and four (the so-called *tetraktys*), and their sum-total, ten (the Decad). The first four numbers seem to be in some way inherent in the One, and come to actuality in the process of its initial limitation of the Dyad. In *Metaphysics* N 7 (1081^b10 ff.), Aristotle seems to describe a process whereby the primal numbers are generated by, first, the Dyad producing the number two, by 'doubling' the One, and then producing the other numbers by adding to two and to each successive number either the One or itself. But the whole process remains obscure to us.[38]

From this action of the primal numbers upon the Dyad, and its reaction on them, all the other natural numbers are generated. This seems the most reasonable explanation, apart from emendation, that can be derived from the important, but obscure, passage of *Met.* A 6 ($987^b34–988^a1$), which has been mentioned above: 'Plato made the

[36] This process is arguably being portrayed, albeit rather cryptically, in the second hypothesis of the *Parmenides* (143A–144A). On this passage see the useful remarks of Turnbull (1998).

[37] A 'Form-Number' is to be distinguished from a mathematical number in that, in Aristotelian terms, it is 'non-addible' (*asymblētos*)—for the good reason that it is *what it is to be* the number in question, three, say, or four. There is such a thing as threeness, or fourness, and the threeness of three cannot be added to the fourness of four. Aristotle, however, has no patience with this notion.

[38] Aristotle is actually criticizing this process in this passage, but from what he says we may, I think, deduce what the process was.

other principle a Dyad, because of the fact that the numbers, *apart from the primal ones,*[39] are generated from it by a natural process (*euphyōs*), as from a mould (*ekmageion*).'[40]

Thus arises, then, the whole system of Form-Numbers, which would appear to be what the Platonic Forms have now become identified with. How many of them are there? The numbers up to four, and indeed the numbers up to ten, certainly hold some sort of distinctively basic position, but the multiplicity of physical entities requires that the basic numbers combine with each other in some way to produce compound numbers which can stand as 'formulae' for the immense variety of physical genera and species. We must not neglect, however, a bothersome passage, *Met.* M 8 (1084[a]11 ff.), where Aristotle seems to be saying that Plato took only the numbers up to ten as constituting the Forms:

> But if the number is finite, how far does it go? Not only the answer but the reasoning should be stated. If number goes up to ten, as some say, first, Forms will soon run out—if three is the archetype of Man (*autoanthrōpos*), for example, what number will the archetype of Horse be? The numbers which are in each case archetypal go up to ten, so it must be one of the numbers in these (these being the real essences (*ousiai*) and Forms), but they will still run out, since the classes of animal will exceed them.   (trans. Annas, slightly altered)

Aristotle is probably here being deliberately obtuse, for polemical reasons, and combining Plato's view that the Decad comprises the sum of number with his doctrine that the Forms were numbers.

---

[39] The meaning of the phrase *exō tōn prōtōn* has been much disputed. The suggestion, first made by the Aristotelian commentator Alexander of Aphrodisias, that it means the *prime numbers,* seems most improbable, but there is no agreement as to what else it might mean. See the judicious discussion of W. D. Ross in his commentary *ad loc.* (i. 173–6). A. E. Taylor's suggestion that the numbers referred to are one and two is tempting, but is thought by Ross to run into the notorious problem that One is not generally regarded as a number. As we shall see, however, when dealing with Speusippus, this is not universally valid. In any case, the whole concept of the *tetraktys* involves One being one of the first four numbers. I would suggest that in fact by *prōtoi arithmoi* Aristotle means (albeit disapprovingly) the *tetraktys,* as these numbers are basic in the system that he is criticizing.

[40] Aristotle here, we may note, deliberately utilizes the term used for the Receptacle by Plato in the *Timaeus* (50c).

Obviously, the numbers of the Decad must generate all other numbers, and there is certainly a hierarchy among the Forms, but Aristotle's criticisms here are unlikely to do full justice to the complexity of Plato's position.[41] That he is being less than fair here is indicated by the contradictory nature of his other references to the same issue: *Met.* M 8 (1073[a]14 ff.), where it is admitted to be uncertain whether the number of the Forms is ten or more than ten; and M 3 (1070[a]18–19), where we find the statement that 'Plato maintained, very soundly (*ou kakōs*), that there are as many Forms as there are natural beings (*hoposa physei*).' Theophrastus, indeed, in his *Metaphysics* (6[b] 11 ff.) seems to envisage a hierarchical arrangement when he speaks of Plato 'making all other things dependent on the Forms, and these on numbers, and proceeding from numbers to first principles'.[42] Here a distinction is actually made between Forms and numbers, seeming to conflict with the testimony of Aristotle that for Plato Forms *were* numbers. The conflict may, however, be averted if we take the numbers here in question as none other than the Decad, the Forms being those secondary combinations dependent on the *primary* numbers comprising the Decad.

Within the Decad, the first four numbers (the *tetraktys*) plainly came to play a major part in Plato's cosmology, as they did in those of his successors. They are the principles providing the link between the absolute unity of the One and the three-dimensional physical multiplicity around us. These four also have a geometrical aspect, though how that is linked to their essential nature is not clear in Plato—for Speusippus, as we shall see (p. 45 below), the geometricals are a separate level of being. At any rate, One is also the point, Two the line, Three the plane, and Four the solid (the last two being represented by triangle and pyramid respectively). We have Aristotle's—albeit disapproving—testimony (*Met.* A 9. 992[a]20 ff.)

---

[41] As we shall see below (p. 52), Speusippus equated the Decad with the paradigm of the *Timaeus,* and we need not suppose that he concocted such an equation entirely on his own initiative. More probably he is representing a late Platonic position which took the Decad as in some way the sum-total of numbers, and therefore of Forms.

[42] That is to say, the One and the Indefinite Dyad, mentioned just above at 6[a] 24–5. See on this passage the useful commentary of van Raalte (1993), 271–5.

that Plato refused to analyse the line into points, but postulated rather 'indivisible lines'—as also did Xenocrates after him (cf. below, pp. 111–15).[43] There has been much dispute as to where these entities fit into his metaphysical scheme, but it would seem reasonable, if Plato is going to postulate indivisible lines, that he should allow indivisible triangles as well, though we have no evidence on this point. It may be only at the level of Soul that the four basic numbers assume their geometrical aspect for Plato; at any rate, the composition of the Soul in the *Timaeus* is intimately bound up with the doctrine of four basic numbers as geometrical entities, and the relations of proportion between them. From the Soul the dimensions are projected upon Matter, in the form of combinations of basic triangles, initially to form the four elements, Fire, Air, Water, and Earth, and ultimately all other physical beings. Thus an uncompromisingly mathematical model of the universe is laid down, which set the tone for all subsequent cosmological speculation within the Academy—though drawing powerful criticism from Aristotle (e.g. at *De Caelo* III 1).

The doctrine of Soul is a central, but very difficult feature of Plato's system. Once again, the dialogues, particularly the *Timaeus,* must, I think be taken in the light of what we can unravel from secondary sources, particularly Aristotle. He is, for instance, quite emphatic[44] that Plato, besides the Forms (or Form-Numbers), postulated the existence of what he called 'mathematicals', or 'objects of mathematics'. These are distinguished from the Forms by being 'many the same' and being combinable with each other—the Forms being each one of kind and 'non-combinable' (*asymblētoi*)—and from physical

---

[43] Aristotle actually asserts that Plato rejected the concept of point altogether, dismissing it as a 'postulate of geometry' (*geometrikon dogma*), and proposing rather that lines were made up of minimal lines. If this is substantially accurate, it may be that Plato argued that there is actually no need to assume such an entity as a point on the ontological level, useful though it may be in geometry, since the number One itself will serve adequately as a first principle of geometricals. One does not, after all, build up a point from minimal points, as one does in the case of the other three dimensions. These issues will find their echoes in Speusippus and Xenocrates, as we shall see.

[44] In *Met.* A 6, 987[b]29, and, more elaborately, N 6, 1080[a]36–[b]36, though in this latter passage he is criticizing Speusippus and Xenocrates as well.

objects by being eternal and immaterial. From other evidence it becomes clear that these mathematicals are particularly connected with the Soul.[45] The most natural conclusion is that the Soul, which Plato is alleged by Aristotle (*De An.* III 4, 429ᵃ27) to have described as the 'place' (*topos*) of the Forms, receives the Forms into itself, and somehow transforms them into mathematicals, then projecting them upon Matter to form the physical world.

When we speak of Soul here, the reference is, of course, to the cosmic entity, the World-Soul, the construction of which is described in *Timaeus* 35A ff., but which otherwise only appears in Book X of the *Laws*. Of this entity the human soul is a microcosm. In its role as mediator between the intelligible and the physical realms, it is composed of aspects which reflect both what is 'above' and what is 'below' it. It is properly at the level of soul that the four Primal Numbers take on the aspect of Point,[46] Line, Plane, and Solid. Aristotle tells us (*De An.* I 2, 404ᵇ16 ff.)[47] that Plato constructed the soul out of these four entities, and made the equation between them and four modes of cognition, intuitive knowledge (*nous*), discursive or scientific knowledge (*epistēmē*), opinion (*doxa*), and sense-perception (*aisthēsis*). This fourfold division seems to be alluded to at *Laws*

---

[45] This evidence is admittedly rather late, consisting of such works as Iamblichus' *De Communi Mathematica Scientia*, chs. 1–4 and 9, and Proclus' *Commentary on Euclid*, Prol. pp. 11, 26–14, 23 Friedlein, but it is based on perfectly sound inferences from the *Timaeus*, and is hardly original to either of those authors. To quote Proclus (p. 13, 6–13): 'We must therefore posit the soul as generative of mathematical forms and *logoi*. And if we say that the soul produces them by having their patterns (*paradeigmata*) in her own essence and these offspring are the projections (*probolai*) of forms previously existing in her, we shall be in agreement with Plato and shall have discerned the true essence of mathematical being.' For a good discussion of this question, see Merlan (1960), ch. 1.

[46] Strictly speaking, as we have seen from Aristotle's testimony above (cf. n. 43), Plato prefers not to postulate a point as such, but rather sees the One itself as manifested at this level, as a first principle of dimensionality. This is of some importance, I think, for our understanding of Speusippus' position (cf. below, pp. 44–5).

[47] What precisely Aristotle is referring to by the phrase *en tois peri philosophias legomenois* is a notoriously controversial matter, but in the context it seems inevitable that it must at least include Plato. He has just asserted, with wicked ambiguity (juxtaposing Plato here with Empedocles), that Plato in the *Timaeus* composed the soul 'out of the elements' (*ek tōn stoicheiōn*).

X. 894A,[48] though in an ontological rather than a properly epistemological context; and something like it would seem to be being used in the Line simile of *Republic* VI, where what may be taken as 'mathematicals' appear at the second level (there termed *dianoia*, 511D), so this scheme may already have been in Plato's mind at this stage. Plainly the Soul is designed as the supreme mediating entity, receiving influences from the intelligible realm and passing them on in modified form—that is to say, extended and multiplied—to bring about the creation of the sensible realm. This is the process described, with many mythological flourishes (of which the Demiurge is the chief one), in the *Timaeus*.

It is indeed on the interpretation of the doctrines presented in the *Timaeus* that much cosmological speculation within the Old Academy can be seen to be centred. The principal problems left by the *Timaeus*, problems which Plato himself, it would seem, declined to solve himself definitively, are the following: (1) whether the cosmogonic process described is to be thought of as taking place at any point in time; (2) the identity of the craftsman god (*demiourgos*), or Demiurge; (3) the identity of the 'young gods' to whom the Demiurge delegates the creation of the lower part of the human soul; (4) the nature of the activity that may properly be assigned to the 'receptacle'; (5) the manner in which any combination of immaterial, two-dimensional triangles can generate a world of material, three-dimensional entities; (6) what relation these basic triangles and combinations of triangles, or indeed the Paradigm which is their source, can have to the system of Forms as they appear in earlier dialogues. On these questions controversy continued throughout later Platonism, beginning with Plato's immediate successors.

---

[48] This is indeed an odd passage. It overtly refers to the generation of three-dimensional physical objects from an ultimate non-dimensional first principle (*archē*), and runs as follows: 'What is the condition which must occur in everything to bring about generation? Plainly it is whenever an initiating principle, receiving increase (*auxē*), comes to the second stage, and from this to the next, and on coming to the third admits of perception (*aisthēsis*) by percipients.' This certainly seems to envisage a process of development from One to line to plane to solid, but it is introduced rather incidentally, and not elucidated.

First of all, as we shall see, Speusippus and Xenocrates maintained that the cosmogonic process described in the *Timaeus* was timeless and eternal, and that Plato had only employed an apparent temporal succession 'for the purpose of instruction'. Aristotle, however, who may here be simply being tendentious,[49] accuses Plato of postulating a temporal beginning for the world, while nonetheless stipulating that it will continue eternally (*De Caelo* I 12; II 2). It is possible, of course, that Plato himself did not make his position clear, preferring to leave his disciples to work out the solution for themselves. At any rate, if the demiurgic account is not to be taken literally, certain interesting consequences would seem to follow. What we seem to be left with is (1) a cosmic Intellect, the contents of which are the matrix of Forms comprising the 'model', or Paradigm, which the Demiurge is said to contemplate, and (2) a World-Soul, which constitutes a conduit for transmitting the Forms, as combinations of triangles, to the material substrate; or perhaps, more radically still, as we shall see when considering the position of Philippus of Opus (below, pp. 183–92), and possibly also that of Polemon (below, pp. 172–3) simply a rational World-Soul, as the active principle in the universe, thus constituting a suitable antecedent to that of the Stoics.

The process by which Soul acts on the 'Receptacle', or Matter,[50] the activity proper to Matter, and the nature of the basic triangles are not problems to which one finds any satisfactory answer in the surviving traces of the works of Plato's immediate successors, but that

---

[49] It is odd, certainly, that one of Aristotle's criticisms of Plato's system is that he neglects the efficient cause, and recognizes only the formal and material ones (*Met.* A 6, 988^{a}7–14). One might ask him what he takes the Demiurge to be. The answer to this, I think, is that Aristotle, despite his polemical resolve to take the *Timaeus* literally, knows perfectly well that it was not so intended, and that the Demiurge is a figment, being no more than the executive aspect of the Forms, or the Paradigm.

[50] The hesitations of modern scholars to identify this 'Receptacle' with the Aristotelian concept of Matter are somewhat undermined, it seems to me, by the fact that Aristotle himself has no hesitation in doing so (e.g. *Phys.* IV 2, 209^{b}33 ff.)—unless, of course, like Harold Cherniss, one assumes that he once again simply misunderstood Plato! Certainly we can make a distinction between a receptacle ('place') *in* which physical objects are formed, and a 'matter' *out of* which they are formed, but I think we must recognize that the distinction was not so clear either to Aristotle or to the Old Academicians.

does not mean that there was none. Aristotle's criticisms of the whole scheme in the *Physics* and the *De Caelo* were powerful, and needed to be answered. It is possible, indeed, that the 'atomistic' speculations of Heraclides of Pontus (see below, pp. 208–11) are an attempt to carry forward somewhat the speculations of Plato on this question.

So much, at any rate for what might be denominated 'physics'.[51] In the sphere of ethics, as I have remarked earlier (p. 18), there are sufficient indications that, for Plato as well as for Aristotle, the virtues are to be regarded as means between two extremes of 'too much' and 'too little', with Justice (symbolized by the Pythagorean *tetraktys*) as the force holding the universe together—a metaphysical concept as well as an ethical one.[52] We have evidence of treatises by both Speusippus and Xenocrates *On Justice* (the latter apparently a dialogue, also entitled *Archedemus*), but we have no idea, unfortunately, as to what they contained.

Important also for later Platonism is Plato's distinction, in *Laws* I 631B–C, between higher, or 'divine' goods—that is, goods of the soul, the virtues—and lower, or 'human' goods—goods of the body, such as health or beauty, and external goods, such as good fame or wealth. The Old Academicians probably adopted this distinction (as did, certainly, Platonists of later periods), but once again all we have is bare titles: *On Wealth, On Pleasure, On Friendship* (Speusippus), *On Virtue* (Xenocrates), *On Anger, On Pleasure, On Love, On Friends and Friendship* (Philippus of Opus), *On Virtue, On Happiness* (Heraclides of Pontus), with no clear indication how these topics are ranked.

On the topic that became a basic feature of ethical theory in later times, that of the overall purpose of life—the *telos,* or 'end of goods'—Plato is certainly on record, in two passages especially

---

[51] It seems to have been Xenocrates, if we may credit the evidence of Sextus Empiricus (cf. below, p. 98), who first formalized the tripartite division of philosophy into the topics of physics, ethics, and logic, but Sextus also declares that Plato himself made the distinction implicitly (*dynamei*). In fact, it seems to be recognized already by Aristotle in such a passage as *Topics* I 14, 105^{b}19 ff.

[52] See on this the useful discussion of Krämer (1959: 86–96).

(*Phaedo* 64E, *Theaet.* 176A–B), as asserting that it consists in the withdrawal of the soul from association with the things of the body so far as possible, and thus in assimilation to the divine. The whole simile of the escape from the Cave in *Republic* VII expresses the same attitude. The formulation 'likeness to God' (*homoiōsis theōi*) became the general definition of the *telos* among later Platonists, but there is no real indication that this was a doctrine adopted formally by the Old Academy. On the other hand, there did arise in the later Academy, with Xenocrates and Polemon, a doctrine of 'living in accordance with Nature', which plainly provided a stimulus to the doctrine developed by Zeno and the Stoics, but which has no very clear ancestry in the dialogues.

On the question of the self-sufficiency of virtue, and the freedom from passion (*apatheia*) of the wise man, another subject of lively debate in later times, Plato's position is somewhat ambiguous. A passage such as *Republic* III 387D–E asserts the good man's self-sufficiency, but seems to envisage him as moderating his passions rather than extirpating them.[53] The problem of when a moderated passion ceases to be a passion at all tends later to become a fruitful source of semantic confusion between Aristotelians and Stoics. As for the Old Academy, at least Xenocrates and Polemo seem, on the evidence of Cicero, as we shall see,[54] while tending to austerity, to have maintained a place for the goods of the body and external goods in the composition of happiness.

In the sphere of logic, the evidence points to Plato's maintaining the system of Division (*diairesis*), as first outlined in *Phaedrus* 265D ff., and even elevating it into a cosmogonic principle. It is the soul's business to bring order out of chaos by making the right 'divisions',

---

[53] A nice passage of similar purport occurs in the rather odd context of the mock funeral speech in the *Menexenus* (247E–248A): 'For that man is best prepared for life who makes all that concerns his happiness (*eudaimonia*) depend upon himself, *or nearly so,* instead of hanging his hopes on other men, whereby with their rise and fall his own fortunes also inevitably sway up or down: he it is that is temperate, he it is that is courageous and wise.' This is in the context of an elucidation of the saying, 'Nothing in excess' (*mēden agan*).

[54] See below, pp. 138–42 and 161–2.

hitting the right means and harmonies. There is no evidence that Plato himself developed anything as elaborate as the Aristotelian syllogistic and system of categories—although Aristotle's ten categories can be regarded as only a somewhat scholastic elaboration of the two basic categories of 'absolute' (= substance) and 'relative' (= all the rest). Plato, on the evidence of his follower Hermodorus,[55] seems to have made use of the basic categories of 'absolute' (*kath' hauto*) and 'alio-relative' (*pros hetera*), which latter was subdivided into 'opposite' (*pros enantia*) and 'relative' proper (*pros ti*), which in its turn was divided into 'definite' and 'indefinite'. Hermodorus is certainly not basing himself here on the evidence of the dialogues, though traces of such distinctions can be discerned in them (e.g. *Soph.* 255C; *Parm.* 133C–D; *Phlb.* 51C–D). The Old Academy seems to have maintained the system of *diairesis;* only in the Middle Platonic period did Platonists fully adopt Aristotelian logic, which they then managed to reclaim for Plato himself.

We do seem to observe, however, in the *Philebus* (15A–16B), a degree of concern on Plato's part that the practice of *diairesis* could tend to cause difficulties for the doctrine of Forms, and this may reflect discussions within the Academy as to whether the process of division was to be regarded merely as a logical instrument for the identification of forms, and their relations with one another, or whether it involved a significant ontological dimension. There is an element of real concern in the question that Socrates is made to raise at *Phlb.* 15B:

whether we ought to believe in the real existence of units (*monades*) of this sort; and secondly, how we are to conceive that each of them, being always one and the same and subject neither to generation nor destruction, nevertheless is, to begin with, most assuredly this single unity, and yet subsequently comes to be in the infinite number of things that come into being—an identical unity being thus found simultaneously in unity and in plurality. (trans. Hackforth)

If we may press the implications of the Epicrates fragment (above, pp. 7–8), as well as other testimony available as to the views of

---

[55] See below, pp. 200–3.

Speusippus (below, pp. 79–82), we may see evidence of development in an ontological direction; and reflections of this might be discerned also in Xenocrates' assertion of the priority of the species to the genus (below, pp. 115–17). But it is hard to get a clear view of such variations in approach.

What we find, then, bequeathed by Plato to his immediate successors is something of a physical plant and a fairly distinctive, though still quite open-ended, intellectual tradition, providing in either case an ample base on which to build. Let us now attempt to see something of what they did with it.

Speusippus and the Search for an Adequate System of Principles

Life and Works

Plato was succeeded as head of the Academy, as we have seen, by his nephew Speusippus, son of his sister Potone and a certain Eurymedon.[1] The circumstances of this succession are unfortunately quite obscure, since such ancient sources as we have—Philodemus' *History of the Academy*[2] and Diogenes Laertius—treat the event as unproblematical. Both Philodemus and Diogenes simply say 'he succeeded' (*diedexato*), without giving any indication of the procedure involved. Plato's last will and testament, preserved by Diogenes Laertius (III 41–3), really throws no light on the matter,

---

[1] This man must have flourished in the latter part of the 5 cent. BC, and been reasonably prominent, to have married a member of Plato's family, but none of the Eurymedons known to the prosopographical record seems to fill the bill (one possible candidate, the general Eurymedon, son of Theucles, died in Sicily in 413, which is rather too early, it is felt, to have generated Speusippus). We know that he owned an estate at Eiresidae adjacent to one of Plato's own—though the Eurymedon actually mentioned as the owner in Plato's will (DL III 42) must be a son, or even a grandson, since Eurymedon himself could not possibly have been alive in 347 BC.

[2] Hitherto known simply as the *Academicorum Philosophorum Index Herculanensis,* but recently claimed, with reasonable plausibility, for Philodemus himself by its latest editor, Tiziano Dorandi.

since Speusippus, although he is named (along with six others) as an executor (*epitropos*), is not bequeathed anything therein, the only named beneficiary being Adeimantus (presumably Plato's nephew, or even grand-nephew, rather than his older half-brother). It is not even clear whether the school was the sort of entity which one could bequeath to anyone; certainly it receives no mention in the will.[3]

Sadly, all we have in the way of 'biographical' information on Speusippus (chiefly from Diogenes Laertius) is a farrago of unreliably attested anecdotes, most of which do not even sound plausible, and none of which would be of much importance in any case. By way of illustration of this, I append a sample:

He set up statues of the Graces in the shrine of the Muses erected by Plato in the Academy. He adhered faithfully to Plato's doctrines. In character, however, he was unlike him, being prone to anger and easily overcome by pleasures. At any rate, there is a story that in a fit of passion he flung his favourite dog into a well, and that pleasure was the sole motive for his journey to Macedonia to be present at the wedding-feast of Cassander.[4]

The various elements in this have been well analysed by Leonardo Tarán.[5] There is no reason to doubt Speusippus' contribution of the statues of the Graces to the shrine to the Muses established by Plato, but it would be precarious to draw any deeply significant conclusions from that. Rumours of his bad temper and proneness to pleasure are plainly malicious, and the latter allegation at least probably has something to do with Speusippus' known doctrine on pleasure, which we will examine in due course; the allegation of bad temper, however, might have some substance—the odd story about throwing his dog down a well has at least the virtue of a degree of specificity, though we have no idea of its provenance—but it conflicts with other evidence to be quoted below. As for his alleged motives for attending Cassander's wedding, the whole story must be dismissed on chronological grounds, since the only known wedding of the Macedonian regent Cassander was to Thessalonike, daughter of Philip II, in 316, long after Speusippus' death. Some fact may lurk beneath the muddy

---

[3] On the questions discussed here see also Dillon (1983).
[4] DL IV 1 (trans. R. D. Hicks).   [5] (1981: 175–80).

waters of this anecdote, but it is not obvious what it could be, or whether it ever really concerned Speusippus in the first place.

The same, we must regretfully conclude, goes for such snippets as the allegation that he had an affair with one of the lady pupils of the Academy, Lastheneia of Mantinea; that he suffered badly from arthritis in his latter years (not intrinsically improbable); or that he committed suicide out of depression (highly improbable).

There is some reasonably good evidence, on the other hand, of his being on good terms with Plato's friend and disciple, Dion of Syracuse, whom he got to know when Dion was living in exile in Athens in the 360s. I quote from Plutarch's *Life of Dion,* ch. 17:

> Dion lived in the city with Callippus, one of his acquaintances, but for diversion he bought a country place, and afterwards, when he sailed to Sicily,[6] he gave this to Speusippus, who was his most intimate friend at Athens. For Plato wished that Dion's disposition should be tempered and sweetened by association with men of charming presence who indulged seasonably in graceful pleasantries. And such a man was Speusippus.   (trans. Perrin)[7]

This tells us something, not only about the relationship between Speusippus and Dion, but, more importantly, about his relationship with his uncle Plato. There are a number of other accounts of relations between the two, of varying degrees of reliability. One, relayed by Plutarch,[8] alleges that Plato

reclaimed his nephew Speusippus from great self-indulgence and debauchery, not by either saying or doing to him anything that would cause him pain, but when the young man was avoiding his parents, who were always showing him to be in the wrong and upbraiding him, Plato showed himself

---

[6] In 357, when he led an expedition back to overthrow the tyranny of his nephew Dionysius II, who had exiled him.

[7] We also learn, from ch. 22 of the same work, that, when Speusippus was in Syracuse in 361/0, accompanying Plato on his third journey there, he sent messages encouraging Dion to mount an expedition to liberate his homeland. Plutarch (or rather his source, Timonides of Leucas, who served with Dion, and composed an account of his campaign, which he dedicated to Speusippus, who was a friend of his) reports that Speusippus 'mingled more with the people [sc. than Plato himself], and learned to know their sentiments', which goes to confirm this impression of his amiability and 'common touch'.

[8] *De Frat. Am.* 491F–492A (= T24 Tarán).

friendly and free from anger to Speusippus and so brought about in him great respect and admiration for himself and for philosophy. Yet many of Plato's friends used to rebuke him for not admonishing the youth, but Plato would say that he was indeed admonishing him: by his own, the philosopher's, manner of life, showing him a way to distinguish the difference between what is shameful and what is honourable.

While one must feel duly cautious about such unattributed anecdotes as this, it is perfectly possible that there is a kernel of truth in it. After all, the fact remains that Plato's nephew did follow him into the philosophic life when he might have done many other things, and this approach to the moral training of the young does, as Tarán points out,[9] accord with Plato's own recommendation at *Laws* V 729B–C. The fact that there is a vaguely similar story told about Xenocrates' rehabilitation of Polemo, as we shall see presently, is really neither here nor there.

Another odd, but popular, little story[10] tells of Plato becoming angry with one of his slaves, and, precisely because he was angry, asking Speusippus to beat the slave for him. Unfortunately for the reliability of this, however, there are fully seven other sources listed[11] which give Xenocrates in this role instead of Speusippus. It is in any case not of much significance.

Other than these, there are the details mentioned in the previous chapter: the famous fragment of Epicrates, depicting the students of the Academy analysing the pumpkin; and the story about Aristotle giving the aged Plato a hard time during Xenocrates' absence, when Speusippus was ill and unable to defend him. In either case, what we can deduce is that already in Plato's lifetime Speusippus was acknowledged as one of the key figures in the Academy, if not already the designated successor. But that is, after all, no more than what one would expect.

From the period of Speusippus' own short reign as head of the Academy (347–339), we have only the information that Heraclides

---

[9] (1981: 216).

[10] Told by Valerius Maximus IV 1, 15, Seneca (*De Ira* III 12, 5–7), and twice by Plutarch (*De Lib. Educ.* 10D; *adv. Col.* 1108A) = T25 Tarán.

[11] In Riginos (1976: Anecdote 113A, p. 155).

of Pontus came first to study with him, before moving on to Aristotle (DL V 86),[12] and the tale of a confrontation with Diogenes the Cynic (DL IV 3), which would not be worth mentioning were it not for the fact that it may attest to the fact that he was afflicted with arthritis in his declining years (he was, after all, over sixty when he assumed the headship).

One other incident from this period, however, may be included, the historicity of which has long been under a cloud, but, I am now convinced, without adequate cause, and that is the matter of Speusippus' *Letter to King Philip*, which would, if genuine, have to have been composed in 343 or 342.[13] It is a document of some interest, though not one which sheds a very creditable light on Speusippus, trying as it does to ingratiate him and the Academy with Philip, through adducing various mythical, and equally doubtful historical, justifications for the legitimacy of Philip's conquests, while attempting to blacken the reputation of the aged Isocrates and his students, in particular the historian Theopompus, who were basking in Philip's favour at the time. It does, however, constitute an example of the sort of politicking in which a head of school felt that he had to indulge in the period of the growth of Macedonian power. It does not, on the other hand, merit much attention in a study of his philosophy.

As regards Speusippus' works, we have a list in Diogenes Laertius' *Life* (IV 4–5), comprising twenty-seven[14] separate items, some involving multiple books (e.g. ten books of *Homoia*, or 'Resemblances'), which Diogenes himself does not claim to be exhaustive (although he gives at the end a total of lines, which may

---

[12] On the probable meaning of this piece of information, see below, Ch. 6, p. 205.

[13] I am influenced in this by the excellent doctoral thesis of Tony Natoli, of the University of New South Wales, which I trust will be published as a monograph before long. He provides an exhaustive survey of the arguments for and against authenticity, as well as a detailed commentary on its contents. Otherwise, the basic edition is that of Bickermann and Sykutris (1928). The letter survives as no. 30 of the *Epistolographi Graeci* collected by Hercher (1871).

[14] After some probable subtractions have been made for dittographies: *Aristippus the Cyrenaic* and *Aristippus; A Reply to Cephalus* and *Cephalus; Cleinomachus or Lysias* and *Lysias.*

be authoritative: 43,475). Diogenes describes them as comprising both treatises (*hypomnēmata*) and dialogues, and this seems to be borne out by the list of titles.

We have first a group of apparently ethical works, beginning with a dialogue *Aristippus,* no doubt attacking the hedonistic doctrines, ostensibly of Aristippus of Cyrene (with whom we may, perhaps, imagine Socrates to be in conversation), but primarily directed against Speusippus' colleague in the Academy, Eudoxus of Cnidus, who maintained also a hedonistic position.[15] There follow treatises *On Wealth, On Pleasure, On Justice, On Philosophy,*[16] and *On Friendship.* As we shall see, Xenocrates also wrote treatises on all these subjects, as on many other subjects treated by Speusippus, either in support or in emulation.

We find then a treatise *On the Gods,* followed by (perhaps) a series of dialogues, *The Philosopher, Cephalus, Cleinomachus or Lysias,* and *The Citizen.* The use of the names Cephalus and Lysias leads one to suppose that Speusippus is dramatizing the well-known orator (whom he would have known) and his father (portrayed delightfully in Book I of Plato's *Republic*), but what these dialogues were about escapes us entirely. As for Cleinomachus, it has been suggested that he may be an eristic philosopher who was a contemporary of Eucleides of Megara, but this does not help us very much, except to suggest that Speusippus should not have approved of him. Both Philippus of Opus and Xenocrates wrote treatises *On the Gods. The Citizen (Politēs)* is a curious title, presumably of political content, not certainly a dialogue. but odd as the title of a treatise.

We find then a treatise *On the Soul,* a basic philosophical topic on which we also find treatises by Xenocrates (in two books), and Aristotle (in three), as well as single books by Theophrastus and Heraclides of Pontus. This no doubt developed Speusippus' distinctive definition of the soul, which will be discussed further presently. A treatise *To*

---

[15] Aspects of this dispute may be preserved, along with ironic comment, in Plato's dialogue *Philebus.* I confess to presuming this in my discussion below of Speusippus' doctrine on pleasure.

[16] Admittedly not clearly ethical in content, but embedded in a list of ethical treatises.

Gryllus follows, presumably addressed to Xenophon's son of that name, who died in the battle of Mantinea in 362, and whom Speusippus may well have known. Aristotle tells us (*ap.* DL II 65 = Fr. 68 Rose) that many people wrote encomia in his honour, and Aristotle himself composed one, as did the rhetorician Isocrates.

There follow a number of rather mysterious titles: *Tekhnōn Elenchos* probably means 'A critical examination of rhetorical treatises', since *tekhnē* can have that meaning; *Hypomnēmatikoi Dialogoi* could mean 'memoirs (*hypomnēmata*) in dialogue form', but more probably 'dialogues for mnemonic purposes', i.e. to help memorizing; and *Tekhnikon* probably has something to do with rhetorical treatises as well. So we may have here a little nest of treatises concerned, critically or otherwise, with the practice and theory of rhetoric—which would not be surprising: Platonic philosophers continued to take an interest in rhetoric to the end of antiquity, despite—or perhaps because of—Plato's strictures in the *Gorgias,* the *Phaedrus,* and elsewhere.

Next we have the well-known *Homoia,* or *On Similar Things,* in ten books, though preceded by the puzzling rubric *dialogoi,* since it is highly unlikely that such a work was cast in the form of a dialogue. The rubric is best assumed to be out of place. It could have described a number of the previous works in the list, most probably the sequence from *Philosophos* to *Pros Gryllon.* The *Homoia* is followed by *Diaireseis kai pros ta Homoia Hypotheseis* ('Divisions, and Hypotheses relating to the *Homoia*'), which sounds as though it is closely related to the *Homoia* itself, perhaps on a more theoretical level, if the *Homoia* was concerned, as on the evidence of the surviving fragments preserved by Athenaeus (Frs. 6–27 Tarán) it seems to have been, with the actual assembling of genera and species. There is a further work *Peri genōn kai eidōn paradeigmatōn* ('On examples of *Genera and Species*'—taking *paradeigmatōn* as governing the other two nouns, but the title is peculiar), which seems to relate to the same topic. Aristotle doubtless learned a good deal from Speusippus in this area, though he is loth to admit it. It is probable[17] that when he

---

[17] As is suggested, reasonably, by Tarán (1981: 66).

refers in the *Parts of Animals,* as he does on two occasions (642^{b}12 and 643^{a}36), to 'the written divisions' he is actually referring to one or other of these works by Speusippus, especially since the context is one of trenchant criticism of dichotomous divisions.

We come next to a mysterious title, *Pros ton amarturon,* 'In relation to the unwitnessed (one)'. This may, however, as Tarán proposes, be explained as yet another rhetorical work, a contribution to a controversy which involved the rhetorician Isocrates, who, shortly after the restoration of the democracy in 403, composed a speech on behalf of one Nicias against a man called Euthynous. Nicias, conceiving himself to be in danger during the rule of the Thirty Tyrants, had deposited a sum of three talents with Euthynous, who was a cousin of his, neglecting to bring anyone with him to witness this transaction. When he came to ask for the return of his money, Euthynous tried to fob him off with only two talents. Nicias had to wait till after the fall of the Thirty to bring suit against Euthynous, and, because of the circumstances, Isocrates was forced to compose a speech based solely on circumstantial evidence and probabilities—a considerable challenge for a forensic orator.[18] Hence the title, *Pros Euthynoun, amarturos.* This speech, which was presumably successful, plainly acquired some degree of notoriety as an *exemplum,* becoming known simply as 'the *Amarturos'*. Diogenes Laertius tells us (VI 15) that Socrates' follower Antisthenes composed a reply to it. This, we may assume, at some later stage Speusippus also did, perhaps as part of an ongoing feud which the Academy and Isocrates' school waged with each other during the middle years of the century.

Following on this, we have some more perspicuous items. First, the *Encomium of Plato,* or, as Diogenes terms it earlier, in his *Life of Plato* (III 2), *The Funeral Banquet (Perideipnon) of Plato,*[19] in which we

---

[18] Lysias is reported as having composed a speech in defence of Euthynous (Fr. 98 Thalheim).

[19] The disparity in the titles is troubling, but not beyond reconciliation. Presumably the encomium was delivered at the funeral banquet. There is also an outside chance that encomium may have been composed by Speusippus as part of a larger work, the *Perideipnon,* which may itself have been cast in the form of a dialogue. We have a mysterious (because rather fragmentary) passage from what is now accepted to be Philodemus' *History of the Academy* (formerly *Index Herculanensis*) VI (ed. Dorandi

are told that Speusippus actually made the claim that his uncle was in fact the son of Apollo, relating a 'miraculous birth' story distinctly uncomplimentary to Plato's father Ariston:[20] 'The story went that Ariston tried to force his attentions on Perictione, who was in her youthful bloom, and failed of his purpose; and then when he ceased from his violence, Apollo appeared to him in a vision; as a result of which he left her unmolested until her child was born.'

This extraordinary story is hard to evaluate, but we must reflect that it is told in the context of a funeral oration, and may therefore best be viewed as a rather sophisticated conceit (surely nobody in the room, in Athens in 347 BC, can have taken it literally?), making use of the 'divine birth' motif borrowed from similar stories already current about the birth of Pythagoras. It would thus be Speusippus' way—he was himself an enthusiastic Pythagorean—of assimilating his uncle to Pythagoras.[21] To make sense of the narrative, I think, we must presume Ariston, rather than indulging in rape, already to have married Perictione, and to be portrayed as pressing his marital rights rather roughly on his timid young virgin wife (who has in fact, unbeknownst to him, already been visited by Apollo!).[22]

Following on this, we have a trio of letters, addressed respectively to Dion, Dionysius (presumably Dionysius II), and Philip (of Macedon). Letters answering to these descriptions survive among the large collection of Greek letters. The first two are probably spurious, but the third, as I have suggested above, may well be genuine. It is certainly hard to see why anyone would have bothered to forge it.

1991), which mentions 'Timolaus of Cyzicus, Calligenes, and Timolas (*sic*) of Athens', whom Speusippus presents as hosting the feast in his *Funeral Banquet of Plato*.

[20] This story is filtered through two later authorities, Clearchus of Soli in his *Encomium of Plato*, and Anaxilaides in Book II of his *On Philosophers*, before it reaches Diogenes himself, but we must presume that the substance of the story is due to Speusippus.

[21] We may note also, if we accept as genuine a funerary epigram for Plato attributed to Speusippus both by Diogenes Laertius (III 44) and the *Anthologia Planudea* (= Fr. 87 Tarán), that he has no hesitation there in identifying him as 'son of Ariston'—though there he does describe Plato's soul as joining 'the immortal order of the Blessed Ones'—to which one may attach what weight one wishes.

[22] St Joseph, it will be recalled, found himself in rather the same situation as regards Mary in the birth narrative of Matthew, 1:18–25.

Then there is a treatise *On Legislation*. Then one entitled *Mathematikos* (*The Mathematician*), which may have contained the remarks on the nature of mathematical postulates discussed below, pp. 82–6. Then what sounds like another dialogue, the *Mandrobolos*, or *Mandroboulos*, about which we know only what we can deduce from a passage of Aristotle's *Sophistical Refutations* (174^b19–27), where Aristotle tells us that a certain Cleophon (presumably not the extreme democrat leader who met his end in 404) in this work resorts to the device of claiming that his opponent's argument, though valid against one sense of a word he is using, is not valid against the sense of it that he intends.

There follow a further dialogue, the *Lysias,* which I presume to be identical with the *Cleinomachus, or Lysias* mentioned above; *Horoi* (*Definitions*), presumably not identical with the surviving pseudo-Platonic *Definitions,* since they are full of Peripatetic and Stoic material, though that work may perhaps be a later reworking of a document of his; and lastly a curious title, *Taxeis hypomnēmatōn,* 'Arrangements, or lists, of commentaries, or memoirs', which can hardly in any case be a title of a treatise of any sort, but rather, if anything, a catalogue-style list of treatises.

There follows a rather garbled numeral giving the total of lines for all the treatises, generally read as 43,475, but which Ritschl, followed by Tarán, reads as 224,075, which certainly seems rather high for the total of works included in Diogenes' list. But Diogenes is not claiming that this is complete, and we know of at least one important work omitted from it—in fact the only work of Speusippus (apart from the *Letter to King Philip*) of which we have any verbatim remains. That is the little treatise[23] *On Pythagorean Numbers,* quoted by the author of the pseudo-Iamblichean *Theology of Arithmetic* (pp. 82, 10–85, 23 De Falco = Fr. 28 Tarán), which will be discussed below, pp. 59–64.

This is a reasonably impressive œuvre (though not by any means as extensive as that of Xenocrates, as we shall see), and it is a solemn thought that barely a line of it, apart from the last-mentioned work,

---

[23] Described by the author who quotes it (ap. *Theol. Ar.* p. 82, 13–14 De Falco), who may be Nicomachus of Gerasa, as a *biblidion glaphyron,* 'a skilful' or 'elegant little book'. Cf. below, p. 60.

and (in my view) the *Letter to King Philip* discussed above, survives to us. If, as I shall argue below, we can add to that the substance of chapter 4 of Iamblichus' *De communi mathematica scientia* (*DCMS*), then the loss becomes a little less complete, but this is a controversial claim, and it is not easy to see in which of the above-listed works Speusippus might have discussed the basic features of his metaphysics as set out in *DCMS* 4. At any rate, let us now turn to a consideration of his philosophical position.

Philosophy

First principles

In embarking on an evaluation of the doctrines of Speusippus, the first unhappy truth that confronts us is that we cannot evade the evidence of Aristotle. I have referred already[24] to the enormous importance which that evidence, biased and allusive as it is, takes on for the Old Academy as a whole—or at least for the Academy prior to 322 BC—but in the case of Speusippus it takes on particular importance, by reason of the fact that we have very little other evidence on his doctrine, and of that evidence that part which is potentially of most importance is unfortunately of rather doubtful status, as we shall see.

First, then, let us attempt to uncover Speusippus' doctrine of first principles, and specifically his theory of the derivation of other levels of being from his first principles of One and Multiplicity. Speusippus, naturally, takes his start from what was at least the later doctrine of Plato, itself much influenced by Pythagorean speculation, which postulates as first principles of all things a One and an Indefinite Dyad (for Plato, if we may credit Aristotle,[25] 'the great-

---

[24] Ch. 1, p. 17.

[25] *Met.* A 6, 987^{b}19 ff.; *Phys.* IV 209^{b}35 ff. Cherniss, of course, would see this as merely confusion on Aristotle's part (cf. 1945: 18–20), since Aristotle proposes in the latter passage to identify the 'great-and-small' with the Receptacle of the *Timaeus* (which he also identifies with his own concept of matter), which would mean that it could not also be regarded as the 'material' or differentiating principle of the forms. I do not see Aristotle as being confused here, merely tendentious.

and-small', or 'the greater-and-smaller'). From the action of the first of these on the second, there derives the system of Forms, conceived as mathematical entities of some sort. Plato himself is not recorded as being very specific as to how this comes about, nor about the relation of forms to numbers (though the first ten numbers, the 'decad', seem to have a privileged status of some sort), or to the 'mathematicals', whatever they were.[26] However, Speusippus seems to have provided somewhat more positive proposals on the mechanics of the derivation of the various levels of being, and this gives Aristotle occasion for astringent criticism. This he delivers in *Met.* Z 1028[b]21–4, and again at various points in Books M and N.

We need to look closely at these passages,[27] since they provide good illustrations, I think, of Aristotle's strategies in criticizing those he did not approve of, while also, if used judiciously, affording adequate clues as to Speusippus' true position. I should state at the outset that I believe that Speusippus *does* have a coherent metaphysical theory, and that it can be derived primarily from the valuable passage preserved by Iamblichus in *De communi mathematica scientia*, ch. 4,[28] with some help from a verbatim extract from his treatise *On Pythagorean Numbers,* preserved in the pseudo-Iamblichean *Theology*

---

[26] All we are told about 'mathematicals' by Aristotle is that they are 'many the same', that is to say, addible (*Met.* A 987[b]14–18), and 'a second kind of number, with which arithmetic deals' (991[b]27–30), whereas formal or eidetic numbers are not. The only sense I can make of this is that, for instance, one may postulate the Form of Three, or Threeness, which informs groups of three, but is not the sort of thing that you can add (either to another number or to itself), because it is *what it is to be three,* and if you try to add another three to it, or rather to the group that it is informing, it 'withdraws', and the Form of Six appears on the scene. But on the other hand one often wants to talk, for instance, of 'three threes making nine', or 'ten threes making thirty', and in this case one might wonder what these 'threes' are that one is manipulating. Plato's answer, I presume, is that these are 'mathematical' numbers, which *are* addible (cf. *Rep.* VII 526A, where mathematicians are portrayed as dealing with this sort of number—certainly not with the forms of the numbers). They are not identical with any sensible particulars, nor yet with forms, and may thus be presented by Aristotle, tendentiously, as a further form of intermediate *ousia,* between forms and sensible particulars; but is not clear to me that Plato necessarily saw them in this way.

[27] Conveniently collected by Tarán (1981), as frr. 29–34.

[28] ed. N. Festa (1891). I have defended Philip Merlan's identification of this chapter (1960: 98–140), as essentially Speusippan, against what seems to me the misguided scepticism of Tarán (1981: 86–107), in Dillon (1984) (repr. in Dillon 1990).

of Arithmetic,[29] and even (despite himself) from Aristotle. The scenario that Aristotle wishes to present to us, and that Tarán seems largely prepared to accept, is of a thinker so inconsequential that he should not have been let out on the streets without a nurse (to borrow a thought from Thrasymachus' abuse of Socrates in *Republic* I). It is not unreasonable, therefore, in the case of a man who shows various signs of having been a philosopher of considerable subtlety, to ask whether one cannot, with a little sympathetic imagination, put together a reasonably coherent theory.

The theory that emerges from *DCMS* 4, and our other sources of evidence, is as follows. Speusippus accepted the doctrine of two opposite principles propounded by Plato (at least in his later years), according to which all things are to be derived from a One and a principle of indefinite multiplicity (termed by Plato the Indefinite Dyad, and perhaps also the 'great-and-small', but by Speusippus himself *plēthos*, 'multiplicity'), but he altered it in an interesting direction. Laying particular emphasis on the status of the first principles as 'seeds' or 'potencies' of all things, he argued that what is itself the cause of some quality in other things cannot have that quality in the same way, so that if the One is the cause of goodness and being for all other things, it cannot itself properly be termed good or even existent (Frr. 42–3 Tarán), any more than an acorn is itself an oak tree. This led him to an interpretation of Plato's first principle which placed it at an extreme of transcendence.[30]

Let us first look at Aristotle's remarks at *Met.* N 1092[a]11–17 (= Fr. 43 Tarán), where he is criticizing the view that what is more developed derives its existence from what is less developed. In this connection, he takes a dig at Speusippus (referred to anonymously, as usual):

---

[29] pp. 82, 10–85, 3 De Falco = Fr. 28 Tarán.

[30] In this connection see the interesting passage preserved in Proclus' *Commentary on the Parmenides*, p. 38, 31–40, 10 Klibansky (= Fr. 48 Tarán), quoted below, pp. 56–7, where Speusippus appears to attribute to the Pythagoreans a One above Being, which is so transcendent as not even to count as a principle, without the additional postulation of the Indefinite Dyad. He must be suspected, however, of putting forward his own views here, under the umbrella of Pythagoras.

Nor is someone correct who compares the principles of the universe (*hai tou holou arkhai*) to that of living things and plants, on the grounds that the more complete always comes from what is indefinite and incomplete (this being his reason for saying that this applies to the primary principles too, *so that the One itself would not even be an existing thing*).[31] For even in this case the principles from which these things come *are* complete; it is a man that produces a man, and it is not true that the sperm is primary.

I think we may reasonably suspect Aristotle of being tendentious here. It is possible that Speusippus did somewhere (though not in the following passage) make a comparison between seeds of natural things and the One, but if he did, it can only have been in respect of the seed's (apparent) simplicity in comparison to the animals or plants which develop from it, as an analogue to the One's (actual) simplicity with respect to everything else in the universe; there could be no implication of incompleteness or imperfection in the case of the One.

We should now look at the beginning of *DCMS* (p. 15, 5 ff. Festa):

Of mathematical numbers[32] one must postulate two primary and highest principles, the One (which one should not even call Being (*on*), by reason of its simplicity and its position as principle of everything else, a principle being properly not yet that of which it is the principle); and another principle, that of Multiplicity (*plēthos*), which is able of itself to facilitate[33]

---

[31] *Hōste mēde on ti einai to hen auto.* Tarán, in his discussion of this passage (1981: 104, and in his comm. ad loc.) makes much of the fact that Aristotle here uses a 'natural result' construction (*hōste* + infinitive), rather than an 'actual result' construction, and that this implies that the consequence presented is a derisive postulate of Aristotle's, rather than a position held by Speusippus (and thus in conflict with *DCMS* 4). While granting, however, that Aristotle is being sarcastic here, we do not have to accept that the 'natural result' construction *excludes* the actual result—which makes the passage in fact good confirmatory evidence for the reliability of *DCMS* 4.

[32] This specification poses a slight problem, since it seems to limit the discussion to numbers, but Iamblichus' topic is, after all, number, so that it is possible that he has indulged in some editorial touching up here. It is also conceivable, however, that Speusippus expressed himself in these terms, since for him numbers are the first level of reality deriving from the union of the first principles.

[33] The verb used is *parekhesthai,* which need not connote any degree of positive activity. I have chosen to render it by 'facilitate'. *Plēthos* for Speusippus is a passive principle, but it does provide the opportunity for 'division', and hence the creation of all other entities (as does any material principle worth its salt, after all)—and is even, if one puts this

division (*diairesis*), and which, if we are able to describe its nature most suitably, we would liken to a completely fluid and pliable matter (*hyle*).[34]

Out of these two—coming together, Speusippus says vaguely, 'by reason of a certain persuasive necessity' (a phrase, I think, intentionally recalling the 'persuasion' of Necessity by Reason in *Timaeus* 48A)[35]—is generated Number, *plēthos* providing the principle of infinite divisibility, and the One imposing limit and quality, to produce the first principle of Number.

It is here, however, that difficulties begin to accumulate. The first product of these two, as I say, is Number. Speusippus appears to have portrayed this as the number One, which gives Aristotle a handle for much malicious criticism. It is a notable fact that neither Plato nor Aristotle appears to have considered 'one' as being properly a number, but rather the root or basis of number, whereas Speusippus, as Tarán shows (1981: 35 ff.), took it—or at least a certain *sort* of one—as the first odd number. However, this should not lead us (as it unfortunately leads Tarán) to confuse this mathematical 'one' either with Speusippus' absolute first principle, or even with the first principle of his second level of reality, which is that of numbers. What Speusippus seems to have postulated is a first principle of number, which, as the representative of the One at the next level of being, is necessarily unitary, and may be termed 'one',[36]

evidence together with that of the passage from Proclus' *Parmenides Commentary* (mentioned above, n. 30), to be regarded as the creative principle in the proper sense, since, as Speusippus there remarks, 'if one postulates the One itself, thought of as separate and alone, nothing else at all would come into being'.

[34] The use of this term, even in a comparison, is interesting, but cannot, I think, be used to tell against Speusippan authorship. Even if it is an Aristotelian coinage in its technical sense (which is not a necessary supposition in any case), there is nothing to prevent his older contemporary Speusippus from borrowing it. The adjective *euplades* ('pliable'), we may note, is found nowhere else in extant literature.

[35] Intentionally, but also rather deviously. Here, after all, the 'persuasiveness' characterizes *anangkē* itself, not *nous*. Speusippus seems here to combine the actions of both, perhaps as a way of rationalizing the mythical element in Plato's account, which we know that both he and Xenocrates were concerned to do.

[36] It is one of Speusippus' problems, I think, to be somewhat short of technical terminology to do justice to his very subtle positions. In the sphere of ethics, also, as we shall see, he seems to have been constrained to describe the median state which he pos-

uniting with the principle of multiplicity once again, this time to produce the series of natural numbers—or perhaps, in the first instance, just the sequence of numbers up to ten—since he exhibits, in his treatise *On Pythagorean Numbers* (= Fr. 28 Tarán), as we shall see, a special reverence for the Decad as, in a way, the summation of number.

However, in some way not clear from the evidence, this union of Number and Multiplicity also generates the first principle of Figure,[37] which is represented (again as the representative of the primal One) as a point (*stigmē*), this 'point' serving as the unitary first principle of all geometrical entities, whether two- or three-dimensional, which unites in turn with a corresponding form of Multiplicity—which he terms *thesis kai diastasis topōn*, 'position and spatial interval' (p. 17, 16)[38]—to generate.

The whole range of geometrical entities are thus generated, but there is also produced an essential geometrical entity which, once again, unites with the principle of Multiplicity to serve as the first principle of the realm of Soul, which, as we know,[39] Speusippus defined as 'the form of the omni-dimensionally extended' (*idea tou pantēi diastatou*). Soul in turn generates all the souls in the universe, but also, by the same means, serves as the first principle of the physical world, or body.

So much, I think, we can discern, on the basis of the data presented in *DCMS* 4, about Speusippus' strategy for generating the totality of existence.[40] It is certainly tortuous and complex, and by no means

tulates between pain and pleasure, and which is neither of them, as itself *hēdy*, 'pleasant', and this gives Plato a stick with which to beat him in the *Philebus* (cf. below, p. 70).

[37] I forbear to say 'plane' or 'solid', because it seems, again on the evidence of *DCMS* 4, that Speusippus lumped lines, planes, and solids together as the next level of reality, the geometrical, though he certainly distinguished them in other contexts.

[38] This seems to correspond to the *diastēma* which Aristotle alludes to in *Met.* M 1085[a]31, in the course of a criticism of Speusippus (below, pp. 46–7).

[39] Admittedly from a rather bald doxographical notice in Iamblichus' *De Anima* (ap. Stob. *Ecl.* I 363, 26–364, 7 Wachs. = Fr. 54 Tarán).

[40] It has been suggested to me by Malcolm Schofield that, since there is actually no evidence for the conceptual device that I have proposed for the linking between levels of reality in Speusippus' universe, he may in fact have left his universe 'episodic', in the way that Aristotle accuses him of, and that this might be a defensible position—Speusippus could have contented himself with an assertion of 'analogy' between the various levels.

without difficulties, and it plainly irritated Aristotle extremely, but I think that it can be shown to be not without some philosophical justification, and based on a creative analysis of difficulties within the Platonic metaphysical scheme that he had inherited.

First of all, there is a problem facing all monistic cosmological systems, particularly those which, like Plato's, postulate a totally simple and uniform first principle, acting on a totally undifferentiated material principle, and that is (as is pointed out at *DCMS* 4, pp. 16, 18 ff.) that, if both elements involved are quite undifferentiated, their union should logically produce, if anything at all, only one thing, or one level of being, not a whole series of such levels, such as we seem to observe in the cosmos as we have it. Therefore, it seemed to Speusippus, one needs to postulate also some mechanism to explain this latter phenomenon. The best he could come up with—and it is this that Aristotle takes delight in satirizing as his *episodic* universe[41]—is the theory that the (logically) first product of the union of the two ultimate principles should then become a principle in its turn, mating, so to speak, in an incestuous union, with its mother (which Speusippus has been careful to characterize, as we have seen, as 'a totally fluid and pliable matter'), and producing the next level of being.

That some such process is being envisaged by Speusippus seems indicated by further remarks of Aristotle in Book M of the *Metaphysics*. First of all, at 1085^a31-^b4 (= Fr. 51 Tarán), we find the following (he has just been criticising Plato):

These thinkers, then, generate magnitudes from this kind of matter, but others [sc. Speusippus] from the point (*stigmē*)—they regard the point as being, not one, but *like* (*hoion*) the one—and another material principle (*hylē*) which is *like* Multiplicity (*plēthos*), but not Multiplicity; yet in the case

I admit to embarrassment about the lack of evidence for the mode of connection between levels, but I still feel that a truly episodic universe would be anathema to a Platonist. There would, at the least, have to be some objectively real link corresponding to this 'analogy', and that is what I am in search of. Here the passage of *Met.* M quoted just below seems to me helpful, if interpreted correctly.

[41] Cf. *Met.* M 1028^b21-4 (Fr. 29a Tarán), $1075^b37-1076^a4$ (Fr. 30), 1090^b13-21 (Fr. 37).

of these principles nonetheless we get into the same difficulties. For if the matter is one, then line, plane, and solid will be the same; because the product of the same elements must be one and the same.[42] If on the other hand there is more than one matter—one of the line, another of the plane, and another of the solid—either the kinds are associated with (*akolouthousin*) one another, or they are not. Thus the same result will follow in this case also; for either the plane will not contain a line, or it will be a line.

This critique, while seeking to ridicule Speusippus' position, also gives us some insight into what it was. What Speusippus does indeed wish to postulate is a sort of *akolouthia* obtaining between the various levels of *plēthos,* or *hylē,* however he may have expressed this. Nor, it seems, was this notion entirely original to him. Somewhat earlier in this book (M 9, 1085^{a}8 ff.), Aristotle criticizes those Platonists (hardly identical with Speusippus, though their identity is uncertain) who propose to derive lines, planes, and solids from what Aristotle chooses to term 'species' (*eidē*) of the 'Great and Small'—'the Long and Short', the 'Broad and Narrow', and the 'Deep and Shallow'—and the first principles (*arkhaí*) corresponding to these. Speusippus was not therefore, it would seem, entirely on his own in worrying about the problem of the mechanics of deriving a multi-layered universe from a pair of totally simple first principles.

Aristotle's polemical strategy here, as so often elsewhere, is to assume that his opponents are using the terms they use in precisely the sense that he would use them himself, and thus reduce their position to absurdity. In the section of Book M immediately following the passage quoted above (1085^{b}4–34 = Frs. 40 and rest of 51 Tarán), he does just that, in particular understanding the concepts 'one,' 'number', and 'multiplicity' in terms of his own system, in a way which renders Speusippus' position quite incoherent. What he does not allow for is that Speusippus is postulating first principles of unity, multiplicity, and number which are not subject to Aristotelian definitions. For instance, for Aristotle, a multiplicity is a multiplicity of *units* (*monades*), and 'number' is also made up of units, whereas in

---

[42] This, of course, was just the problem which we must suppose Speusippus to be trying to address.

Speusippus' system there are such entities as primal Multiplicity and the first principle of number of which this does not hold true. It is therefore, as I say, hardly fair of Aristotle to employ arguments making these assumptions. Nevertheless, such a passage as this is most useful for discerning something of Speusippus' theory, if read with due caution and discernment.

The second aspect of Platonic doctrine that plainly caused Speusippus some trouble was the notorious Theory of Forms. Aristotle testifies[43] to the fact that the difficulties in the theory, even in the final form which it reached in Plato's thought, were what led Speusippus to abandon the Forms as such, and postulate instead simply a system of numbers, and then of geometrical figures, as the proper objects of knowledge (for which he fully accepted the need). What were these difficulties? They seem to have been for Speusippus very much the ones that have been brought against the theory by critics ever since, beginning with Aristotle. Not only is it very difficult to decide of what things there are forms, and what degree of 'similarity' they may have to the particulars which they 'inform', but also how exactly the forms, and especially forms of different degrees of generality (in particular genera and species) relate to each other.[44] In face of these problems, Speusippus plainly thought that the theory was not worth preserving in anything like its traditional Platonic form, but yet was concerned by the problem which had led Plato to postulate it in the first place, the need for there to be eternal and

---

[43] At *Met.* M 9, 1085^{b}36 ff. (= Fr. 35 Tarán), where he speaks of Speusippus seeing the 'difficulty and artificiality (*dyskhereia kai plasis*) attendant on the postulation of forms'. It is interesting in this connection, and has been drawn attention to in a stimulating article by Schofield (1971), that Aristotle, when mentioning Speusippus' 'difficulties' with Platonic doctrine, repeatedly uses the noun *dyskhereia*. Schofield puts this together with Plato's slightly curious characterization of the 'enemies' of *Philebus*, and suggests that this, in both adjectival and nominal form, may have been a favourite word of Speusippus', and that this is used both by Plato and Aristotle, to identify—and perhaps to tease—him. We may note in this connection that the verb *dyskherainō* is used, in a significant context, at *DCMS* 4, p. 17, 10.

[44] Cherniss (1945: 41–3) may well be right in suggesting that it was in fact the development of the method of *diairesis* that presented what seemed to Speusippus insuperable 'difficulties' with the system of superordinate and subordinate forms of genera and species.

unchanging objects of knowledge.[45] He found adequate candidates for these, however, in the systems of numbers and geometrical figures, which did not have the same problems of diversity and hierarchy to which the traditional forms were subject.[46] This does not necessarily mean, however, as Aristotle would have us believe, that he simply gave up on the Forms. There was still a paradigmatic and creative function to be performed in the universe which could not be reasonably attributed to purely mathematical entities (as Aristotle takes pleasure in pointing out). Speusippus was quite cognizant of this, however, and seems to have attributed this function to the World-Soul, as I shall explain presently. He is not to be regarded, therefore, as having simply abandoned the Forms; rather, he restructured and rationalized them.

If we examine Aristotle's polemical strategy in response to these innovations of Speusippus, we can see him, first of all, endeavouring to score points by emphasizing the apparent series of separate first principles to the exclusion of the linking process that I have postulated for Speusippus. Let us consider first *Met.* Z 1028ᵇ15 ff. (= Fr. 29a Tarán):

Some people consider the limits of bodies, such as the surface and line and point and monad, to be substances (*ousiai*), and indeed more so than body and the solid. Further, some [sc. the Pythagoreans] hold that nothing such as this exists independently of perceptible objects, while others think that there are a multiplicity of such entities, and that they are actually *more* real, since they are eternal, as for instance Plato holds that there are forms and mathematicals, as two distinct levels of substance, and then as a third the substance that consists of perceptible bodies, while Speusippus postulates even more substances, beginning with the One, and then first principles (*arkhai*) of each level of substance, one for numbers, another for volumes (*megethē*), and then that of the soul; and in this way he strings out (*epekteinei*) the levels of being.

---

[45] Cf. *Met.* N, 1090ᵃ2–ᵇ5 (= Fr. 36 Tarán).

[46] No doubt larger and more complex numbers are in some way subordinate to the basic numbers of the Decad, and particular types of Triangle are subordinate to triangle in general, but this is an altogether simpler scenario than we face with the traditional Forms. At any rate, it does not seem to have disturbed Speusippus.

As I say, this is cleverly laid out. First Plato is presented as producing the 'mathematicals' as a separate level of being between forms and physical particulars,[47] and then Speusippus is brought on as developing this tendency to absurd lengths—the verb *epekteinei* I would take as pointedly satirical.

This odd propensity of Speusippus is returned to later, in Book M 8, 1083ᵃ20 ff. (= Fr. 34 Tarán), in the context of a refutation of the Platonist concept of idea-numbers (that is, numbers incomparable with one another). Aristotle's particular complaint against Speusippus here is that, since he abandoned the idea-numbers, and retained only mathematical numbers, he cannot then declare 'One' to be a sort of idea of number, and not postulate ideas of all the other natural numbers as well:

But again, what certain others have to say about numbers is not well said either. These are those who do not accept the theory of Forms either as such or as some sort of numbers, but believe in the existence of mathematicals, and hold that numbers are first among beings, and that the first principle of them is the One itself (*auto to hen*). For it is bizarre (*atopon*) that there should be a One that is first among the ones, as those persons say, and not a Two for the twos, nor a Three for the threes; for they are all in the same logical situation. If, then, this is the situation as regards number, and one postulates the existence of mathematical number alone, then the One is not a principle (for then such a One would have to be of a different nature from all the other ones; and if this were the case, then there would have to be a primal Two different from the twos, and similarly for all the other numbers in turn). But if the One is a first principle, it would have to be rather as Plato used to maintain was the case in relation to numbers, that there was also a primal Two and a Three, and these numbers would not be commensurable (*symblētous*) with one another. But again, if one makes that postulate, as has been said, many impossibilities result. And yet it is necessary that either the latter or the former situation obtain, as, if neither is the case, there is no possibility that number be separable.

[47] The justice of this I leave aside for the present, but have commented on it above in Ch. 1, n. 23. While not accepting Cherniss's position that Aristotle is simply misunderstanding data derivable from the dialogues, I do think that he is distorting Plato's true position on 'mathematicals' for polemical purposes. I do not believe that they were intended to form a separate *level* of being analogous to Speusippus' various levels.

If my reconstruction of Speusippus' doctrine is even approximately correct, we can see Aristotle here being wickedly misleading about that doctrine, in order to set up Plato and his nephew as holding two equally implausible positions. I am not concerned here to defend Plato's theory of idea-numbers; my concern is only with Speusippus. What Aristotle is doing in his case is, first, to present him as abandoning the Forms in favour of entities which he seeks to identify with Plato's 'mathematicals'; and then to suggest that Speusippus tries to elevate the ordinary mathematical number 'one' to the status of a first principle, not only of numbers, but of everything.

We can see from what has emerged already, I hope, how misleading this is. Speusippus may indeed have involved himself in some terminological difficulties, but it seems clear enough that he is postulating three distinct entities: a supreme 'One', or Unity, the first principle of all things, a secondary 'One', or Unit, which is the immediate product of the primal One and Multiplicity, and serves in turn as the first principle of Number—and thirdly, the purely mathematical 'one', which (unlike both Plato and Aristotle) Speusippus regarded as the first odd number, and which is on the same metaphysical and logical level as all the other numbers.

As for abandoning the Forms (whether as numbers or *haplōs*), this, as I have said, would seem to be a further gross over-simplification. Certainly, Speusippus seems to have unhitched the concept of Form *in its causative aspect* from either the mathematical or the geometrical levels of reality, but he does this only to establish it firmly at the level of Soul, which he (following, as I think, his non-literal interpretation of the *Timaeus*) takes as the immediate transmitter of form to the physical universe.[48] Soul, let us recall, he defined as the 'form of the omni-dimensionally extended (*idea tou pantēi diastatou*)'. If we give due weight to that admittedly very compressed and elliptical definition, we must, I think, interpret it as the 'executive aspect', so to speak, of the Essential Living Being, or Paradigm, of the *Timaeus*

---

[48] This I find to be more or less the conclusion come to by Krämer (1964:209–10, and n. 48).

(which in itself, Speusippus, as emerges from the surviving portion of his treatise *On Pythagorean Numbers* (= Fr. 28 Tarán), wished to identify with the Decad—and with the geometrical equivalent of the Decad). This system of numbers, projected already at the next level of being as geometrical entities, is finally set in motion by the Soul, and is projected in turn upon the 'Receptacle' of Matter in the form of the basic triangles and basic geometrical figures described (rather schematically and poetically) in the *Timaeus*.[49]

Forms, then, in the strict sense, manifest themselves only in the World-Soul (which is itself a sort of super-form), not at any higher level. What they do, presumably, is to constitute that three-dimensionality which Aristotle condemns as the 'Pythagorean' version of the basic substance of things,[50] and for which his own doctrine of 'matter' is designed as a substitute. Aristotle's denunciation of geometricals as invisible and insubstantial (being rather *quantities,* if anything) would, I think, leave Speusippus unmoved. For him, it is precisely the projection of these entities, in the form of combinations of the five 'Platonic' regular solids (which, we learn, he discussed in the first part of his treatise *On Pythagorean Numbers*)[51] onto the field of force described by Plato in the *Timaeus* as 'the Receptacle' that produces what *appears to us* as the physical world. It is as 'solid' as we are, but our bodies too, it must be remembered, are made up of immaterial triangles. It is as the source, or matrix, of all these combinations, then, that the World-Soul is denominated the *idea* of three-dimensionality.[52]

---

[49] Leonardo Tarán, I am sorry to say, manages to be remarkably perverse in his discussion of Speusippus' doctrine of the soul (in the course of his exegesis of his Fr. 54 (pp. 365–71)—while, as usual, making many useful observations. He is no doubt correct in criticizing Philip Merlan for claiming rather too much for the accuracy of Iamblichus as a doxographer, but it is *not* the case that one must choose between the definition provided by Iamblichus (which was also, on the evidence of Plutarch (*Proc. An.* 1023B = Posidonius, Fr. 141a Edelstein–Kidd), adopted by Posidonius), and the evidence of Aristotle. Aristotle in fact provides *no* positive evidence about Speusippus' doctrine of the soul, and the negative evidence that he provides (e.g. in Fr. 29) need not bear the interpretation that Tarán puts upon it.

[50] e.g. in *Met.* B 5, 1101^{b}27 ff.

[51] ap. *Theol. Ar.* p. 82, 17–18 De Falco. See below, p. 60.

[52] It is interesting, perhaps, that at the very end of antiquity, the Christian philoso-

It is only at the level of soul, after all, Speusippus wishes to assert (and this is another assertion for which Aristotle satirizes him[53]), that 'goodness' may properly be said to manifest itself (*DCMS* 4, p. 18, 2 ff.).[54] The full significance of this remarkable doctrine needs some thought to elucidate. Speusippus wished to deny 'goodness' both to the primal One, and even to the mathematical and geometrical levels of reality, not because they were *bad,* but simply because he felt that the term had no real meaning at those levels.[55] So what, then, would be the 'real' meaning of 'good' at the cosmic level for Speusippus? It seems to me that it is closely allied to the creative, or 'demiurgic', activity of the World-Soul, and in this connection I think that the well-known characterization of the Demiurge as 'good' by Timaeus at 29E (*agathos ēn*. . .)[56] is profoundly relevant. In Speusippus' 'deconstruction' of the myth of the *Timaeus,* the function of the Demiurge breaks down fairly naturally into (a) an archetypal aspect, which is transcendent Intellect (the contents of which,

pher John Philoponus, steeped though he was in Aristotle, seeks to dispose of the Aristotelian doctrine of matter in favour of a Neopythagorean (and, I would suggest, Speusippan) doctrine of three-dimensionality as the ultimate substrate of bodies. See on this the penetrating study of de Haas (1997).

[53] Cf. *Met.* N 4, 1091^{a}29–^{b}3 = Fr. 44 Tarán (cf. also 1091^{b}30–5 = Fr. 45). Again, it is unreasonable of Tarán to argue (1981: 102; 341–2) that Aristotle's evidence is at variance with that of *DCMS* 4, simply because there it is stated that *to kalon* arises first at the level of numbers, and *to agathon* later, while Aristotle simply speaks of both *kalon* and *agathon* arising 'later'. Aristotle is not concerned with exactly at what point in his universe Speusippus wished to introduce each of these two qualities; he regards his position as essentially absurd, and is criticizing him globally.

[54] The report of his views at this point (and at this stage of the chapter it *is* only a report) is unfortunately elliptical, but his position can readily be deduced, especially with the help of Aristotle's (albeit hostile) evidence. All that is said is that *evil* only arises, as a sort of by-product of good, at the lowest level of the universe (the physical world). What is not said, but inevitably implied, is that good has first appeared at the next stage above, and that is soul.

[55] Plato, of course, had notoriously presented his supreme principle as the Good in the *Republic,* as the object of all striving, and as that which gave existence and knowability to all the rest of true being, but Speusippus ventures to reject this as a misuse of the term. One of his objections, which is a good one (*DCSM* 4, p. 15, 23 ff. confirmed by Ar. *Met.* N 1091^{b}30–5), is that, if the first principle is 'good', this would logically make its counterpart, Multiplicity, or the Indefinite Dyad (which after all stands as an opposite to it, *evil*—and that would quite misrepresent its position.

[56] Cf. also 29^{a}3 and 30^{a}1–2.

in Speusippus' terms, would be the system of numbers and geometricals[57]); and (b) an 'executive' function, which would be most naturally transferred to the World-Soul. It is this latter that would most properly be described as *agathos,* as being the agent of all order and tendency towards perfection in the physical universe, and this, it seems to me, is the rationale behind identifying Soul as the first level of being that can properly be characterized as 'good'.

Even as nothing is said of the soul in *DCMS* 4 (since such a topic is not relevant to Iamblichus' purpose there), so nothing is said of any lower level of being than soul[58]—except an incidental remark at the end of the extract (p. 18, 9–12 Festa), à propos the origin and nature of evil in the universe. Speusippus declares that there is nothing either ugly or bad (*oude aiskhron oude kakon*) in the higher reaches of reality—the realm of the One, of Number, or of Figure, 'but only at the lowest level, among the fourths and fifths, which are combined from the lowest elements, does evil come into being—and even then not principally (*proēgoumenōs*), but as a result of a falling-away from and failure to control what is in accordance with nature.'

This, brief and elliptical as it is, provides much food for thought. However we may distinguish the 'fourths and fifths', we seem to discern here a five-level universe, two more levels being postulated below the level of Figure. Since there is no other mention in this document of Soul, one might feel that we must identify the fourth level with that, but there are difficulties. I cannot see that Speusippus (or anyone else) would have described Soul as 'combined from the lowest elements', and, though one might allow for the incidental arising of evil at the level of the *embodied* soul, one would hardly contemplate it arising at the level of pure soul. So the 'fourths and fifths' must, I think, be regarded as lower levels of being than pure soul, and this in turn would entail that Speusippus is not counting the One and

---

[57] We must recall once again, in this connection, that Speusippus identified the Paradigm of the *Timaeus* with the Decad (Fr. 28 Tarán).

[58] It may be that Speusippus himself had not much to say about the derivation of the lower, physical levels of reality. So, at least, Theophrastus alleges at *Met.* 6^b5–6, in the passage mentioned above (Ch. 1, p. 21), where Speusippus is assimilated to those Platonists who 'go to a certain point and then stop' in their exposition of the development of all things from the first principles.

Multiplicity themselves among the levels of being—a somewhat paradoxical, but not entirely surprising conclusion, in light of his view of the One as 'not even yet a being' and, as a principle, 'not being such as are the things of which it is a principle'.[59]

Soul, then, may be taken as occupying the third rank in Speusippus' universe. What can we take the 'fourths and fifths' to be? They must be bodies of some sort, since they are composites of elements, so there is no question of anything like prime matter being regarded as a level of being, any more than is the One. This would not in any case be coherent with Speusippus' doctrine, since he identifies a 'material' principle at every level of being, and, as I have suggested above, has no use for Aristotelian-style matter, 'prime' or otherwise. Nor, I think, can we see here a distinction between the heavenly and sublunar levels of being, since one could hardly describe the heavenly bodies as being composed of 'the lowest elements'. On the whole, I would suggest that the distinction here being made is between animate and inanimate physical beings, both of which are so composed, but the former of which are informed by soul, while the latter are informed merely by a lower offshoot of soul which could be termed a principle of cohesion—something like an ancestor of the Stoic *hexis*. Only at these levels do badness and ugliness manifest themselves, as deviations from nature, and instances of the imperfect dominance of matter by form.

If this is so, it presents an attitude to evil in accord with the doctrine of the *Timaeus,* where the 'errant cause' inherent in the Receptacle ensures that nothing in the physical world can go quite right all the time. However, we are left with the problem of how the system that we have seen unfold in the first three levels is continued on into the fourth and fifth. I can only suggest that Soul, as formal principle, unites with Multiplicity once again to produce the class of individual embodied souls, and also a lower formal principle— 'Nature' (*physis*), as Plotinus would later term it—which is a kind of

---

[59] An indication in favour of this is that at p. 17, 25–6, the matter proper to numbers is referred to as 'first', and that proper to lines, planes, and solids is denominated 'second'. The original Multiplicity, therefore, although being itself described as 'a sort of moist and pliable matter' (p. 15, 12–13), is not being counted in this calculation.

lower soul, and this in turn, uniting with Multiplicity, produces, finally, the inanimate creation.[60]

I produce this scenario simply in an effort to grant coherence to the system which we find presented in *DCMS* 4, but since Aristotle does not anywhere in his writings dignify this level of the Speusippan universe with even a mention, there is not much to go on.

Some further light is thrown on Speusippus' metaphysical scheme by a curious little notice preserved in Proclus' *Commentary on the Parmenides* (VII, pp. 38, 32–40, 7 Klibansky).[61] Let us look at this *testimonium* in its context:

For if the first One participated in Being in some way, although it is higher than Being and produces it, it would be a one which took over the mode of reality which belongs to Being. But it is not *a* one, and is the cause not just of Being but of everything, though of Being before the rest. And if everything must participate in its cause, there must be a 'one' other than the simply One, in which Being participates; and this 'one' is the principle of beings. This is also how Speusippus understands the situation (presenting his views as the doctrines of the ancients).[62] What does he say?

'For they held that the One is higher than Being and is the source of Being; and they delivered it even from the status of a principle. For they held that, given the One, in itself, conceived as separated and alone without other things,[63] with no additional

---

[60] Some light may conceivably be thrown on this by a rather baffling report in Damascius' *Commentary on the Phaedo* (p. 177, 1–7 = Fr. 55 Tarán) that Speusippus and Xenocrates postulate immortality also for the irrational soul (*alogia*). What this could mean, as far as concerns Speusippus, is merely that he postulated a distinct level of irrational soul as a component of his universe.

[61] This is preserved, unfortunately, only in William of Moerbeke's Latin translation, but William is a very literal translator, so the original Greek terminology is always discernible. It is certainly curious that Proclus should at this stage suddenly quote Speusippus by name, having strenuously eschewed reference to any of his predecessors throughout the previous extent of the commentary, but he does refer by name to Xenocrates back at p. 888, 36 Cousin, and that renders the reference to Speusippus here a little less odd.

[62] That is to say, the Pythagoreans. This is interesting testimony to what seems to have been a characteristic feature of Speusippus' presentation of his doctrines (on which more below, p. 53), a concern to link them with the teachings of Pythagoras—as interpreted by him.

[63] This phrase may actually be an intentional reminiscence of *Parm.* 143^{a}6–8: 'Now take just this "One" which we are saying has being, and conceive it just by itself alone,

element, nothing else would come into existence. And so they introduced the Indefinite Dyad as the principle of beings.'

So he too testifies that this was the opinion of the ancients about the One: it is snatched up[64] beyond existence, and next after it comes the Indefinite Dyad. Here too, then, Plato proves this One to be beyond the existent and beyond the unity that is in the existent and beyond the whole One Being.

This passage is of interest, not just for Speusippus' doctrine of the role of the Indefinite Dyad, or Multiplicity, in generating the other levels of the universe, but also, perhaps, for a suggestion that it might provide as to how Speusippus may have interpreted the second part of Plato's *Parmenides,* and specifically the relation between the first and second hypotheses. The possibility that an 'ontological' (as opposed to a logical) interpretation of the hypotheses of the *Parmenides* might go back all the way to the Old Academy, and specifically to Speusippus, instead of arising in Neopythagorean circles some time in the late first century AD,[65] is a dangerously radical one, but I think that we must entertain it as a possibility in the light of this passage.[66]

We must ask ourselves, after all, why Speusippus should be brought into this discussion by Proclus at all. What relevance has the Indefinite Dyad to the 'one' of the second hypothesis? A possible explanation is that Proclus found in some source to which he had access (possibly the commentary of Porphyry or of Iamblichus on the same dialogue) a reference to Speusippus' doctrine of first principles arising from his exegesis of the first two hypotheses of the *Parmenides.* The scenario would be the following: the 'one' of the first hypothesis is indeed so hedged about by negativities as to be, by itself, incapable of generating anything further. In the second hypothesis, on the other hand, we find a process set out in which a 'one' undergoes a process of self-division, initially into 'one' and

apart from the being which we say it has'—which would strengthen, in my view, the possibility that Speusippus has indeed got the second hypothesis in mind here.

[64] This is Chaldaean terminology (cf. *Or. Chald.* Fr. 3, 1 Des Places), introduced by Proclus, not to be imputed to Speusippus.

[65] As is the conclusion come to by Dodds (1928).

[66] I am indebted here to the bold speculations of Halfwassen (1993).

'being', which generates, first, such basic categories as 'sameness' and 'otherness', and then the whole realm of numbers (cf. especially 143A–144A). The passage is worth quoting:

> Now suppose we take a selection of these terms, say 'being' and 'different', or 'being' and 'one', or 'one' and 'different'; in each case we are selecting a pair which may be spoken of as 'both'. I mean: we can speak of 'being', and again of 'one'. We have thus named each member of a pair. And when I say 'being and one' or 'being and different' or 'different and one', and so on in every possible combination, I am in each case speaking of 'both'. And a pair that can properly be called 'both' must be *two*. And if a pair of things are two, each of them must be *one*.
>
> This applies to our terms: since each set forms a couple, each term must be one. And if so, then, when any one is added to any pair, the sum will be *three*. And three is odd, two even. Now if there are two, there must also be *twice times*, if three, *three times*, since two is twice times one and three is three times one. And if there are two and twice times, three and three times, there must be *twice times two* and *three times three*. And, if there are three which occur twice and two which occur three times, there must be *twice times three* and *three times two*. Thus there will be even multiples of even sets, odd multiples of odd sets, odd multiples of even sets, and even multiples of odd sets. That being so, *there is no number left, which must not necessarily be*.
>
> Therefore, if a one is, there must also be number.   (trans. Cornford)

One may surely see in this passage the derivation of the set of natural numbers from the action of the Dyad on the One. I would suggest, then, that Speusippus (whether or not based on authorization from his uncle I forbear to speculate) interpreted the subject of the second hypothesis of the *Parmenides* as being, not the Indefinite Dyad as such, but rather the portrayal of the results of the action of the Indefinite Dyad on the original One.[67] The role of the Dyad is to initiate a process of 'splitting', by which, initially, unity is distinguished from being, and, then, by the adducing of the principles of

---

[67] In fact, Plotinus' later identification of the subject of the second hypothesis as Intellect (in his system) can be viewed simply as a variation of this, since Plotinus' *Nous* can under a certain aspect be viewed as the Indefinite Dyad; cf. in particular *Enn.* V 1, 5, where *Nous* is characterized not only as the Indefinite Dyad, but even as Speusippus' particular term, Multiplicity—and that in the context of identifying a subject for the second hypothesis.

'sameness' and 'otherness', there is generated the whole system of numbers. What ontological values, if any, Speusippus may have assigned to the remaining hypotheses we can have no real idea, but, since he seems to postulate a five-level universe (if we may draw this conclusion from the mention of the 'fourths and fifths' in *DCMS* 4), one might hazard a guess that he was prepared to identify the first five hypotheses (taking 155E–157E as the third, as was done by all later ancient Platonists) with the five levels, or at least basic features, taking these as: (1) the One by itself; (2) Multiplicity, acting on the One to generate the whole mathematical realm, figures as well as numbers; (3) Soul; (4) animate beings; (5) inanimate beings. This would imply that the last four hypotheses produce purely negative conclusions, as is implied by their format. But we are no doubt straying too far into the realm of pure speculation here. We do not even know, after all, how Plotinus identified the hypotheses after the first three; and yet he certainly assigned a value at least to those.

At any rate, we seem here to catch a glimpse of how Speusippus envisaged at least the initial cosmogonic process getting under way. Let us turn now, finally, by way of rounding off the examination of his metaphysics, to his treatise *On Pythagorean Numbers*,[68] for the light that it might cast both on his metaphysical scheme in general, and on his theory of mathematics in particular.

The form in which what we have of this treatise is preserved, as mentioned above, is rather troublesome. The *Theologoumena Arithmetikēs* is an anonymous work,[69] of the late antique or possibly

[68] One might speculate as to the true significance of this title, especially as one of the topics dealt with was the five Platonic figures of the *Timaeus,* which are not, properly speaking, numbers. It would seem that Speusippus is concerned to father his own doctrines and those of Plato on 'the Pythagoreans'. This, I would suggest, is one, at least, of the roots of the phenomenon termed 'Neopythagoreanism' (of which more below).

[69] There is no evidence in the manuscript tradition to connect the work with Iamblichus. The tentative identification was based on a promise which Iamblichus gives at the end of his commentary on Nicomachus' *Introduction to Arithmetic* (p. 125, 15 ff. Pistelli) of a more comprehensive treatment of the philosophy of arithmetic, but this work is certainly not it. On the other hand, the work as we have it is largely made up of excerpts from Nicomachus and Anatolius, who was one of Iamblichus' teachers, so that there is an outside chance that it may represent an Iamblichean work in an unfinished form (Iamblichus is not accustomed to quote his authorities by name in the finished volumes of his Pythagorean sequence).

early Byzantine period, largely made up of a series of extracts from arithmological works by Nicomachus of Gerasa and Anatolius of Laodicea. The extract from Speusippus occurs in the course of a passage apparently borrowed from Nicomachus,[70] which gives it a provenance in Neopythagorean circles of the second century AD, precisely the milieu in which, if anywhere, we might expect to find some surviving acquaintance, however minimal, with Speusippus' work. Nicomachus (if it is he) first gives a summary in his own words of the first half of the work—which he describes (a trifle patronizingly, perhaps!) as a 'well-turned' or 'subtle little book' (*biblidion glaphyron,* p. 82, 13–14[71])—and then presents an extract from the second part, which, he tells us, was exclusively concerned with the Decad, which Speusippus regarded as the summit of all number.

On his account, the first half of the book comprised the following:[72] 'In the first half of the book, he very elegantly expounds linear numbers, polygonal and all sorts of plane numbers,[73] solid numbers, and the five figures which are assigned to the elements of the universe, discussing both their individual attributes and their shared features, and their analogousness and correspondence.'

The item of chief interest here is the five regular solids. It is not at all clear from this whether Speusippus is remaining true to Plato in the *Timaeus* (47E–57C) in assigning the fifth regular solid, the

---

[70] Nicomachus is, admittedly, not explicitly identified here as the author, but since the second part of the entry on the Decad is identified as *Anatoliou,* it seems not improbable. There are many details of language, however, that cannot be matched in the surviving works of Nicomachus, so it may have been worked over by a later hand.

[71] *Glaphyros,* we may note, is a favoured term of Nicomachus for characterizing such things as elegance in mathematical procedures, cf. *Introd. Ar.* I 16, 4; I 19, 8; I 23, 4; II 19, 4; II 23, 6 Hoche. On the other hand, the word is also used freely by Iamblichus in the same sense (ten times in the *In Nic.* alone), so this is less than decisive for identification of authorship.

[72] I make use, with some modifications, of the translation of Waterfield (1988)—the only translation of the whole work into any modern language.

[73] Tarán (1981: 263) argues, reasonably, that Speusippus, like Nicomachus after him, regarded triangular and pentagonal numbers as plane numbers, whereas Euclid (*Elem.* VII, Def. 17) makes a distinction between polygonal and plane numbers. For Speusippus, as we shall see, two is the first linear number, three, as triangle, the first plane number, and four, as pyramid, the first solid number, whereas for Euclid four is the first plane and eight the first solid.

dodecahedron, to 'the universe as a whole', or whether, like his colleagues Philippus of Opus and Xenocrates (though in their different ways)[74] he is postulating a fifth element, aether, to which to assign it. Tarán (1981: 265) tries to get round the problem by suggesting that this phrase 'may be a parenthetical remark of the author of the excerpt and need not represent anything in Speusippus' book at all,' but this is surely an unjustified assumption. On the whole, it seems most natural to conclude that Speusippus too postulated a fifth, celestial substance to answer to the dodecahedron, and, what is more, that he was prepared to attribute all this, quite anachronistically, to 'the Pythagoreans'.

The other problem is whether we are to take the last phrase, which speaks of individual attributes (*idiotēs*) and shared features (*koinotēs*), analogousness (*analogia*) and correspondence (*antakolouthia*),[75] as referring to the five regular solids (which would be more natural), or to the various types of number mentioned before them—or both. On the whole, it would seem most natural to take them as referring to both. After all, Speusippus could well have discussed such topics as the *idiotēs* of the triangles which make up the cube (cf. *Tim.* 55B–C), which render earth non-exchangeable with the other elements, as well as the analogies and correspondences between the various classes of numbers and the Platonic figures. We may assume, then, that every sort of property of and relationship between the numbers from one to nine, and the figures corresponding to them, were discussed in this part of the work.

The description of the contents continues as follows:

---

[74] Philippus (cf. p. 193 below), in the *Epinomis*, chooses, oddly, to insert aether between the celestial fire and air, whereas Xenocrates accepts it as the substance of the heavens.

[75] On *antakolouthia*, Tarán very pertinently remarks (1981: 268) that the more usual, later meaning 'reciprocal implication' (as in the case of the Stoic theory of the *antakolouthia* of the virtues) is not apposite here, since 'higher' entities, such as the monad, are not reciprocally implicated with 'lower' ones, such as the point, so that the meaning 'correspondence' (found also, perhaps significantly, used by Iamblichus, *In Nic.* p. 39, 1–2—though not, unfortunately, in what survives of Nicomachus himself) is what is needed.

Next, in the remaining half of the book, he goes straight on to deal with the Decad, which he shows to be the most natural (*physikōtatē*) and perfective (*telestikōtatē*) of existent things, because it is, in itself, and not based on our conceptions or because we postulate that it happens to be so, a sort of productive form (*eidos ti tekhnikon*) of the finished products (*telesmata*) in the world, and set before the god who created the universe as a completely perfect paradigm.

There are many interesting points here, both of terminology and of doctrine. As becomes progressively more obvious, what is being described here is the Paradigm of Plato's *Timaeus,* though in terms distinctive of Speusippus. But let us attend first to details of terminology. First of all, the adjective *physikōtatē* would seem to denote that the decad is the sum-total or quintessence of all natural things, while the rare adjective *telestikōtatē* indicates, as does *tekhnikon* below, that it is the agent responsible for bringing all things to realization.[76] As for the use of the rather loaded Platonic term *eidos,* it is not clear if it is to be taken in the fully technical sense of 'form', or simply in the sense of 'sort' or 'type', but I see no compelling reason not to take it in its technical sense. If so, however, we must observe that this *eidos* is given an active, demiurgic role in the universe, and thus the description of it as being 'set before the god who is the creator of the universe' must be taken as figurative language based on the *Timaeus,* which, as we know, Speusippus did not in any case take literally.

It is at first sight somewhat confusing, certainly, to find Speusippus making use of the machinery of creator god and paradigm, especially since he appears to wish to father all this doctrine on 'the Pythagoreans'. If anything, the demiurgic role in Speusippus' universe should, as I have suggested above, be fulfilled by the World-Soul, with the help of the psychic analogues of the content of the geometrical realm of existence. However, if we bear in mind that it

[76] *Telestikos* in this sense is actually attested only in the pseudo-Aristotelian *Physiognomonica* (813ᵃ4) and, interestingly, in the earlier part of this section of the *Theol. Ar.* (p. 81, 10), whereas *tekhnikos* in an active sense, characterizing a thing rather than a person, is more or less confined otherwise to the Stoic use of it to describe the creative divine fire (*pyr tekhnikon*)—other than the use of it to characterize the divine *nous* earlier in this treatise (p. 79, 5–8).

was Speusippus' understanding that Plato himself was speaking figuratively in the *Timaeus,* he may well have felt entitled to adopt this same figurative language for himself.

After all, it is highly unlikely that Speusippus, any more than Plato, would have wished to excise 'God' (*ho theos*) from his system; the only problem was to decide just where to situate him. On the whole, the evidence, such as it is, seems to favour the World-Soul as the most properly 'divine' element in the Speusippan universe (even as it appears to be, after all, in Book X of Plato's *Laws,* which would have been Plato's own last word on the subject). We have a snippet from Cicero's *De Natura Deorum* (I 13, 32 = Fr. 56a Tarán), admittedly from the recklessly polemical mouth of the Epicurean Velleius, which points in this direction. Having just disposed of Plato himself. Xenophon, and Antisthenes, he continues: 'Very similarly Speusippus, following his uncle Plato, and speaking of a certain force that governs all things, and is endowed with soul (*vim quandam dicens qua omnia regantur, eamque animalem*), does his best to root out the notion of deity from our minds altogether.' This *vis animalis* is most reasonably interpreted, I think, as being a garbled reference to the World-Soul, in which case the connection being made with Plato is not entirely unjustified, at least with reference to the *Laws.*

Another straw in the wind may be a doxographic reference from Aetius (*Placita* I 7, 20 Diels = Fr. 58 Tarán): 'Speusippus [declares God to be] Intellect, which is not identical with the One or the Good, but has a nature peculiar to itself (*idiophyēs*).' This distinguishes 'God' (and Intellect) from Speusippus' highest principle (inaccurately given also the Platonic title of 'the Good'), but it does not clearly identify it with any other level of Speusippus' universe. However, if we put two and two together, we may reflect that, in the *Timaeus* (the mythological trappings of which, as we recall, Speusippus would deconstruct) the Demiurge is at 47E clearly identified with *Nous,* and both at 30B and at 46E the principle is laid down (in a way very confusing for those who persist in taking the *Timaeus* literally) that '*nous* cannot be present to anything without soul', or 'the one and only existent thing which has the property of acquiring *nous* is soul'. So it would seem very probable that 'God' is to be identified with the

World-Soul in its rational, demiurgic aspect—and it is this that contemplates the Decad, which is in turn best seen as the sum-total of the realm of Number, reproduced analogically, first as the realm of Figure, and then, with the principle of motion added, as the contents of Soul itself.

The actual verbatim quotation from Speusippus, while very good to have, does not actually advance our knowledge of his doctrine very significantly. In it, Speusippus is concerned to exhibit the perfection of the Decad in as many ways as he can, and this becomes an exercise in arithmology rather than mathematical theory in any modern sense. However, he does in the process illustrate what he means by *analogia* and *antakolouthia* as between the first four numbers and the geometrical figures corresponding to them, at one point (p. 84, 11–12) describing the point, line, triangle, and pyramid as 'primary and first principles of the classes of entity proper to each' (*prōta kai arkhai tōn kath' hekasta homogenōn*)—an important reminder of how Speusippus viewed the role of these primary figures. Strictly speaking, the point must be regarded as the first principle of the whole geometrical realm, even as the monad is of the realm of number, but plainly all four basic figures have an archetypal role, analogous to that of the first four numbers (the *tetraktys*) in the realm above.

Ethics

We have now surveyed, as sympathetically as we can, what can be known or conjectured of the structure of Speusippus' universe. From metaphysics, or 'physics', let us now turn to ethics. Once again, the evidence is fairly exiguous, and once again, we have to contend with tendentious testimony from Aristotle.

The basic text on Speusippus' ethical doctrine is a passage of Clement of Alexandria's *Stromateis*,[77] which we may reasonably quote in full, since we have little enough else to go on in reconstructing his position:

---

[77] II 133, 4 = Fr. 77 Tarán.

Speusippus, the nephew of Plato, declares that happiness (*eudaimonia*) is a perfect state in the area of what is natural, or the state of [possession of][78] goods, which is a state for which all men have a [natural] impulse, while the good aim at freedom from disturbance (*aokhlēsia*). It would be the virtues that are creative of happiness.

We have here a very summary (but, we hope, basically accurate) sketch of Speusippus' doctrine. He recognizes that men in general strive for happiness, but seems to introduce as a qualification of this that the good aim at 'freedom from disturbance'. There must be some ellipse, though, here, I think, arising from Clement's compression of his source. The state (*katastasis*) for which all men have a natural impulse may be *eudaimonia,* but Speusippus may well have gone on to say that most men believe, foolishly, that this lies in the acquisition and enjoyment of sources of pleasure, while only the wise understand that it really resides in attaining 'freedom from disturbance'. In that case, Speusippus would grant this much to the proponents of hedonism (such as Aristippus, founder of the Cyrenaic school, or his own colleague Eudoxus of Cnidos), that pleasure is indeed a natural object of striving for all living creatures, but he would deny that this proves what it is claimed to prove: that pleasure is the good for man. Speusippus wishes to maintain that for man, as a rational being, pleasure as an end must be transcended, with the aid of dialectic, and supplanted by a rational striving for *aokhlēsia*.

Speusippus appears to have used a number of arguments to support his position (which seems to have been developed in opposition to that of his colleague Eudoxus),[79] one of which in particular

---

[78] This represents a rather waffling attempt to render what seems to be a variation between two senses of *hexis* here, 'state' and 'possession'. It may seem hardly credible that Clement should use the same word in two different senses in the space of one line, but the ambiguity may be more apparent in English than in Greek.

[79] His position was no doubt set out primarily in his treatise *On Pleasure,* perhaps in response to Eudoxus' exposition of his doctrine; but his dialogue *Aristippus,* as I have suggested earlier, very probably also dealt with the same theme, this time featuring Socrates' disciple Aristippus, perhaps in conversation with Socrates. However, here too Eudoxus would no doubt have been the real aim of his criticism. As will emerge, I see the *Philebus* as Plato's ironic commentary and judgement on this ongoing dispute between two of his most distinguished followers. There is no reason to assume that the views of either of these men were published later than the composition of the *Philebus*.

comes in for trenchant criticism from Aristotle.[80] Speusippus wished to argue that, just because pain is admittedly an evil, it does not follow that pleasure, as its opposite, is a good, since both may be evils, opposed (as extremes) to some third thing (sc. a mean between them), which is a good—even as the greater may be opposed both to the less and to the equal. Aristotle cannot very well object to this argument as such, since it is integral to his own doctrine of virtue as a mean between extremes, but he tries to pick holes in it on the specific ground that, if something is an evil, it is to be avoided (*pheukton*), and men do not in fact seek to avoid pleasure—quite the contrary—while they do seek to avoid pain.

This is not, however, an argument which Speusippus need feel defeated by. His response could well be that pleasure is indeed a thing to be avoided, even though men in general do not recognize this. What men are seeking is in fact happiness, and they wrongly imagine this to be attainable through pleasure, or even to consist in pleasure. What all too few of them realize, but which all *should* recognize, is that the state which constitutes true happiness is that in which the soul has reached the perfect balance between pleasure and pain, which is attained by the scientific application of limit (*peras*) to the unlimited spectrum of more and less which runs from extreme pain to extreme pleasure, either condition constituting a grave disturbance of the organism, and of the soul which presides over it. It is this median state which Speusippus denominates 'freedom from disturbance' (*aokhlēsia*)—and which, it could be argued, such otherwise opposed later philosophers as Zeno and Epicurus both recognized as an ideal as well, Zeno with his concept of 'joy' (*khara*), as opposed to 'pleasure', and Epicurus with his concept of 'katastematic', as opposed to 'kinetic', pleasure.

To a certain extent, this whole argument might seem to turn on a semantic quibble as to what constitutes pleasure, but this is not necessarily the case. Speusippus would not wish to deny, I think, that his

---

After all, by the generally agreed date of the dialogue (*c.*355 BC), Speusippus was already in his fifties, and Eudoxus (born *c.*390) had probably already died, in his mid-thirties.

[80] At *EN* VII 14, 1153^b1–7 (= Fr. 80 Tarán), and X 2, 1173^a5–28 (= Fr. 81 Tarán).

preferred state of *aokhlēsia* is in some sense pleasant; his objection to 'pleasure', in its usual connotation in Greek, is rather that it essentially describes a *process,* and an open-ended, disorderly one at that, while what he is aiming at, and recommending, is a *steady state* (*hexis*). He is to some extent, perhaps, constricted by a lack of suitable terminology, and this leads him to fasten on this rather negative-sounding term for his ideal state, though without, I am sure, intending anything merely negative. Either of the later terminological distinctions mentioned above, Stoic or Epicurean, would have pleased him, I believe, if they had been brought to his attention.[81]

This brings us to a very vexed issue, the identity of 'the enemies of Philebus' in *Phlb.* 44A–D. A great many scholars have taken up positions on this question, many in favour of the identification with Speusippus, notably Wilamowitz,[82] A. E. Taylor,[83] I. Düring,[84] H.-J. Krämer,[85] and most recently Malcolm Schofield;[86] on the other hand, Leonardo Tarán, in his introduction to the fragments,[87] proposes to dismiss the identification as based on misunderstandings and inadequate evidence. He begins, however, with what seems to me to be a misconception of his own:

Because of his extreme anti-hedonism, several scholars have ascribed to Speusippus the doctrine espoused by Philebus' enemies in Plato's homonymous dialogue (44B–D), according to which pleasure is merely the cessation

---

[81] It is interesting, however, that, in the *Philebus,* Plato makes use of the verb *khairein* repeatedly (five times between 43^{d}3 and 44^{a}5, together with *kharmonai* once, at 43^{d}7), when presenting the position of the 'ill-conditioned', or 'hard-to-please ones' (*hoi dyskhereis*), whom Schofield (1971), has given good grounds for identifying with Speusippus.

[82] (1919: 2: 272–3).

[83] (1928: 455–6), and (1937: 409–10, 423, with n. 1).   [84] (1966: 457, n. 157).

[85] (1971: 205–9, with n. 88).   [86] See above, n. 43.

[87] Tarán (1981: 78–85). August Diès, in his Budé edition of the dialogue (pp. lvii–lxii), also rejects it, but for reasons which Tarán rightly dismisses ('not consistent with what we know of Speusippus' character from the sources'). Hackforth too (1945: 87–8) finds it impossible to reconcile the position of the *dyskhereis* with what he feels he knows of Speusippus' doctrine, and opts cautiously for Grote's suggestion that they were 'Pythagorizing friends' of Plato. But, as I shall argue, he was wrong to make an absolute distinction between the assertion of the *dyskhereis* that pleasures are nothing but escapes from pain and the belief of Speusippus that pleasure is real, but an evil.

of pain. This conception of pleasure as *something purely negative*[88] can hardly have been part of Speusippus' doctrine, however, since for him the neutral state between pleasure and pain coincides with the good. This neutral state he must have identified with the freedom from disturbance (*aokhlēsia*) which for him is the necessary condition of virtue and happiness. Hence, according to Speusippus the virtuous man must free himself from both pain and pleasure; and if pleasure were nothing but the cessation of pain, he would not have considered it an evil, nor would he have thought that the virtuous man must avoid it as such.

It seems to me that Tarán's mistake here is to take Plato too literally, even as he frequently seems to me to take Aristotle too literally in his attacks on Speusippus.[89] There is certainly nothing *negative* about Speusippus' doctrine on pleasure, but that does not mean that his uncle's satirical presentation of it might not seek to present it as negative—even as he is doubtless distorting in various ways the hedonist arguments of Eudoxus.

The dispute between Speusippus and Plato, after all, might be viewed as at least partly a semantic one. The mere cessation of pain could, certainly, be presented as a type of pleasure; but it need not be, and Speusippus chose not to present it as such. He wishes to reserve the term 'pleasure' to describe one of the equally reprehensible extremes which flank his ideal state, whereas Plato, it would seem, wishes to extend the notion of pleasure to take in also the state which Speusippus sees as transcending both pleasure and pain, and even to give it the title of 'true' or 'pure' pleasure.[90]

[88] My italics.

[89] As a notable instance of this one might take his interpretation of Aristotle's criticism of Speusippus at *Met.* N 4, $1092^{a}11$–17 (= Fr. 43 Tarán), discussed above, pp. 42–3. Another example is his treatment of Theophrastus' polemical criticism of Speusippus (*Met.* $11^{a}18$–26 = Fr. 83 Tarán) for limiting the good to a little patch in the middle, with vast stretches of evil on either side of it, which is a malicious conflation of his doctrine that 'good' only arises at the level of soul (cf. above, p. 53), the One not being properly describable as 'good', with his ethical doctrine of the good lying between the twin evils of pain and pleasure. Tarán takes this far too seriously (1981: 444–9).

[90] Interestingly enough, in Book VII of the *Laws* (792C–D), somewhat later than the *Philebus* (but not much), Plato is quite prepared to propound a median state between pleasure and pain, which he terms 'benignity' (*to hileōn*—a word normally used more of gods than men), and declares to be 'the very condition (*diathesis*) of God himself'. This rather Buddha-like state is very like what I conceive Speusippus to be envisaging.

This would not be the only area, we may note, in which Speusippus ventures to oppose what he feels to be a looseness in terminology on his uncle's part. On the other hand, he himself was left with a problem of terminology. It is unfortunate that Speusippus felt constrained to employ a negative term, *aokhlēsia,* to describe his ideal state, instead of, perhaps, the term *to hileōn* that Plato himself comes up with in *Laws* VII,[91] or the later Stoic term *khara,* but that does not mean that he intended anything negative by it. Indeed, he undoubtedly wished to claim that this state was productive of profound satisfaction, not to say joy. He may, however, for want of a better adjective, have been constrained to describe it as *hēdy,* 'pleasant', though denying that it involved any form of *hēdonē,* and this gives Plato the chance to score a point off him, which he does not fail to take.[92]

Let us now, in this connection, take a close look at a crucial passage of the *Philebus,* and see if we can divine just what sort of position is being criticized there. We may begin at 43C. Socrates has just secured Protarchus' agreement that not all changes in our constitution produce pleasure or pain, but only fairly considerable ones. He continues (43c8–d10):[93]

SOCR.: In that case, the form of life I mentioned just now would become a possibility again.

PROT.: What one is that?

SOCR.: The one we said would be without distress or enjoyments (*kharmonai*).

PROT.: Certainly it would.

SOCR.: To sum up, then, let us posit three forms of life, one of pleasure, one of distress, and one of neither. What would you say on the subject?

PROT.: Just what you have said, that there are these three lives.

---

[91] Cf. n. 90 above.

[92] An interesting reflection of how difficult it is to avoid using parts of *hēdys* when one is in search of a positive value word may be seen at *Phlb.* 66A—where indeed Plato may be making some linguistic play with this fact, as is suggested by Diès in the introduction to his Budé edition (p. lxxxix).

[93] I borrow here the the translation of Gosling (1975).

Speusippus

SOCR.: Now not being in distress would hardly be the same as enjoying one-self (*khairein*), would it?

PROT.: Of course not.

SOCR.: So when you hear people say that the pleasantest (*hēdiston*) thing is to live all one's life free from distress, what do you think they are saying?

PROT.: They seem to be saying that not being in distress is pleasant (*hēdy*).

Let us pause here for a moment. Somebody, or some class of person, is being accused of claiming that the life without pain is the most pleasant (*hēdy*) of all. If this is Speusippus, then one would like to think that he is being deliberately misrepresented; otherwise he is being notably careless in his language. Speusippus does, admittedly, have a problem, as I have suggested above. He needs some positive value word to characterize his ideal psychic state, but he must be wary of employing words of the same root as *hēdonē* for that purpose. The fact, however, that Plato also uses *khairein* repeatedly[94] in this passage to describe this state might indicate that this was in fact the preferred term of the supporters of this position, who would thus be anticipating the Stoics in their technical use of this term. In that case, though, one might ask why they did not go all the way, and employ an adjective derived from the same root to characterize the preferred state, instead of falling back on *hēdys*. All one can suggest is that the available adjective, *khartos,* is somewhat rare and poetical,[95] and *hēdys* is much readier to hand.

Let us continue, however (43^{e}1–44^{b}3):

SOCR.: Take any three things now, say one gold, one silver, one neither, just to have fine names.

PROT.: All right.

SOCR.: Could the one that is neither possibly become either gold or silver?'

PROT.: How on earth could it?'

SOCR.: Similarly, it would be a mistake for anyone to believe and therefore

---

[94] As remarked above, n. 82.

[95] Though in fact Plato does make use of it once, as a synonym of *hēdys* (along with *terpnos*) at *Protagoras* 358A.

70

to say that the midway life was either pleasant (*hēdys*) or distressing—at least if we are to be strict.

PROT.: How could it be?

SOCR.: Yet we find people who say and believe these things.

PROT.: Certainly.

SOCR.: Do they then think that they are enjoying themselves (*khairein*) on the occasions when they are not in a distressed condition?

PROT.: That's what they say, at any rate.

SOCR.: So they believe they are then enjoying themselves (*khairein*), or they wouldn't say it.

PROT.: Certainly.

SOCR.: Yet they are making a false judgement about enjoyment (*khairein*)— if, that is, enjoyment and lack of distress are two quite different things.

PROT.: But they turned out to be quite different things.

SOCR.: We have a choice, then. We could hold, as we did just now, that there are three alternatives, or that there are only two, first distress, which we could say was an evil for men, and secondly release from distress, which, being no more nor less than good,[96] we should call pleasurable (*hēdy*).

I think we can see various instances of unfair argumentation in this passage. First of all, to produce gold and silver as examples of two extremes between which there is to be a third thing which is neither of them seems profoundly tendentious. Gold and silver are not, after all, *opposites*; and they are selected in such a way that any other item in the same class (presumably, of metals) is going to be worse than they are—unless, perhaps, we are to think of the fabled orichalc!

Further, Socrates is attempting to convict the protagonists of this position of wishing both to condemn pleasure and to commend their chosen intermediate state as something *pleasant*, which it would certainly be inconsistent for them to do, without allowing that they may

---

[96] 'My rendering of *auto touto agathon on*, which seems to be rather under-translated by Gosling (1975) as 'being itself good'.

have wished to claim that their intermediate state was characterized by a condition of mind far superior to pleasure, precisely as being the result of the imposition of limit and order on the disorderly and unlimited spectrum of sensations of which pleasure is, so to speak, one 'wing'. They may have had difficulty in finding an adjective to describe this (and so may have incautiously fallen back on *hēdys*), but it rather looks, on Plato's own evidence, as if their preferred verb/noun for it may in fact have been *khairein/khara*.

This, after all, would by no means be the only time that Plato's Socrates was less than fair to a position of which he disapproved. But let us press on. Socrates now (44^b4-^c2) gets round to identifying a group which he describes as 'the enemies of Philebus', who are characterized as being 'experts in natural science' (*deinoi ta peri physin*) and being afflicted with a certain 'crankiness arising from a not ignoble nature' (*tis dyskhereia physeōs ouk agennous*):[97]

PROT.: Why are we raising this question at this stage, Socrates? I don't see what you are getting at.

SOCR.: Don't you know the real enemies of Philebus here?

PROT.: Who are you referring to?

SOCR.: People with a considerable reputation as experts in the science of nature,[98] who deny any real existence to pleasures.[99]

PROT.: How do they do that?

Socr.: According to them, what Philebus and his friends call pleasures are nothing but cases of release from distress (*lypōn apophygai*).

---

[97] I borrow the translation of Gosling here, with some amendments.

[98] The real meaning of the appellation *deinoi legomenoi ta kata physin* is a troublesome question. It does not necessarily refer, as it is often taken to do, to expertise in, or enthusiasm for, what we would call 'natural science', though it may include that. It can just as well refer to what we would term 'the human sciences', including ethics. I take it, though, to be a good-naturedly teasing reference to Speusippus' well-known concern to give a comprehensive account of the relations of all branches of knowledge to one another, attested by Diogenes Laertius (IV 2; see below, pp. 79–82).

[99] There is some problem here as to what the Greek, *to parapan hēdonas ou phasin einai*, really means. Gosling translates 'who completely deny that they [sc. the pleasures arising from the cessation of distress] are pleasures'. This would admittedly make better sense, but it is not the most natural meaning of the Greek, I think. I give a translation compatible, I hope, both with the Greek and with what I take to be its real meaning.

The question to be addressed is whether the position stated here is in any way compatible with what appears from our other evidence to have been Speusippus' doctrine. On the face of it, one would be compelled to doubt it. After all, Speusippus is not attested as having denied the *existence* of pleasures; rather, he declared that they were just as much of an evil as pains, which would seem to recognize their existence at least to the same extent.

But then, one asks oneself, could anyone in his right mind have denied the existence of pleasures? Surely what we have here from Plato is the conclusion of a polemical argument against pleasure. The argument, I submit, would go something like this (and a complementary argument could in theory be employed against the existence of pain, except that there was no need to wean people from an irrational attachment to pain!). Any pleasure you care to name, if you analyse it, can be discerned as the result of freeing the organism from some form of distress or other, resulting from a disequilibrium in one direction. What is called 'pleasure' is simply the tilting of the balance in the other direction. So pleasures do not have a substantial existence, in that their manifestation is always a by-product of the removal of pain. You do not experience a sensation of pleasure except in the context of the relief of some painful organic imbalance or other.[100]

Now this is a pretty tendentious argument, but at least it is not manifestly absurd, as an outright denial of the existence of pleasure would be; and I think that it is a position that Speusippus could have taken up, consistently with his known views. The great problem that it leaves him with—and this is where, perhaps, his 'crankiness' (*dyskhereia*) comes in—is that he is forced to deny that what Plato would wish to term 'pure pleasures' (51A ff.), such as those of smell or hearing, where there has been no previous distress, or indeed most pleasures of the mind, are to be described as pleasures at all.

But of course this is just what Speusippus wishes to deny, and it is

---

[100] We seem to get a version of this argument in the admittedly rather casual remark of Socrates at the beginning of the *Phaedo* (60B), as he sits up on his bed and rubs his legs after they have been released from the irons, that pain and pleasure seem in a way to be Siamese twins, 'joined together in one head'.

here that his semantic dispute with his uncle becomes acute. Plato, at *Phlb.* 52^{c}1–^{d}1, actually makes very much the distinction that Speusippus must have made, but he makes it between 'impure' and 'pure' pleasures, whereas Speusippus would have made it between 'pleasures', which he would regard as intrinsically unmeasured and disorderly, and sensations arising out of his ideal state of equilibrium:

> So now we have an orderly sorting out of the purified pleasures from what should be called unpurified cases. As a further point we ought to attribute to violent pleasures disorderliness (*ametria*), and to those that are not, orderliness (*emmetria*). Those that admit of great degrees and intensity, whether becoming such commonly or only rarely, we should put in the category mentioned earlier of that which is indeterminate (*to apeiron genos*) and which in varying degrees of more and less permeates both body and soul; the others we should put in the category of ordered things.

Socrates goes on (52^{d}5 ff.) to argue that the disorderly and indeterminate class of pleasures can properly be declared 'false', and only the ordered ones 'true', for very much the same reasons that 'the cranks' back in 44B–C were criticized for denying the substantial reality of pleasure. Even there, we may note, the position of the cranks is not absolutely rejected; they are rather treated, ironically, as 'inspired prophets' (*manteis,* 44^{c}5), who have grasped an intimation of the truth through a certain natural talent, but have not worked it out dialectically. This, it seems to me, is a very suitable form of put-down for Plato to use when dealing with a bumptious nephew. In fact, their two positions are not that far apart; it is just that Plato does not see the sense of denying the title of 'pleasure' to those states of the human organism which he has identified as 'pure' pleasures, whereas for Speusippus the essential distinction between these states and what he wants to designate 'pleasures' is precisely that they are *states,* and the others are *processes,* or motions, admitting of indefiniteness and of 'more and less'.

Plato's contention is that the position of the 'cranks', while doing them credit in a way, has not been properly thought out. It seems to me, on the other hand, that there is a certain amount to be said for it, even if it presents difficulties. After all, if we bear in mind Speusippus' Pythagoreanizing world-view (which is not, indeed, very different from that presented in the *Philebus*), it is important that, in the sphere of ethics, one postulates the existence of perfect states, representing the imposition of *peras* on the disorderly substratum of *apeiria,* and that it is such states that generate *eudaimonia.*[101] The problem of how to describe the by-products of such states, which may include such experiences as the enjoyment of the smell of roses, the sound of birdsong, or of a string quartet of Beethoven, as well as of philosophizing, is something that he may not have quite solved, though it seems possible, as we have seen, that he made some use of the verb *khairein* in this connection.

To complete our exegesis of *Phlb.* 44B–D, however: we may derive from it (or rather from its continuation, 44E–45D) a further polemical argument against pleasure which may well have been advanced by Speusippus. Socrates, at any rate, with his usual irony, thanks the 'cranks' warmly for supplying him with it.

The argument goes as follows. If we want to get a clear view of the nature of a given thing, we should look at it in its most extreme or unadulterated form. In the case of hardness, for example, we should examine the hardest things we can find, if we wish to acquire an accurate idea of what hardness is. In the case of pleasure, then, we look for the most extreme forms of pleasure, if we wish properly to comprehend the nature of pleasure. But then we are led to admit that people suffering from illness, either physical or mental—the argument glosses over the question whether all illnesses qualify in this regard, or only certain ones—experience more pleasure in more extreme forms (as a relief from their various pains or distresses) than healthy people. Thus it is argued that it is the most unbalanced natures that experience the most extreme pleasures. And so it is indicated (I hesitate to say *proved*) that pleasure is essentially connected with imbalance in the organism, and is thus the antithesis of a desirable state.

---

[101] We may note that one of the arguments that Aristotle, in *EN* X 2 (1173ª15–17) = Fr. 81a Tarán, represents Speusippus as making against pleasure being a good is that it is 'unbounded' (*aoriston*), while the good is bounded.

I see no reason not to accept that Plato is in fact borrowing this argument from Speusippus, and using it for his own purposes. He makes Socrates thank the 'cranks' for it, as I say. If anything, it brings home to us how close their positions really were. This does not, however, mean that Plato was any the less displeased with his nephew for taking up a position on his 'right', so to speak, on such a sensitive question as the status of pleasure. Mainly, though, he seems to have regarded this super-austerity of Speusippus as evidence of deficiency in logical rigour. The sensations of the virtuous and self-controlled have enough in common with those of the dissolute and intemperate to merit being given the same generic name. A more correct way of evaluating them is to make the distinction that he works out in the latter part of the dialogue between 'adulterated' and 'pure', 'false' and 'true' pleasures, rather than being left with a class of sensations for which no proper name at all had been developed. This, after all, is just the role that the 'heavenly tradition' set out in *Phlb.* 16–19 is meant to fulfil, making the correct distinctions within the previously vague and amorphous concept denominated 'pleasure'.

It may after all turn out, though, that Speusippus has the best of this argument. The Stoics were second to none in logical rigour, and they, it seems to me, sided in retrospect with Speusippus. The Stoic theory of *eupatheiai,* or 'equable states', after all, is precisely developed to provide a set of sensations, including pleasurable ones, which are appropriate to a wise man who is quite free from passions, and that is the sort of Pythagorean sage that Speusippus seems to be envisaging. For the Stoics, the experiences of the sage are not to be assimilated to those of the vulgar, despite superficial resemblances between them, and that is surely very much the position of Speusippus before them.

There is not much other evidence remaining as to the ethical position of Speusippus, but a passage of Plutarch, *On Common Conceptions, Against the Stoics* 1065A (= Fr. 79 Tarán), provides us with the information that Speusippus (and Xenocrates after him) accepted that such things as health and wealth were not 'indifferent' in the Stoic sense, but could be 'goods' (even though minor goods, compared to those of the soul) if properly employed.[102] We may reasonably conclude, I think, that both Speusippus and Xenocrates would have assented to Plato's views as expressed in *Laws* II 661A–C (cf. also V 728D–729A), to the effect that those things popularly regarded as goods, such as health, beauty, and wealth, are goods for the good man, but potentially great evils for the rest of mankind; and this presumably remained the official position of the Old Academy. Again, the difference with the Stoics is very largely a semantic one; once one recognizes, as did at least the later Stoics, that, among the 'indifferents', there are some to be 'preferred' and others to be 'dispreferred', one is very much back at the Old Academic position. But such terminological niceties are the very stuff of inter-school disputes.

Epistemology and Logic

Let us turn to look now at some aspects of Speusippus' epistemology, and then at what we know of his contributions to logic.

We may take our start from a report of Sextus Empiricus (*Adv. Math.* VII 145–6 = Fr. 75 Tarán) as to Speusippus' doctrine of the criterion of truth, or of knowledge.[103] This is sandwiched between a report of Plato's doctrine, and of that of Xenocrates (to which we will come in due course), and is most interesting. Its provenance I would discern (despite the characteristically sceptical strictures of Tarán 1981: 431–2) as being in all probability a work of Antiochus of Ascalon,[104] and this will colour the technical terminology employed, but there is little reason to doubt the basic accuracy of the

---

[102] Speusippus, as we have seen, composed a treatise *On Wealth* (as, indeed, did Xenocrates), in which he doubtless discussed its proper use.

[103] The origin of this formulation, *kritērion tēs alētheias,* is not clear. It is not to be found in Plato or Aristotle, but appears in the earliest Epicurean and Stoic sources. It is not likely, therefore, to have been used as a technical term by Speusippus.

[104] Certainly the 'Platonists' referred to by Sextus at VII 143, in the course of his account of Plato's doctrine, are post-Stoic, and concerned to present Plato's doctrine as the ancestor of the Stoic doctrine of the 'cognitive impression' (*kataleptikē phantasia*), which is precisely the concern of Antiochus. In fact, we find casual mentions of Antiochus, and of his chief doxographic work *Kanonika,* both at 162 and at 201, which is just the way in which compilers like Sextus allow us to know the identity of their sources.

account.[105] What we find is an account of what Speusippus terms 'cognitive sense-perception' (*epistēmonikē aisthēsis*), which is quite distinctive, and deserves some discussion. But first let us look at the passage in full:

Speusippus' view was that, since there are things which are sense-perceptible and others which are intelligible, of those that are intelligible the criterion is cognitive reason (*epistēmonikos logos*), while of sensible things it is cognitive sense-perception. And cognitive sense-perception he conceived to be that which participates in the truth which accords with reason. To take an example: the fingers of the flute-player or harper possess an artistic activity (*tekhnikē energeia*), which is, however, not brought to fruition primarily (*proēgoumenōs*)[106] through the fingers themselves, but is fully developed as a result of training under the co-operative guidance of reasoning (*logismos*); and the sense-perception of the musician, while it possesses an activity capable of grasping the harmonious and the non-harmonious, nevertheless is not self-produced (*autophyēs*) but is acquired by reason. Even so, cognitive sense-perception naturally derives from reason the cognitive experience which it shares, and which leads to the unerring discrimination (*aplanēs diagnōsis*) of its proper objects (*hypokeimena*).

We need to probe carefully the theory being developed here, particularly as regards the status being accorded to the rational cognition of the physical world, a topic with which Speusippus is plainly much concerned. If we think of the hands of the skilled pianist, for example, flashing across the keys, we can say that there is a purely physical facility in the fingers, built up by fairly mechanical practice, which is certainly necessary for the skill of the pianist to be realized (and which the onset of arthritis, say, would impede or destroy). This would presumably answer to the basic physical efficiency of the sense-organs in receiving their proper objects. But what makes the

---

[105] The preceding account of Plato does, admittedly, give a rather slanted account of his doctrine in the *Timaeus*, in the direction of upgrading the evidence of the senses, with the introduction of the Stoic concept of *enargeia*, which is not employed by Plato in the dialogue—though for the doctrine cf. the mention of 'firm and true opinions and beliefs' at 37B.

[106] It is worth noting that this comparatively rare word (otherwise earliest attested in Theophrastus, *De Igne* 14) turns up also at Iamblichus, *DCMS* 4, p. 18, 11 (quoted above, p. 54).

movement of the fingers purposeful and truly artistic is the *intellectual* power of the pianist, directing them in obedience to his conception of the *form* of the composition. Even so, our perception of the physical world, our discernment and identification of objects (*pragmata*), groups of objects, and situations within it, is a function, not of 'raw' *aisthēsis*, but rather of *logos* directing *aisthēsis*—that is to say, *epistēmonikē aisthēsis*.[107]

Not unconnected with this doctrine, I think, is Speusippus' remarkable claim that knowledge of any given physical object requires knowledge of its differentiae in respect of everything else. This doctrine is communicated to us, critically, by Aristotle at *An. Post.* 97ª6–22 (= Fr. 63 Tarán), but as usual he criticizes Speusippus from the perspective of his own philosophical system, not from that of Speusippus:

There is no necessity for someone practising definition and division to know the totality of existents. And yet some people declare that it is impossible to know the differentiae between each thing and the rest without knowing each thing severally. [The argument goes that] without knowledge of the differentiae it is not possible to know each thing; for if something is not differentiated[108] from something else, it is the same as that thing, and if it is differentiated from it, it is other than it.

First of all, this is false; for a thing is not 'other' in respect of every differentia. There are many differentiae, after all, which belong to things within the same species, but not essentially nor in themselves. And then, when one fastens on a pair of contraries and the differentia which distinguishes them, and assumes that everything falls on this side or that [of the dichotomy], and assumes that what is being sought is on one side or other, and that this is the object of one's knowledge, it makes no difference whether one knows or doesn't know how many other things the differentiae are predicated of. For it is obvious that if, proceeding along these lines, one comes to what is no longer distinguished by a differentia, one will then have the account of the essence (*logos tēs ousias*[109]).

---

[107] The mention of *aplanēs diagnōsis* seems to be a reference to the 'circle of the other' in the soul, as described in *Tim.* 37c, which, when 'moving in a straight course', causes 'opinions and beliefs which are firm and true'.

[108] The verb is simply *diapherei*, but to represent adequately the point being made, this more elaborate translation is required.

[109] That is, the Aristotelian term for what a definition is of.

Here Aristotle does seem to be on strong ground in his criticisms, but, once again, it is worthwhile, I think, to try to unravel what may have been Speusippus' motivation in making such a remarkable assertion.[110] First, I think, we must recognize that Speusippus' purposes in practising definition are significantly different from those of Aristotle. Aristotle has a biologist's interest in classifying objects in the physical world into their natural kinds; furthermore, for him it is the individual combination of form and matter that represents primary substance, and only essential differentiae are necessary to establish this. For Speusippus, the true realities are numbers and geometrical figures, and it is only these that are truly knowable. Physical essences he seems to have regarded as analogous to monads or points, being merely the focus of all the relations that make each of them different from everything else. When he declares that, to attain *knowledge* of any one of these entities, one would have to be able to give a full account of the relations (of both similarity and difference) in which it stands to every other physical object, it seems best to suppose that he is just stating an impractical ideal, to make clear why it is impossible in practice to have *epistēmē* of physical objects. In the case of the number seven, after all, or of the equilateral triangle, it is not difficult to enumerate the totality of relationships of similarity and difference in which it stands with other entities of its class;[111] but in the case of the average plant, animal, or other natural object the task is much more complex. Yet Speusippus is plainly not advancing this difficulty in order to argue for complete scepticism as regards the physical world. We know, in fact, that he was a most industrious classifier of natural kinds, author of two works on the subject, the *Homoia* ('Similarities'), in ten books, and *Divisions and Hypotheses in*

---

[110] Barnes (1975: 234–6), gives a good analysis of the form of Speusippus' argument, showing that Aristotle is unfair in making a distinction between 'essential' and 'inessential' differentiae. Speusippus, as he says, could have inserted the word 'essentially' after each occurrence of 'differ' in his argument, and still have maintained his point. Falcon (2000) seeks to argue that Speusippus is not liable to Aristotle's refutation because he did not practise the method of division; but this seems to me most improbable. His article, however, contains much of interest.

[111] Admittedly, the series of natural numbers is infinite, but the *sort* of relationships that seven, say, would have with all other numbers can be stated fairly easily.

relation to the Similarities, and (mainly thanks to Athenaeus) we have a number of brief reports of classifications that he made, chiefly in Book II of the *Homoia.*[112]

Aristotle plainly studied this work fairly closely, though mainly to disagree with it. He criticizes Speusippus (a) for employing a rigid dichotomic scheme in his divisions even when this is not suitable; (b) for using privative terms (such as 'wingless', 'bloodless') in the course of these dichotomies, since these cannot properly provide a positive characterization; and (c) for making inapposite distinctions between natural species on the basis of such non-essential features as habitat (as when he links water-birds with fish on the basis that both are 'water-animals', as opposed to 'land-animals', under which he included land-based birds).[113]

Speusippus' procedure, as I say, does seem on the evidence available to us to have been considerably less scientific than that of Aristotle, and the rigid practice of dichotomy does have obvious drawbacks, but we have to reflect, as I say, that Speusippus' purpose in engaging in this classificatory activity was probably very different from that of Aristotle. The actual title of his main work, *Homoia,* as well as what Aristotle tells us about his procedure, that he was enquiring in each case into 'in what respects a given thing is similar, and in what respects it is different' *(ti tauton kai ti heteron),*[114] gives us some indication, I think, as to what his real purpose may have been.[115] We may recall that, in the *Timaeus* (37A–C), where the func-

[112] On this feature of Speusippus' thought, Arthur Lovejoy, in the opening chapter of *The Great Chain of Being* (1936), in the course of his listing of characteristic 'philosophical' states of mind, makes this acute observation, which seems to me relevant to Speusippus (p. 10): 'Again, there is the organismic or flower-in-the-crannied-wall motive, the habit of assuming that, where you have a complex of one or another kind, no element in that complex can be understood, or can, indeed, be what it is, apart from its relations to all the other components of the system to which it belongs.' Speusippus is very much a 'flower-in-the-crannied-wall' man, I think.

[113] Cf. his extended critique in chs. 2 and 3 of Book I of *De partibus animalium,* 642^{b}5–644^{a}11 (=Fr. 67 Tarán).

[114] Cf. *Anal. Post.* II 13, 97^{a}6–22 (= Fr. 63a Tarán), together with the Anon. Comm. on *Anal. Post.* pp. 584, 17–585, 2 Wallies (= Fr. 63b), who adduces the testimony of Eudemus. Tarán's discussion on this topic is most useful (1981, 64–72, and comm. ad frr.).

[115] It is significant in this regard, I think, that Theophrastus, in his *Metaphysics* (6^{a}23 ff.), commends Speusippus' successor Xenocrates for the comprehensiveness of his

tion of the soul in cognizing the physical world (as well as the intelligible world) is being described, its elements of Identity and Difference are brought into play, and when its 'circle of otherness' (*ho tou thaterou kyklos*) is functioning correctly (*orthos ōn*), it conveys back accurate reports to the whole soul, and this results in 'opinions and beliefs that are firm and true' (*doxai kai pisteis bebaioi kai alētheis*). It seems to me that all of Speusippus' considerable efforts in the area of classification of similarities and differences had as their true purpose the purification of the soul, by helping its 'circle of otherness' to be *orthos,* and not the sort of scientific sorting-out of natural kinds which was so important to Aristotle; and his remark about the impossibility of ever arriving at a full enumeration of the *diaphorai* which distinguished any physical object from all others, which so incensed Aristotle, was simply a reassertion of what we are repeatedly reminded of by Timaeus in his account, that the study of the physical world can only ever be an *eikōs logos.*[116]

A similar issue concerning the relations between the cognition of the physical and intelligible worlds seems to arise out of a view of Speusippus', reported by Proclus in his *Commentary on the First Book of Euclid's Elements,*[117] on the distinction between a problem and a theorem, in connection with the theory of mathematics, and specifically of geometry. The basis of his complaint is that he takes the term *problēma* to connote 'the bringing into being of something not previously existing', whereas *theōrēma* is more proper to the study of objects which exist eternally. It is worth quoting the passage in full:

account of all levels of reality, whereas he makes no mention of Speusippus in this connection. This would seem to indicate that Theophrastus did not see Speusippus as being much interested in the classification of physical reality as such.

[116] It has been suggested, most acutely, by Cherniss (1944: 60 n. 50) that 'the determination of *tauton* and *heteron* as a means of division and its connection with the principle of *homoiotēs* were adopted by Speusippus from Plato', but with a necessary difference in significance 'consequent upon the absence of a doctrine of ideas'. I would go along with this, while not accepting that Speusippus totally abandoned the 'ideas', because I feel that his view of the relationship of physical individuals to the matrix of quasi-mathematical formulae which comprised the world of Forms for him called for taking individuals as constituted by a network of relationships of 'likeness' and 'unlikeness'.

[117] *Comm. in Eucl.* pp. 77, 15–78, 10 (= Fr. 72 Tarán). I borrow, with minor alterations, the translation of Morrow (1970: 63–4).

Again, the propositions that follow from the first principles he [sc. Euclid] divides into problems and theorems, the former including the construction of figures, the division of them into sections, subtractions from and additions to them, and in general the characters that result from such procedures, and the latter concerned with demonstrating inherent properties belonging to each figure. Just as the productive sciences have some theory in them, so the theoretical ones take on problems in a way analogous to production.

Some of the ancients, however, such as Speusippus and Amphinomus[118] and their followers, insisted on calling all propositions 'theorems', considering 'theorems' to be a more appropriate designation than 'problems' for the objects of the theoretical sciences, specifically because these sciences deal with eternal things. There is no coming to be among eternals, and hence a problem has no place here, proposing as it does to bring into being or to make something not previously existing—such as to construct an equilateral triangle, or to describe a square when a straight line is given, or to place a straight line through a given point. Thus it is better, according to them, to say that all these objects exist and that we look on our constructions of them not as making, but as understanding them, taking eternal things as if they were in the process of coming to be. Hence we can say that all propositions have a theoretical and not a practical import.

This position of Speusippus seems to have something of a polemical edge to it. After all, it is not at all clear that the term *problēma* must denote something that is being postulated as being brought into being. Plato, indeed, is quite prepared to use it in *Republic* VII (530B) to refer the theorems of geometry and mathematical astronomy. The truth seems to be, as Proclus lets us know just below, that Speusippus' contemporary Menaechmus, a pupil of Eudoxus, a distinguished mathematician and associate (at least) of the Academy, took the position that *all* mathematical enquiries may be described as *problēmata,* and that Speusippus is here indulging in some intra-school oneupmanship with a follower of his former rival—as well as once more 'correcting' his uncle.

Nevertheless, there is possibly a serious philosophical point behind this terminological squabble. As we have seen, Speusippus is

---

[118] We have no idea who Amphinomus was, but he is reasonably supposed by Morrow and Tarán to have been a contemporary or virtual contemporary of Speusippus, though whether himself a member of the Academy is uncertain.

insistent on the non-literal, non-temporal interpretation of the *Timaeus,* and in that connection his point is that the apparent description of temporal creation is to be regarded as analogous to the diagrams of the geometers, who appear to generate, say, a figure from a line, but only do this for sake of 'clarity of exposition'.[119] This would be the general principle of which that is a particular application.

Another significant passage from Proclus' commentary (p. 179, 12–22 = Fr. 73 Tarán) reports Speusippus making a distinction between our knowledge of principles (*arkhai*) and of those propositions which derive from them. First principles are characterized by simplicity (*haplotēs*), indemonstrability (*to anapodeikton*), and self-evidence (*to autopiston*),[120] and the mode of their comprehension is thus to be distinguished from that of what follows from them. Once again, the passage is worth quoting:

Principles must always be superior to their consequences in being simple, indemonstrable, and self-evident. In general, says Speusippus, in the hunt[121] for knowledge in which our understanding is engaged we put forward some things and prepare them for use in later enquiry without having made any elaborate excursion, and our mind has a clearer contact with them than sight has with visual objects; but others it is unable to grasp immediately and therefore advances on them step by step and endeavours to capture them by their consequences. For example, drawing a straight line from a point to a point is something our thought grasps as obvious and easy, for by following the uniform flowing of the point and by proceeding without deviation more to one side than to another, it reaches the other point.[122] Again, if one of the two ends of a straight line is stationary, the other end moving around it

---

[119] Aristotle, *De Caelo,* 279^{b}32 ff. (= Fr. 61 Tarán), where we are told by a scholiast ad loc. that he is referring to both Speusippus and Xenocrates.

[120] Of these epithets, only the third is of doubtfully classical provenance, being attested no earlier than Hero of Alexandria (2nd cent. BC), but in any case it is not to be supposed that Proclus had direct access to a work of Speusippus. His probable direct source for the history of mathematics is generally agreed to be Geminus (1st cent BC), or possibly Aristotle's pupil Eudemus.

[121] It is interesting that Speusippus should make use of the same metaphor as Plato, of the hunt (*thēra*), for the process of dialectical enquiry, cf. *Phd.* 66A; *Theaet.* 198A; *Polit.* 285D; *Phlb.* 65A.

[122] Presumably what Speusippus is here asserting is the immediate apprehensibility of the basic principle that a straight line is the shortest distance between two points.

describes a circle without difficulty.[123] But if we should wish to draw a one-turn spiral (*helix monostrophos*), we need a rather complicated device, for the spiral is generated by a complex of motions; and to construct an equilateral triangle will also require a special method for constructing a triangle. Geometrical intelligence will tell me that, if I think of a straight line one end of which is fixed and the other revolving about it, while a point is moving along it from the stationary end, I describe a monostrophic spiral; for when the end of the line which describes a circle has reached its starting point at the same time as the point completes its movement along the line, they coincide and make such a spiral. And again, if I describe two equal circles and join their point of intersection with the centres of the circles and draw a straight line from one centre to the other, I shall have an equilateral triangle. It is far from true, therefore, that these things can be done at first glance and by simple reflection; we should be content to follow the procedures by which the figures are constructed.

In what work Speusippus may have discussed this topic we cannot be certain, but the *Mathematikos* seems a good candidate. One can observe here a striking similarity in subject matter to the last chapter of Aristotle's *Posterior Analytics* (II 19), where Aristotle raises the question of how we can come to know first principles (*arkhai*), since they cannot be arrived at by demonstration (*apodeixis*), such as leads to scientific knowledge (*epistēmē*). Aristotle concludes that they can only be known by immediate intuition (*nous*). He doubtless had Speusippus' discussion in mind.

Lastly, in the area of logic, we may take note of an area wherein Aristotle has no great quarrel with Speusippus, but where he seems to be less than straightforward in acknowledging his debt to him, preferring rather to attack him on relatively minor points of dispute. This is on the subject of the division of names (*onomata*). Aristotle's own distinction at the beginning of the *Categories* between homonyms and synonyms is well known—though this is in fact a

---

[123] I take the force of the adverb *apragmateutōs* (a relatively late word) here to be 'without having to engage in any chains of reasoning'. It is immediately and intuitively obvious that, if one end of a straight line is led round the other which remains stationary, a perfect circle will result.

distinction between types of *thing* rather than of words[124]—but it is less well known that he is here adapting a series of distinctions made already by Speusippus. We know this from Simplicius' commentary ad loc.,[125] who is himself reporting the testimony of the earlier Peripatetic commentator Boethus (1st cent. BC). According to Boethus, Speusippus divided names dichotomously, first into *tautōnyma* and *heterōnyma* ('identical words' and 'different words'); then *tautōnyma* into *homōnyma* and *synōnyma,* by which he means respectively identical words which have different and unrelated meanings (e.g *kuōn,* standing for 'dog', 'dog-fish', and even 'dog-star'), and identical words with identical meanings;[126] and then *heterōnyma* into *idiōs heterōnyma* ('strictly different', that is to say, quite unconnected, such as 'grammar', 'man', and 'wood') and *polyōnyma* (different words with the same meaning, such as *aor, xiphos, phasganon,* all meaning 'sword'[127]). Lastly (though here Boethus or Simplicius seems to have slipped up slightly in his reporting), he seems to have divided *polyōnyma* into *idiōs polyōnyma* and *parōnyma* (that is to say, words different but related to each other by derivation or other contiguity).

Aristotle does not explicitly criticize Speusippus' division of names (though he does so implicitly at the beginning of the *Categories,* by giving the designation of *synōnyma* to members of different species, such as 'man' and 'ox', which have the same generic name, 'animal'), but he does attack a distinction which Speusippus seems to have made on the basis of this division. Speusippus took an interest in the analysis of the sources of ambiguity.[128] Speusippus,

[124] I agree with Tarán (1978), and (1981: 406–14), as against Barnes (1971), that Speusippus is concerned here with words, not things.

[125] *In Cat.* p. 38, 19–24 Kalbfleisch = Fr. 68a Tarán.

[126] For this reason, Speusippus' definition of a homonym (also reported by Boethus, ap. Simplicius, ibid., p. 29, 5–12), 'that of which the name is the same, but the definition (*logos*) is different', is quite adequate for his purposes. Aristotle's addition, 'the definition *of being which corresponds to the name*' is only necessitated by his peculiar innovations.

[127] These are what the Stoics later (and even Aristotle himself on occasion, when he is not innovating, but following accepted Academic usage, e.g. *Rhet.* 1404^b37 ff.) called *synonyma.*

[128] I am much indebted here to Leonardo Tarán's sound discussion of the question at (1981: 72–7, and 414–18).

we can gather from Aristotle, *Soph. El.* 170ᵇ12–171ᵇ2 (= Fr. 69a Tarán),[129] divided all arguments into those addressed to the word (*pros to onoma*) and those addressed to the concept (*pros tēn dianoian*),[130] and in connection with the former kind of arguments he maintained that all sophistical refutations are based upon ambiguity (*para to ditton*). He therefore devoted himself to investigating ambiguity as a means of avoiding and refuting fallacies.

Aristotle (ibid.) rejects this classification of Speusippus' (cf. also *SE* 177ᵇ7–9 = Fr. 69b Tarán), and denies that all sophistical refutations are based upon ambiguity:

No real distinction, such as some people propose, exists between arguments used against the word and those used against the concept; for it is absurd to suppose that some arguments are used against the word and others against the concept, and not the same in both cases. For what is failure to use the argument against the concept except what happens when a man does not apply the term in the meaning about which the man questioned thought that he was being questioned when he made the concession? And this is equivalent to using it against the word; whereas to use it against the concept is to apply it to the sense about which the man was thinking when he made the concession. If, then, when one word has more than one meaning, both the questioner and the man questioned were to think that it had only one meaning—as, for example, 'being' or 'one' have several meanings, but both the answerer answers and the questioner puts his question on the supposition that there is only one meaning and that the argument is that 'all things are one'—will the argument have been directed against the word and not rather against the concept of the man questioned?   (trans. Forster, adapted).

Of the examples mentioned here, 'one' is shrewdly chosen, if Speusippus is being aimed at, since, as we have seen, he had various uses for the word, and thus could be accused of ambiguity in that connection. In general, though, as Tarán very reasonably argues,

---

[129] Speusippus is, admittedly, not named here, but Cherniss (1944: i, n. 47), has given excellent reasons for making this identification.

[130] I prefer to translate *dianoia* here as 'concept', rather than 'thought', as is done by Tarán (and Forster, in his Loeb trans.). Speusippus' distinction is presumably between the 'true' underlying concept in the mind of the disputant, as opposed to the possibly ambiguous word or words that may be employed in the argument.

Speusippus

Aristotle is engaged in point-scoring by disregarding the nature of Speusippus' distinction between arguing 'against the word' and 'against the concept', and addressing it on his own terms. Speusippus seems really to have been concerned with a distinction between a disputation where both participants have gained an accurate conception of what is being argued about, and one in which verbal ambiguities are being exploited. He would not have been oblivious to the fact that there were various kinds of ambiguity, but he wants to claim that all sophistical refutations are based on ambiguity of one sort or another. The distinctions that Aristotle makes are doubtless more sophisticated than those of Speusippus, but at the same time he obscures the very considerable amount that he learned from his senior colleague.

Conclusion

This survey has, I hope, revealed a philosopher of some idiosyncrasy of viewpoint, perhaps, but by no means lacking in coherence or breadth of vision. Speusippus was certainly not the equal of Aristotle as an original mind, but neither was he an entirely unworthy heir to Plato's physical and intellectual establishment. He is, as we have seen, by no means a slavish follower of the doctrines of his uncle; indeed a number of his innovations in doctrine were not to find an echo in the Platonic tradition before the Neopythagoreans of the first and second centuries AD. It is only with his successor, indeed, that Platonism begins to settle down to some sort of 'orthodoxy'—although even Xenocrates, as we shall see, is by no means devoid of original thought.

If one had to select the most original, and ultimately the most influential, aspect of Speusippus' theorizing, the choice would have to fall on his doctrine of the nature of the first principle—and that did not come into its own again (and even then on rather different premisses) until the time of Plotinus. But other aspects of his thought, such as his doctrine on happiness and the nature of pleasure, his theory of the nature and role of the World-Soul, and a number of his logical formulations, seem to have proved stimulating both to his rival Aristotle and, later, to the founders of Stoicism.

Xenocrates and the Systematization of Platonism   3

Life and Works

We have touched on some aspects of Xenocrates' life, and in particular the manner of his succession to the headship of the Academy, in
the course of Chapter 1. Other details, though, are hard to come by.
He is declared to have been the son of one Agathenor, and to have
come from the Megarian colony Chalcedon on the Propontis.
Chalcedon had spent most of the fifth century as a member of the
Athenian League, and had, in 389, in Xenocrates' boyhood, been
induced back into alliance with Athens by Thrasybulus (with the
help of a fleet of forty ships). Presumably, coming as he did from a
relatively remote part of the Greek world, Xenocrates—or his
father—got to hear of the Academy in much the same way and at the
same time as Aristotle's father did, through some philosophical-ped-
agogical grapevine that had established itself during the 370s. As he
was born in 396,[1] it would presumably have been in the mid-370s
that Xenocrates arrived in the Academy, since Diogenes Laertius

---

[1] Diogenes Laertius (IV 14) tells us that he was 82 when he died in 314, and there
seems no reason to disbelieve this.

tells us that he had been a pupil of Plato's 'from a youth' (*ek neou*). For glimpses of his life, we are dependent, as we were in the case of Speusippus, and will be in the case of Polemo, more or less exclusively on anecdotes of doubtful reliability, mostly relayed by Diogenes Laertius. As with Speusippus, we can distinguish, within the witless muddle that is Diogenes' narrative, both a 'hostile' and a 'favourable' tradition, though a number of the stories could be interpreted either way.[2]

Apart from the stories related in the first chapter,[3] that from Aelian relating Aristotle's harassment of the aged Plato and Xenocrates' defence of him, which can be dated to the last years of Plato's life, perhaps around 350, and that concerning the famous courtesan Lais' attempt to seduce him,[4] which seems to assume his headship of the school, and so could be dated later than 339, the anecdotes concerning him that can be dated cluster round two incidents in his life: first, his visit to Syracuse, accompanying Plato (and Speusippus), probably on the second trip in 367 (rather than the third in 361); and secondly, his participation in an embassy to the Macedonian regent Antipater in 322, after the Athenian defeat in the Lamian War.

As regards the visit to Sicily, the main story[5] concerns a relative triviality, but with enough circumstantial detail to suggest that it may have some basis in fact. Dionysius II, it seems, organized a drinking

---

[2] For a good discussion of the possible provenance of these traditions, see Leo (1901), and Isnardi Parente (1981).

[3] pp. 4 and 10 above. Another very popular story, concerning the conversion of Polemo, is most appropriately dealt with in the next chapter, pp. 158–9. It too must refer to the last period of his life, after 339.

[4] Or rather Phryne, following the version of Valerius Maximus (IV 3, ext. 3 = Fr. 26 IP), in preference to that of Diogenes Laertius (IV 7), since even Lais the Younger is chronologically too early to consort with Xenocrates, while Phryne fits very well. As Valerius presents the story, it has a plausible ring to it; it seems to have begun as a student prank, devised by Xenocrates' pupils, who make a bet with Phryne that she cannot seduce their master, and win. It then becomes an *exemplum* illustrating his self-control.

[5] Preserved most fully in Philodemus, *Acad. Hist.* VIII–IV Dorandi (= Fr. 1 IP), but also in DL IV 8. The story probably goes back to Timaeus of Tauromenium. It requires the assumption, since the Anthesteria takes place in February, that Plato and his entourage, arriving in Syracuse in the early autumn of 367, stayed through at least until the following spring—but this could reasonably be assumed in any case.

contest to celebrate the Choes, the second day of the Anthesteria—perhaps in honour of his distinguished guests, since there is no other evidence that this was a Dorian as well as an Ionian festival—and Xenocrates won the prize, which was a garland of gold (in place of the usual one made of olive leaves). On leaving the palace, Xenocrates hung this garland on a statue of Hermes, in just the way one would have done in Athens with a simple olive one—thus demonstrating in a spectacular way his indifference to tyrannical wealth and luxury. Apart from the edifying nature of the tale, it places Xenocrates satisfactorily among the inner circle of Plato's disciples already at this stage of his career. As we have seen in the previous chapter, there is anecdotal evidence indicating Speusippus' presence on this expedition also, but he was Plato's nephew, and much Xenocrates' senior.

Another, less plausible (because less circumstantial) snippet of story, relayed by Diogenes (IV 11), has him defending Plato against a threat from Dionysius (presumably after relations had turned nasty). Dionysius threatens Plato that someone will cut off his head, whereat Xenocrates steps up and declares, 'Not before you cut off mine!' All one can derive from this is testimony both to his bravery and to his loyalty.

The story of his participation in the embassy to Antipater is more significant, for various reasons. First of all, we find Xenocrates, now head of the Academy for some seventeen years already, appearing as a widely respected figure in Athenian society, and a suitable candidate to be drafted onto an embassy by popular acclaim, at a critical juncture in the city's fortunes.[6] Though a metic from the Hellespont, Xenocrates appears in these stories as a strong partisan of Athenian independence from Macedon, and a formidable opponent for Antipater. Plutarch's narrative is worth reproducing at some length,

---

[6] Though Phocion, who was heading the embassy, was an old friend, and companion in the Academy in former days (Plut. *Phoc.* 4, 1), Plutarch does not say that it was he who chose him, but rather the people, gathered in assembly, and this is significant. There are other anecdotes also attesting the high regard of the Athenians for him, as we shall see.

for the impression it gives of Xenocrates' standing with the Athenian people:[7]

Accordingly, Phocion returned to Athens with these demands,[8] and the Athenians acceded to them, under the necessity that was upon them. Then Phocion went once more to Thebes, with the other ambassadors, to whom the Athenians had added Xenocrates the philosopher. For so high an estimate was set upon the virtue of Xenocrates, and so great was his reputation and fame in the eyes of all, that it was supposed that the human heart could harbour no insolence or cruelty or wrath which the mere sight of the man would not infuse with reverence and a desire to do him honour.

However, as it turned out, this was not so. Antipater, who was actually a good friend of Phocion's, received the rest of the delegation very civilly, but would not let Xenocrates speak at all. Now Antipater was not generally an unreasonable man, so we may assume that he knew something which made him intolerant on this occasion.[9] In fact, by a curious reversal of roles, the metic Xenocrates finds himself on this delegation as the champion of intransigent Athenian nationalism, while the rest of the delegation are pro-Macedonian and thoroughly flexible. As Xenocrates is reported to have remarked: 'Antipater does well to feel shame before me alone for his ruthless designs against the city.' When the terms were announced, the rest of the delegation agreed to them (though Phocion put in a half-hearted plea against the garrison in the Piraeus), but Xenocrates commented that Antipater 'had dealt with them moderately if they were slaves, but severely if they were free men'.

Later, when the moderate oligarchy had been established, either

---

[7] I borrow here the translation of Bernadotte Perrin, in the Loeb Classical Library edition.

[8] Sc. surrender of anti-Macedonian leaders, notably Demosthenes and Hypereides; institution of a moderate oligarchy, limiting the franchise to those with property of over 2,000 drachmae; and the acceptance of a Macedonian garrison in the Munychia, the citadel of the Piraeus.

[9] A hostile spin on the story, relayed by Philodemus (*Rhet.* p. 67 Crönert = Frr. 37–9 IP), but deriving ultimately from Demetrius of Phaleron, suggests that Antipater shut him up because he was boringly pedantic; but Antipater may also have declined to listen to one who was not an Athenian citizen speaking on behalf of Athens.

Phocion (who was a personal friend, despite differences on political questions) or Demades—depending on which authority one believes[10]—offered to propose Xenocrates for citizenship, but he turned down the offer, saying that he could not take part in an administration for the prevention of which he had served on an embassy.[11]

This raises the interesting question of Xenocrates' political position.[12] Was his objection to the pro-Macedonian regime that of a democrat, or simply that of an Athenian nationalist, who objected, for instance, to the Macedonian garrison? Surely, one protests, the head of the Platonic Academy cannot have been a partisan of Athenian democracy? But if one thinks about it carefully, why not? A faithful Platonist may be a totalitarian, in the sense of advocating a state totally structured towards the inculcation of virtue, but that does not mean that he need favour oligarchy, in the sense of a limited franchise. After all, whatever the state of the *Republic* (which I would persist in taking less than seriously as a political blueprint, in any case) may be, the state of the *Laws,* Plato's final word on the subject, is a democracy of sorts, to the extent that there is no disfranchised underclass (apart from slaves—and indeed metics, such as was Xenocrates). There is a property qualification, in the form of the basic allotment, but all citizens are intended, and required, to meet that. So the 2,000 drachma property qualification could well have been offensive to Xenocrates, as well as the garrison. At any rate, the anti-Macedonian, democratic faction plainly thought that

[10] Plutarch, *Phocion,* 29, 4, says Phocion; Philodemus, *Acad. Hist.* VIII, attributes the offer to Demades. If the latter is true, one would have to assume that Demades, not being a personal friend, is trying to get Xenocrates on side, and neutralize his opposition, for purely political reasons; but this in itself attests to the importance of Xenocrates' political status.

[11] There is a story (in a number of variants) about Xenocrates being arrested for not paying the *metoikion,* or metic's tax (of 12 dr. p.a.), which in one variant (that in Plutarch's *Phocion*) was what led Phocion to moot his being granted citizenship; but since the story is also told, with circumstantial detail, featuring Lycurgus, who died in 325/4 (Ps. Plut. *Lives of the Ten Orators,* 842B), and also featuring Demetrius of Phaleron, who only came to power in 318 (DL IV 14)—in which variant the Athenians have actually sold Xenocrates as a slave for non-payment of the tax, which seems unlikely—we cannot attach it securely to any particular period.

[12] This has been usefully discussed by Maddoli (1967), with whom I am in broad agreement.

Xenocrates was on their side, and his anti-Macedonian remarks entered Athenian popular folklore, which is why we know of them.[13]

Xenocrates was sufficiently concerned with political philosophy to compose either one or two works on the subject (depending on whether or not the titles *Peri Politeias* and *Politikos* in Diogenes' wretchedly muddled list are one and the same work), so that he must have expressed some views on the ideal constitution. We have no idea what these were, but we can perhaps extrapolate from his attested political positions, and from general probability, to the conjecture that they were not far different from those of Plato in his later years.[14]

Other anecdotes reveal other aspects of his personality. A Pythagorean affinity is suggested by the curious tale of his St Francis-like sheltering of a sparrow that flew into his bosom while fleeing from a hawk (DL IV 10), as also by the report that, because of

---

[13] These, we may note, are not his only recorded brushes with Antipater. A certain Myronianus, in his *Homoia* (ap. DL IV 8), tells of him rejecting a gift of money from Antipater (presumably at some time prior to 322). This is not intrinsically improbable, since Macedonian rulers liked to have significant figures on their payroll (there are many stories of Antipater's pressing gifts on Phocion, unsuccessfully, and on Demades, successfully), and Xenocrates' refusal may have been a first cause of offence. We also have a tale of Xenocrates' ostentatiously taking his time before returning a greeting from Antipater until he had finished what he was saying to someone (DL IV 11)—presumably when Antipater was in Athens as an emissary of Philip after Chaeronea in 338. Whether or not such stories are authentic, they at all events reflect Xenocrates' image with the Athenian public.

[14] His political views, as well as his moderation, come into a much-repeated, but doubtful, story of his being sent a gift of fifty talents by Alexander (Frr. 23–29 IP), and returning it, declaring that he had no need of it. This may be connected with a request by Alexander (reported by Plutarch, *Adv. Col.* 1126c–D) for a treatise on kingship, such as we find listed among his works, under the title *Basic Principles (stoikheia) of Kingship, for Alexander, in four books*. It is not, I think, absolutely beyond the bounds of possibility that Alexander, temporarily at odds with Aristotle over the incident of Callisthenes (cf. DL V 10), sent such a request, and even such a present, to Xenocrates.

There is also the problem of a work of his entitled *To Arrhybas*. The probability is that the recipient of this, which was probably a protreptic epistle, was the king of the Molossians who was dispossessed by Philip in 343, and took refuge in Athens, where he received honorary citizenship, and may have had a connection with the Academy. A suitable time for the composition of such an epistle would have been on the return of Arrhybas to his kingdom in 331/0.

extreme trustworthiness, the Athenians exempted him alone from taking an oath when giving evidence in court (DL IV 7): Pythagoreans, notoriously, did not take oaths, and the only plausible basis for this otherwise most improbable story is that Xenocrates may have pleaded some such conscientious objection when called upon to give evidence in a court case, and got away with it. As we shall see, devotion to the teachings of Pythagoras is an important feature of his philosophy. The report that he allotted one hour in each day to silent meditation is a further Pythagorean trait,[15] as is his general reputation for calmness and uniformity of expression.[16]

Apart from anecdotes proper, there are a number of sayings attributed to the philosopher that are worth dwelling on, for the insight they give into his character and way of thinking.[17] One that is widely reported[18] concerns the proverbial prospective student who applies for entry into the Academy. Xenocrates asks him whether he has studied geometry. No, he has not. Has he studied astronomy? Again, no.[19] 'Then,' says Xenocrates, 'off with you. You give me no handles for philosophy.'[20] If this can be accepted as evidence for his views on education, it would seem to betoken a stricter level of entrance requirements than that imposed by Plato himself—if, that is, we can extrapolate from the scheme of 'preliminary sciences' set

[15] DL IV 11, and Stobaeus, *Anth.* III 33, 11 (= Fr. 62 IP). Stobaeus provides the additional information that he divided up the day systematically into various tasks—also a Pythagorean trait.

[16] Pythagorean also is the vegetarianism implied in his remark reported by Plutarch, *De esu carn.* 996B (= Fr. 53 IP): 'The Athenians punished a man who had flayed a ram while it was still alive; yet, in my opinion, he who tortures a living creature is no worse than he who slaughters it outright.'

[17] As will have been observed, I am in favour of accepting the basic authenticity of anecdotes and sayings, in the absence of obvious chronological or other contradictions, as I am a believer in the power of oral tradition in a 'face-to-face' society such as was ancient Athens.

[18] Frr. 56–60 IP.

[19] The story in its various existing forms includes also 'the poets', *mousikē*, and even *grammata*, 'letters', but I would agree with Margherita Isnardi Parente (comm. ad loc., p. 303) that these have probably been added to the original, to accommodate it to the Hellenistic concept of the 'preliminary sciences', the *enkyklios paideia,* which in later times were certainly deemed a necessary prelude to philosophical study.

[20] An alternative version, equally well-turned, is 'The fleece is not washed by the fuller.'

out in *Republic* VII, which are often assumed to correspond with what was taught to the more junior students of the Academy. But on the other hand, there is the famous, though no doubt mythical, notice posted above the entrance to the Academy, 'Let no one unversed in geometry enter here (*mēdeis ageōmetrētos eisitō*)!'—if only we could be sure when that slogan was invented!

The other message to be derived from the story is the basic importance accorded to geometry and astronomy, which takes on special significance in view of aspects of Xenocrates' philosophy which we will have occasion to examine below, as well as the great importance accorded to both, but especially to astronomy, in the *Epinomis,* which I take to be a work of Philippus of Opus, and an important statement of at least one strand of Old Academic thought.[21]

Other sayings may be dealt with more briefly. He is reported[22] to have said that 'it makes no difference whether you intrude into another man's house with one's feet or with one's eyes; for it is equally wrong to look where one should not or to enter where one should not'—a sentiment worthy of Jesus himself! And again, when jeered at by Bion of Borysthenes, he said that he would make no reply: 'for neither does tragedy deign to answer the banter of comedy'.[23]

As for his works, fully seventy-six are given in Diogenes' list (IV 11–14). It begins with six books *On Nature,* followed by six books *On Wisdom* (using the term *sophia,* which should denote theoretical wisdom). Then comes *On Wealth,* presumably a work on practical ethics; then *The Arcadian (Arkas),* presumably a dialogue, but with no clue as to subject matter; then a work *On the Indeterminate (peri aoristou),* which could be about anything from metaphysics to logic or even

[21] See below, Ch. 5, pp. 182–3.

[22] By Plutarch, *De curios.* 521A (= Fr. 63 IP) and Aelian, *VH* XIV 42 (= Fr. 64 IP).

[23] DL IV 10. Bion, who ultimately attached himself to the Cynic movement, but who is declared by Diogenes Laertius (IV 51) to have been originally a follower of the Academy, fills here the same role in the anecdotal tradition as Diogenes did vis-à-vis Plato. There seems to be a variant of this story in Valerius Maximus (VII 2, ext. 6 = Fr. 61 IP), with an anonymous provocateur. Xenocrates is there asked why he does not reply to abuse, and says: 'I have sometimes regretted speaking, but never remaining silent.'

grammar.[24] And so it goes on, ethics, physics, and logic being thoroughly mingled.

Apart from those mentioned, the most significant works would seem to be: *On Being, On Fate,*[25] *On Virtue, On Ideas, On the Gods, On the Soul, On the Good, On the State,*[26] *Solution of Logical Problems,* in ten books, and *On Genera and Species.* Since not a line survives of any of these works,[27] we do not have much indication of their contents, but it may be taken as significant that he writes a treatise on the theory of Ideas or Forms, another on Being, and another on the Good. We shall see presently how these concepts may be fitted into what we know of his metaphysics. It was presumably in his treatise *On the Soul* that he advanced his interpretation of the composition of the soul in the *Timaeus,* rather than in any explicit commentary on that dialogue.

He was not, it would seem, a very graceful stylist, if we may take that as the true meaning of the anecdote relayed by Diogenes (IV 6) about Plato urging him 'to sacrifice to the Graces',[28] and this may partially explain the complete loss of his works.[29] It is a considerable

---

[24] Heinrich Dörrie (1967: 1515), makes the ingenious suggestion that *Arkas* and *peri tou aoristou* be linked together, as alternative titles of the same work, since that is the case with a similar title later in the list (the suggestion being that an *ē* was corrupted into an *a'*), but this would in any case tell us very little more about the content of the work.

[25] This title (if it is Xenocrates' own) at least shows that the technical term *heimarmenē* was already in use by Xenocrates' time, though we cannot assume that he was conversant with anything like the full force of Stoic determinism.

[26] It is not clear whether the treatise *Peri politeias* is really distinct from the *Politikos* (*The Statesman*) listed somewhat below it, but it perfectly well could be. There are also the books to Aristotle *On Kingship* mentioned above.

[27] All that we have by way of verbatim quotation is a few lines, preserved by Simplicius (= Fr. 53 H/264–6 IP), from a work (not listed by DL), entitled *On the Life of Plato,* which, among other things, appears to have contained a sketch of Plato's philosophy (including a rather adventurous interpretation of the *Timaeus,* cf. below, n. 112).

[28] Admittedly, Diogenes relates this rather to his constantly dignified and gloomy demeanour, but the later author Eunapius (*Vit. Phil.* 458), in applying it to Iamblichus, takes it to refer to style.

[29] We may note among these what appear to be a number of dialogues: the *Arcas* above-mentioned; *Callicles*—possibly, if we accept Dörrie's suggestion, subtitled *On Practical Wisdom* (*Peri phronēseōs*); and *Archedemus,* certainly subtitled *On Justice.* The Callicles of the second work may just possibly refer to the same character as the intellectual thug pilloried in Plato's *Gorgias,* whereas Archedemus may be the same person as that described in Xenophon's *Memorabilia* as a rhetor of limited means but upright

misfortune, however, since it seems probable that it was Xenocrates' purpose in this considerable array of treatises to systematize the teachings of Plato in a way that constitutes the true foundation of a 'Platonist' system of philosophy.

Philosophy

First Principles; Physics

We may now turn to consider Xenocrates' distinctive philosophic contributions. By way of introduction, we may note that Xenocrates is credited (by Sextus Empiricus)[30] with being the first to distinguish the three branches of philosophy universally recognised in the Hellenistic and later periods, Physics, Ethics, and Logic—though not, of course, always in that order. This text is worth looking at, since what exactly Sextus is claiming for Xenocrates is not absolutely clear:

These thinkers,[31] however, seem to have handled the question incompletely, and, in comparison with them, the view of those who divide philosophy into Physics, Ethics, and Logic is more satisfactory. Of these Plato is, virtually (*dynamei*), the pioneer, as he discussed many problems of physics and of ethics, and not a few of logic; but those who most expressly adopt this division are Xenocrates[32] and the Peripatetics, and also the Stoics.

Sextus then goes on to report three different analogies for philosophy, the garden, the egg, and the animal (this last contributed by

principles employed by Crito, on Socrates' advice, to get rid of sycophants who were bothering him.

[30] *Adv. Log.* I 16 (= Fr. 1 /82 IP).

[31] That is to say, various Presocratics whom he has just been mentioning.

[32] Sextus actually uses the expression *hoi peri ton Xenokratēn*, but this, as is generally agreed, need mean no more than Xenocrates himself. As for the Peripatetics, Aristotle himself actually seems to recognize a tripartition of philosophy in *Topics* I 14, 105^b19 ff., where he distinguishes between ethical, physical, and logical propositions (*protaseis*), but Sextus does say 'Peripatetics', not 'Aristotle', and lists them after Xenocrates. On the other hand, Aristotle's use of this tripartition would seem to indicate some recognition of it already in the Academy under Plato.

Posidonius), but he seems to credit these definitely to the Stoics, rather than to Xenocrates or the Peripatetics.

What, on the other hand, are we to make of the 'virtual' attribution of the tripartition of philosophy to Plato himself? We find this attributed to him earlier, after all, by Cicero (following Antiochus of Ascalon), in *Acad.* I 19: 'There already existed, then, a threefold scheme of philosophy (*philosophandi ratio triplex*) inherited from Plato: one division dealt with conduct and morals, the second with nature and its secrets, the third with dialectic and the judgement of truth and falsehood, correctness and incorrectness, consistency and inconsistency, in discourse.' Margherita Isnardi Parente, in her commentary on the passage from Sextus,[33] makes the reasonable suggestion that the attribution to Plato may very well be originally made by Xenocrates himself, in the course, perhaps, of a work such as *On Philosophy (Peri Philosophias)*, which is attested for him by Diogenes Laertius (IV 13). It would be very much of a piece with his general tendency to formalize Plato's teachings, about which we will have more to say presently.

As regards the order of topics, from a comparison between the Cicero passage and the passage from Aristotle's *Topics* noted above (n. 32), one might conclude that Xenocrates' preferred order was Ethics–Physics–Logic, and that Sextus is adopting the Stoic order. Certainly Antiochus preferred to take Ethics first, and it is reasonable to assume that he does that because he felt it to be the proper Old Academic order.[34]

Nevertheless, despite Xenocrates' probable preferred order of topics, I prefer, for the sake of consistency, to begin with first principles, and thus with what Xenocrates would have classed as 'physics'.

Xenocrates, like Plato and Speusippus before him, postulated a pair of supreme principles, which he seems to have termed the Monad and the Dyad,[35] the former also characterized as 'Zeus and

---

[33] (1982: 309–10).

[34] Unfortunately, Diogenes' ordering of Xenocrates' works (IV 11–14) gives us no clue here, being to all appearances quite chaotic.

[35] Aetius, *Placita*, I 7, 30, p. 304 Diels (= Fr. 15 H/213 IP). On the interpretation of this rather troublesome doxographic testimony see further below.

odd (number) and Intellect', the latter being the principle of multiplicity and unlimitedness (*apeiria*), corresponding to Speusippus' *plēthos*. The term *apeiria* is attested to by Plutarch in the first chapter of his work *On the Creation of the Soul in the Timaeus*,[36] where he is discussing Xenocrates' doctrine of the soul, to which we shall come later, although he also employs the term *plēthos* to characterize it:

The former [sc. Xenocrates and his followers] believe that nothing but the generation of number is signified by the mixture of the indivisible and divisible being [sc. in *Tim.* 35A–B], the One being indivisible and Multiplicity divisible, and Number being the product of these when the One bounds Multiplicity and imposes limit upon unlimitedness, which they also term the Indefinite Dyad.

We may note here Plutarch's use of all three of the favoured terms for the second principle, Multiplicity (*plēthos*), Unlimitedness (*apeiria*), and Indefinite Dyad (*aoristos dyas*), the context being such as to suggest that Xenocrates employed these terms himself—and indeed there is nothing improbable in such a supposition. His distinctive term for it, however, seems to have been a rather poetical one, replete with Pythagorean overtones, 'the Everflowing' (*to aenaon*).[37] Aetius, our doxographic source for this information, explains this term with the phrase *aenaon tēn hylēn ainittomenos dia tou plēthous*, which might be rendered 'by "everflowing" alluding to matter, by reason of its multiplicity'. However, it is possible that there is more than one dimension to this word. No doubt there is on the one hand a reference to the famous Pythagorean Oath:[38]

---

[36] 1012D–1013B (= Fr. 68 H/188 IP). In general, as we shall see, Plutarch is, apart from Aristotle, our chief source for Xenocrates, and was himself much influenced by him in certain areas, such as the tripartition of reality, and the theory of daemons.

[37] Aet. *Plac.* I 3, 23, p. 288a Diels (= Fr. 28 H/101 IP). It is true, as Isnardi Parente points out (Comm. ad loc., pp. 336–7), that *aenaos* can mean simply 'everlasting', and may even have meant that in the Pythagorean context from which Xenocrates is borrowing, but that sense of the word does not seem to be as apposite as 'everflowing' for the principle which Xenocrates is seeking to characterize. We may also note Plato's use of the term *aenaos ousia* at *Laws* X 966ᵉ2 to characterize the substance of the physical world.

[38] Given by Aetius shortly before the present extract, at I 3, 8, p. 282 Diels; also by Sextus Empiricus, *AM* VII 94.

Nay, by the man I swear who bequeathed to our head the Tetraktys,
Fount containing the roots of nature ever-flowing (*physis aenaos*)[39]

which can be reasonably assumed to antedate Xenocrates (though
the evidence for it is all much later), but there is also the intriguing
possibility[40] that Xenocrates is indulging in some thoroughly
Platonic word-play (much in the spirit of the *Cratylus*), and taking
aenaon to contain the terms *a-en,* 'not-one', and even *a-on,* 'not-
being'. If that is so (and I find it a perfectly plausible suggestion), that
would explain Aetius' otherwise rather odd expression *dia tou
plēthous:* the point would be that that is why the second principle can
be called 'not-one'.[41]

We may see here, then, evidence both of Xenocrates'
Pythagoreanizing proclivities and of his love of word-play and etymologizing. But there may be more to be derived from this bald doxographic notice. If Xenocrates is making an allusion to the
Pythagorean Oath, may he not be invoking also the concept of the
tetraktys, the sequence of the first four numbers, and of the succession
of point, line, plane, and solid, which, when combined together,
make up the Decad? Certainly Plato and Speusippus were much
intrigued with this Pythagorean concept; it is inconceivable that
Xenocrates was not also. For the former two, the *tetraktys* symbolized
the totality of numbers, and of geometrical figures, which make up
the Paradigm of the *Timaeus;* for Xenocrates, I would suggest, it
must have done the same. Xenocrates' first principle is a Monad, but
it is also (unlike that of Speusippus) an Intellect (*nous*), and an intellect, I would submit, must have contents: it must *think.*

We may adduce here a further doxographic notice, admittedly
from a rather late source, Favonius Eulogius, a pupil of St
Augustine's, who wrote a treatise on Cicero's *Somnium Scipionis.*[42]

---

[39] Or 'everlasting'; see n. 37 above.

[40] Raised by Isnardi Parente, loc. cit.

[41] Even as, at least in later times, Apollo was identified with the monad, as being 'not-
many', *a-polla,* e.g. Plutarch, *De E* 393B–C. This etymology is certainly much older than
Plutarch.

[42] *Disp. de Somn. Scip.* V 6, p. 17, 16 ff. van Weddingen (= Fr. 16 H/214 IP). There is
a useful discussion of this passage in Krämer (1964: 42–4).

He, however, was able to draw much of his information from Cicero's contemporary, Varro, and there is no serious reason to challenge the substance of his testimony. He declares that it was the view of Xenocrates that 'Number is Intellect and God (*estque numerus animus et deus*); for there is nothing else but what is subject to Number.' This is simply stating, in a compressed and oversimplified way, what must have been the doctrine of Xenocrates, that the divine intellect, though itself characterized as a monad, comprehended within itself the totality of number, symbolized by the *tetraktys,* and it is in accordance with this (which is a rationalized version of the Paradigm, or essential Living Being, of the *Timaeus*) that it fashions the world.

Having got this far, though, we must turn back to a closer consideration of the troublesome doxographic notice of Aetius which is the main basis for our knowledge of Xenocrates' theology.[43] The text, as transmitted, runs as follows:

Xenocrates, son of Agathenor, of Chalcedon, [holds] as gods the Monad and the Dyad, the former as male, having the role of father, reigning in the heavens,[44] which he terms 'Zeus' and 'odd' (*perittos*)[45] and 'intellect', which is for him the primary god (*prōtos theos*); the other as female, in the manner of the Mother of the Gods (*mētros theōn dikēn*), ruling over the realm below the heavens, who is for him the Soul of the universe (*psychē tou pantos*).

Aetius' account of Xenocrates' theology goes on somewhat further, and we shall return to it, but it is this first passage that concerns us at present. There is much of interest and value in it, but it should be plain that there is something badly wrong with it.[46] The difficulty concerns the characterization of Xenocrates' second principle, the

---

[43] I have dealt with this passage in more detail in Dillon (1986). I am not, however, so confident now of the conclusions I came to then. See also Baltes (1988).

[44] The phrase *en ouranōi basileuousan*, 'reigning in the heavens', is plainly inspired by the scenario in the myth of the *Phaedrus* (246E), where Zeus is presented as 'the great leader in the heavens' leading the heavenly ride. Formerly I was insistent that this was figurative language, and not to be taken as implying that Xenocrates' first principle is in any sense immanent in the cosmos; now, however, I am not so sure (see below).

[45] That is to say, *numerically* odd.

[46] Matthias Baltes has made a gallant defence of the text as it stands, in the most useful article mentioned above (n. 43), but it seems to me that the difficulties are insuperable.

Dyad. This is presented both as 'the Mother of the Gods', but then as occupying a subcelestial rank, and identified as the Soul of the universe.

However, as we can see from the continuation of the extract from Plutarch's *De Proc. An.* quoted above (1012E), Xenocrates viewed the World-Soul, not as the Dyad itself, and secondary principle of the universe, but rather as the *product* of Monad and Dyad—along with the addition of 'sameness and difference', which transforms Number (which, as we have seen, is the primary product of the union of the two principles) into Soul, by the addition of motivity and mobility (*to kinētikon kai to kinēton*). So to portray the secondary, dyadic principle as itself 'the Soul of the universe' is a gross distortion of Xenocrates' metaphysical system.

Something has therefore gone wrong with Aetius' reporting. I was at first[47] inclined simply to posit a lacuna in the text,[48] between *mētros theōn* and *dikēn,* taking *dikēn* as actually a proper name, Dikē, 'Justice', the assessor of Zeus in Hesiod,[49] who could be identified also, on the theological level, with Athena, and could much more properly represent the World-Soul. In that case, a whole line would have dropped out of the text at some stage, containing further characterizations of the Dyad, parallel with those of the Monad, the whole running something like this: 'the other, as female, <holding the rank of Mother of the Gods, which he terms 'Rhea' and 'even' (*artios*) and 'matter' (*hyle*); and as offspring of these he postulates> Dikē, ruling over the realm below the heavens . . .'.

I still think that something like this must have been in the original from which Aetius in drawing, but I am now inclined to think that the confusion is worse than a mere lacuna in Aetius' text, and that Aetius himself may be trying to make sense of an already garbled text. At all events, if this be accepted as the cause, whether immedi-

[47] Dillon (1977: 26); (1986: 49).

[48] There are two considerable lacunae in the later part of the text, which have been filled satisfactorily by scholars.

[49] *Works and Days* 256–7. This idea is actually that of Boyancé (1948), and I think that it is correct, though there remains the troublesome fact that Aetius employs *dikēn* in its adverbial sense ('in the manner of') fully seven times in the surviving extracts of his work—always, however, otherwise with inanimate objects.

ate or remote, of the confusion, the text can be made to yield some most interesting data. My supplement, however, needs defence at various points. It is reasonable, I think, to balance *perittos* with *artios* (or *artia*),[50] and hardly controversial to balance *nous* with *hylē,* in view of Aetius' identification of *to aenaon* with *hylē* in Fr. 28 H/101 IP; but what is the defence for pairing Rhea with Zeus, in place of his proper spouse, Hera?

And yet it is Rhea, not Hera, who is normally identified as 'mother of the gods'. On the other hand, she is, in 'orthodox' mythology, the mother of Zeus as well, not his spouse. But it is just here that we must tread carefully. Xenocrates is not confining himself to mainstream mythology. Along with Pythagoreanism, another of Xenocrates' intellectual enthusiasms was Orphism, as we shall see further below. In the Orphic tradition, Rhea is both mother and daughter of Zeus, and in both capacities he has intercourse with her.[51] The attraction of Rhea for Xenocrates was doubtless etymological, since he would connect the stem *rhe-* with 'flowing', also represented by *aenaos*. In place of the Orphic Persephone, or Kore, however, Xenocrates will, if my reconstruction is correct, have postulated the figure of Dikē, already connected with Zeus by Plato, in the *Laws* (715E), in an Orphic context, and herself in turn readily connected with Athena, and a fine symbol of the rational World-Soul. Where does all this leave Hera, though? She figures nowhere else, after all, in Aetius' account.[52] I would suggest that Xenocrates simply assimilated her to her own mother Rhea—as indeed she is in the Orphic tradition.[53] After all, in the so-called Rhapsodic or

[50] Depending on whether or not one wishes to understand *arithmos,* 'number'.

[51] We are indebted for this information to the author of the Derveni Commentary on the Orphic Poems (col. xxvi), who tells us: 'He [sc. Zeus] wanted to unite in love with his mother [sc. Rhea, but also Demeter]'; but cf. also Fr. 58 Kern (from Athenagoras, *Pro Christ.* 20), which tells us that Zeus mated with Rhea in snake form, and produced Persephone, with whom he also mated.

[52] The suggestion that she might have fitted into the first lacuna, as the divine power presiding over the air (in accordance with later Stoic allegorizing), is rendered implausible by the adjective *aeidē,* 'unseen', used to characterize this deity. The missing figure must in fact be Hades.

[53] As we learn from col. xxii of the Derveni Papyrus, where it is stated baldly that 'Earth, Mother, Rhea, and Hera are one and the same.'

'Protogonos' Theogony, Zeus also mates with Hera (Frs. 132, 153, 163 Kern), and this vagueness would suit the fluidity of the material principle, as Xenocrates conceived of it.

This leaves Dikē, as symbol of the World-Soul, and repository of the Forms, in whatever mode Xenocrates conceived of them. To explore this problem further, it becomes necessary, I think, to adduce various pieces of later evidence, notably from the Roman antiquarian Varro, and the Jewish Alexandrian philosopher Philo, both of the late first century BC. Varro,[54] in his *Antiquities* (in the process of expounding the Mysteries of Samothrace), identifies Jupiter (Zeus) with the creator god, Juno (Hera) with matter, and Minerva (Athena) with 'the ideas' (as sprung from the head of Zeus). Now Varro is in philosophical matters a faithful follower of the Platonist Antiochus of Ascalon, who was himself much concerned to revive, within the Platonist tradition, the dogmatism of the Old Academy (albeit tinged heavily with Stoicism, which he saw as the truest successor of that dogmatism), and it is a reasonable conjecture that neither Varro nor Antiochus fabricated out of the whole cloth the image of Athena as symbolizing the Forms in the mind of God, but derived it from the Old Academy, and specifically from Xenocrates, who was the great systematizer of Platonic doctrine—merely substituting for Xenocrates' concept of the World-Soul the Stoic doctrine of the Logos. In Xenocrates' conception, then, the World-Soul, symbolized by Athena, would receive the Forms, as quasi-mathematical formulae, from the mind of the supreme god, and project them upon the world—very much the scenario derivable from a non-literal interpretation of Plato's *Timaeus,* such as we know Xenocrates to have propounded.

But of course in the Aetius passage we do not have Athena: we have (if my conjecture is correct) Dikē. Can these figures be brought into equivalence? The answer is that they can, without too much difficulty.[55] Athena is in fact honoured in the Orphic tradition, as well as in more orthodox mythology, for performing a number of the

[54] ap. Aug. *CD* VII 28.

[55] Not that it is absolutely necessary that they should. Xenocrates is plainly capable of making creative use of Greek mythology. On this more will be said below.

same sort of tasks as Dikē is assigned, but it is really only in the works of the Platonizing Jewish philosopher, Philo of Alexandria, that we find both Dikē and Athena performing the same role, as the Logos of God (which inherited the role of the Old-Academic World-Soul). Philo's evidence needs a little interpretation, since for tactical reasons he is unwilling to mention Athena by name, but in a notable passage in his *De opificio mundi* (100), in the course of an encomium of the number seven (a propos the Lord's consecrating of the seventh day), he says the following: 'For this reason other philosophers liken this number to the motherless Victory (*nikē*) and Virgin (*parthenos*), who is said to have appeared out of the head of Zeus, while the Pythagoreans liken it to the leader of all things (*hēgemōn tōn sumpantōn*).'

While avoiding the actual name of Athena, he makes it clear to any reasonably educated and alert reader to whom he is referring, by using two of her chief epithets, *nikē* and *parthenos,* while also describing her as 'motherless' and sprung from the head of Zeus. She is cast here as the *Logos* of God, as is Dikē in many passages,[56] and has the role of projecting the Forms or *logoi* upon the physical world. The 'other philosophers' mentioned in this passage could be taken as referring to the Stoics, but, while not excluding them,[57] I would suggest that the context makes a reference to Platonists more appropriate; and the adducing of 'the Pythagoreans' points in the same direction: for Neopythagoreans, such as Varro—or closer to home for Philo, Eudorus of Alexandria—Athena, as the number seven, the Hebdomad, constitutes the primary projection of the supreme deity, the Monad.

For Philo, then, Athena/Dikē as the Logos of God is part of the Greek philosophical tradition upon which he is drawing, and that tradition is an essentially Platonist one, tinged with Stoicism and enlivened with Neopythagorean mysticism and number-theory. It is, admittedly, going beyond our exiguous evidence to see Xenocrates, as interpreted and 'modernized' by Antiochus, at the back of this

[56] e.g. *Mut.* 194 (where she receives the significant epithet *aeiparthenos*, 'ever-virgin'); *Conf.* 118; *VMos.* II 53; *De Dec.* 177; *Spec. Leg.* IV 201.

[57] The Stoic Cornutus (*Theol.* 35, 6; 36, 3), for instance, makes her the symbol of the Logos.

amalgam, but it is not an unreasonable extrapolation. As we shall see when we examine the rest of Aetius' testimony, he credits Xenocrates with having 'provided to the Stoics' the whole set of divine symbols for the elements and other powers in the universe, having himself borrowed them from Plato.

Where would this, then, leave us? I would suggest that we can, on the basis of this, credit Xenocrates with a metaphysical scheme that involves a *Nous*-Monad as primary divine principle, a 'female' material principle, characterized as an Indefinite Dyad, and a World-Soul, as creative repository of the Forms, and projector of them onto the physical plane, sprung from the primal Intellect.[58]

It is notable, in connection with the nature of the first principle, that Xenocrates (whether tacitly or otherwise—we have no means of knowing) has rejected the radical position of Speusippus, and identified his Monad firmly as an Intellect (*nous*). Whether this is in response to criticisms by Aristotle, or simply the result of his own analysis of the Platonic data, we have again no means of knowing, but the result is that, for later Platonism, there is little difference observable between the first principle of Platonism and that of Aristotle as set out in *Metaphysics* Λ—the 'Unmoved Mover', an Intellect thinking itself. The only difference—and it is a significant one—is that the contents of the Intellect of Xenocrates' first principle are specified as the Forms (seen as mathematical entities), and that his Monad exercises a more active providential role in the universe than Aristotle's God, whose activity is entirely self-centred, and who serves only as an object of striving for all the rest of creation.[59] We see here, as elsewhere, Xenocrates exhibiting far more concern than Speusippus to remain true to what he conceives to be the doctrine of Plato, though here it involves reconciling the Good of the *Republic* with the Demiurge-*plus*-Paradigm of the *Timaeus*—and indeed the system of first principles presented in the *Philebus*.

---

[58] On all this, see the detailed discussion of Krämer (1964: ch. 1: 'Die Nus-Monas als Weltmodel'), with which I find myself largely in agreement.

[59] There is a most interesting critique of this concept by none other than Aristotle's own senior pupil Theophrastus, in the first few chapters of the little aporetic work of his entitled (perhaps wrongly) the *Metaphysics*.

Our next problem, then, is to try to discern what Xenocrates did with the Platonic Forms. Here we are faced at the outset with a canard of Aristotle's which has enjoyed a far greater currency than it deserves. More or less any history of philosophy that one looks at, in dealing with the Old Academy, will state, on the basis of Aristotle's evidence, something to the effect that 'Plato maintained the existence of both Forms and mathematicals, while Speusippus rejected the Forms and postulated only numbers, and Xenocrates identified the Forms with the numbers'. This is based primarily on the programmatic passage in *Met.* M, 1076^{a}20 ff., which we have had occasion to discuss before,[60] where Aristotle says that 'some [sc. Plato] recognize these as two classes—the Forms and the mathematical numbers—and others [sc. Xenocrates] regard both as having one nature, and yet others [sc. Speusippus] hold that only the mathematical substances are substances.'[61] As we have seen, Aristotle deliberately muddies the waters by bringing into the story Plato's apparent postulation of a separate ontological status for the objects of mathematics (i.e. intelligible and non-material, but 'many the same'), whereas what is relevant to the discussion of the philosophical positions of Speusippus and Xenocrates is rather the relation of the Forms to Number.

In Xenocrates' case, the situation seems to be that, to quote Aristotle at *Met.* H 1028^{b}24 ff. (= Fr. 34 H/103 IP), 'he holds that the Forms and numbers have the same nature (*tēn autēn ekhein physin*), and that other things—lines and planes—are dependent upon them; and so on down to the substance of the heavens and the sensible realm.'

What are we to make of this? We start with a fairly straightforward identification of Forms with numbers (such as is confirmed in the later passages from *Met.* N),[62] but after that, the relationship pos-

---

[60] Above, pp. 22 and 49.

[61] Cf. also *Met.* H 2, 1028^{b}18 ff. (= Xenocr. Fr. 34 H/103 IP), where Plato and Speusippus, at least, are actually mentioned by name; and N 9, 1086^{a}5 ff. (= Fr. 34 H/110 IP), where Xenocrates is criticized for identifying ideal with mathematical numbers.

[62] I say straightforward, but the precise form that this may have taken is a far from straightforward question. Plainly, we are dealing with nothing as crude as the notorious system of the Pythagorean Eurytus, mentioned satirically by Theophrastus (*Met.* 6^{a}20

tulated with lines, planes, and solids is far from clear; and even less so that with the heavens and the sensible world. However, if we take the former two propositions together, the solution may lie, once again, in the nature of the Pythagorean *tetraktys,* which, as I have suggested above, may be seen in Xenocrates' system as the active counterpart (as constituting the contents of the *Nous*-Monad) to the *aenaos physis,* which is the material principle. We have evidence from other passages of Aristotle that the sequence of the first four numbers, besides serving as the basis for the whole sequence of natural numbers, also was seen as presiding over the sequence of point, line, plane, and solid.[63] Something like this scenario seems to have been envisaged by Plato himself in his latter years, if we can trust Aristotle, so there is nothing here that is outstandingly original to Xenocrates. If anything, he would seem to be drawing back, as in other respects, from the radical position of Speusippus, perhaps in response to Aristotle's satirical characterization of Speusippus' scheme as an 'episodic universe'. On the other hand, how he (or indeed, how Plato before him) addressed the problem that Speusippus is trying to solve by postulating distinct first principles for each level of reality is far from clear. We are woefully short of detail on this, but it would seem as though the number three, for example, would serve both as the first odd number, and as a basis, through combination with the number two and itself, for all subsequent numbers, and as the first principle (in the form of the archetypal triangle) of all plane figures. Xenocrates would then, under the heading of 'number', be subsuming all the three dimensions as well.

---

ff.), who identified the 'number' of man or horse as the number of pebbles out of which he could make a picture of either; but how Xenocrates would arrive at the 'number' of man, horse, justice, or courage, or example, is quite obscure. Possibly everything was in principle assigned a number, rather like a table of atomic elements. In this way, Forms of species, for example, could be combinations or multiples of the numbers of their genera. But we have really very little to go on here.

[63] Or, to be more accurate (since the monad for Aristotle is not properly a number), two, three, and four generate line, plane, and solid, while the monad as point serves as fount or root of these. This arrangement is attributed already to Plato by Aristotle, as we have seen (above, pp. 21–3), at *Met.* A 9, 992^{a}10 ff. The interesting passage in *De Anima* I 2, 404^{b}16 ff. would seem to bear on the same question, though it is primarily concerned with the level of soul.

This whole issue, it must be said, constitutes a good example of Aristotle's polemical strategy. He tries to nail Xenocrates in particular on the following contradiction. Plato, he maintains, postulated both form-numbers and mathematical numbers. Of these, only the former could count as Forms, and shared with other Forms the characteristic that they were not combinable with any other Form, including other form-numbers. Now if one wishes, as Aristotle claims Speusippus does,[64] to dispense with the Forms altogether, well and good; at least he has avoided this contradiction. But Xenocrates wishes to retain the system of Forms, mathematicize them, and then treat these form-numbers as if they were mathematical numbers, e.g. add the Form of Two to the Form of Three to make the Form of Five. This will not do:

> Others [sc. Xenocrates], wishing to preserve both Forms and numbers, but not seeing how, if one posits these [sc. the Monad and the Dyad] as first principles, mathematical number can exist beside form-number (*eidētikos arithmos*), identified form-number with mathematical number—but only in theory, since in practice mathematical number is done away with, because the hypotheses which they propound are of a peculiar nature (*idiai*) and not mathematical. (*Met.* M 1086ᵃ6–11).

How is Xenocrates to answer this? I think that he would perhaps argue that the conflict that Aristotle is trying to set up between form-numbers and mathematical numbers is irrelevant. By postulating the theoretical derivation of all later numbers (and geometrical forms) from the *tetraktys,* Xenocrates is not intending to claim that they ever *were* so derived, or that processes of addition and multiplication take place in the realm of the Forms. The number twenty-four, for instance, may theoretically be derived from $2 \times 2 \times 2 \times 3$, but it is an integral number in its own right, and always has been, and as such is not combinable with anything else: it is just the essence of 'twenty-four-ness'. All the 'mathematicals' ever were, after all, were a postulate of Plato's to explain what those entities were with which one is dealing if one makes a calculation such as $2 \times 2 \times 2 \times 3$, or if one compares two equilateral triangles; they were not physical objects, and

---

[64] e.g. *Met.* M 1086ᵃ3 ff.

they were not Forms, but something intermediate between the two. There may indeed be problems with Xenocrates' theory of form-numbers, but this should not be one of them.

This brings us to a notorious problem in relation to Xenocrates' metaphysical system, that of the postulation of so-called indivisible lines (and planes and solids), for which he is once again satirized by Aristotle.[65] At *Met.* N 3, 1090^{b}21 ff., we find the following complaint:

> Those who posit the Forms [sc. Xenocrates] escape the difficulty [sc. of Speusippus' 'episodic universe'], because they construct spatial magnitudes (*megethē*) out of Matter and a number—Two in the case of lines, Three, presumably, in that of planes, and Four in that of solids; or out of other numbers, for it makes no difference. But are we to regard these magnitudes as Forms, or what is their mode of existence? And what contribution do they make to things? They contribute nothing, just as the mathematicals contribute nothing. Moreover, no mathematical theorem applies to them, unless one chooses to interfere with the principles of mathematics and invent peculiar theories of one's own (*idias tinas doxas*).

Aristotle is in a thoroughly sarcastic mood here. Note, as in the quotation from *Met.* M 9 above, the reference to *idiai doxai*, at variance with the principles of mathematics. What is it that so disturbs him about the postulate of indivisible minima in connection with lines, planes, and solids, and what could induce Xenocrates to make such a postulate? To take the second question first, it would seem that what provoked Xenocrates to this theory was a problem that he had inherited from Plato, and to which he was unwilling to apply the solution arrived at by Speusippus. The problem is simply the fact that there are in the universe, as products of the first principles, not only numbers, but also geometrical figures. How is this variety to be explained, given the essential simplicity of both the Monad and the Dyad?

Plato, if we may believe Aristotle,[66] postulated 'varieties' or subclasses of the 'Great-and-Small', suggesting that we derive lines from

---

[65] e.g. *Phys.* VI 1, 231^{a}21 ff.—an extended critique, running through to 233^{b}15; *Cael.* III 1, 299^{a}6 ff.; *Met.* N 8, 1084^{a}37 ff.; *Met.* H 3, 1090^{b}21 ff.

[66] Though there is a considerable element of satire in his account, *Met.* A 9, 992^{a}2 ff.

111

the 'Long-and-Short', planes from the 'Wide-and-Narrow', and solids from the 'Deep-and-Shallow'. But this is almost whimsical language,[67] and, particularly after Aristotle's trenchant criticism of it, both Speusippus and Xenocrates plainly felt that they had either to abandon it, or firm it up into something like a scientific theory. Speusippus, therefore, proposed his theory of distinct, 'analogous' first principles for each level of reality (which was in turn satirized by the relentless Aristotle), and Xenocrates, retreating from that, seems to have postulated instead that, of the primary numbers making up the *tetraktys,* along with their roles as foundation of the natural numbers, Two should do duty as the Form of Line, Three as the Form of Plane, and Four as the Form of Solid.[68]

This in turn, however, necessitated the postulate that each level of geometrical reality have as its basis indivisible minima out of which more complex figures are constructed. This would seem to cut across the principle that solids can be analysed into planes, planes into lines, and lines into points, but it can be seen rather as complementary to it. Certainly they can, but for a line ever to come to be, one needs more than a collection of points; one needs also the Form of Line, and it is that that necessitates that any given line should be constructed, not from points, but rather from minimal lines.

It is this notion, and the corresponding concepts of minimal planes and solids, that Aristotle indignantly declares to be counter to the principles of mathematics. In this he is technically correct. He, of course, rejects the whole concept of a hierarchy of levels of reality descending from a Monad and Dyad, so he has very little sympathy with the efforts of his former colleagues in the Academy to solve the problem they have set themselves. Indeed, he sees these efforts as introducing mystical Pythagorean flummery into the scientific discipline of mathematics.

---

[67] Though Aristotle does in fact go on here to 'credit' Plato with the postulation of a 'first principle of line' (*arkhe grammēs*), which Aristotle equates with an 'indivisible line'. This is the only passage, however, in which he attempts to father this theory on Plato himself. The truth may be that this was a notion that Plato entertained, but did not definitively adopt.

[68] We find confirmation that this was his solution in a passage of Themistius (*Paraphr. in Aristot. De An.* p. 11, 19 ff. = Fr. 39 H/260 IP), where Themistius claims to be quoting from Xenocrates' treatise *On Nature.*

However, Xenocrates did present a number of arguments in defence of his position, and we know more or less what they were, thanks to the efforts of a later member of the Peripatos,[69] who composed a short treatise, *On Indivisible Lines,* in refutation of him, but prefaces his refutation with a summary of his arguments. They run as follows:

(1) 'If 'much' and 'big', and their opposites 'few' and 'little', are similarly constituted, and if that which has pretty well[70] infinite divisions is not small, but big, it is evident that 'few' and 'little' will have a limited number of divisions; if, then, the divisions are limited, there must be some magnitude which has no parts, so that in all magnitudes there will be some indivisible unit (*ti ameres*), since in all of them there is a 'few' and a 'little'.   (968^{a}4–9)

This actually does not seem too bad an argument, based as it is on the problems inherent in the concept of infinity. It could be seen as a reaction (as might the fourth argument, below) to the puzzle propounded in the previous century by Zeno of Elea: the argument that 'if things are many, they must be both small and great: so small as to have no size, and so large as to be infinite.'[71] The postulation of minima could be designed to counter this line of argument. If even the smallest magnitude is infinitely divisible, it will have an infinite number of parts, and will then be infinitely large; but we make a distinction between what is 'large' and what is 'small'; so then we must recognize that what is 'small', in order to be distinguishable from

---

[69] It is generally agreed that the author of the little treatise is not Aristotle himself, but he is probably not too much later, since the impulse to write in refutation of Xenocrates would not have survived very far into the third century BC. The fact also that Xenocrates is not mentioned by name in the treatise would seem to betoken the familiarity proper to a contemporary. Theophrastus is attested (DL V 42) to have composed a work with this title, and, despite the hesitations of most scholars, I can see no compelling reason to deny it to him. Some of the arguments against Xenocrates are rather simple-minded, but many are sound enough (assuming straightforward Peripatetic mathematical principles), and the whole does not seem unworthy of Theophrastus.

[70] The *skhedon* here is important, and its significance is ignored or misinterpreted by many commentators. What Xenocrates means to suggest is that *it is the popular perception that* what is big consists of a (more or less) infinite amount of parts.

[71] Zeno, Fr. 29B1 D-K.

what is 'large', does not have an infinite number of parts. Therefore there must be minimal parts.[72]

This is really only skirmishing, however. A more pertinent argument follows:

(2) Moreover, if there is a Form of Line, and the Form is primary among the entities synonymous with it,[73] and if the parts are prior by nature to the whole, the Line Itself (*autē hē grammē*) would be indivisible, and in the same way also the Square, the Triangle and the other figures, and in general the Plane Itself and Body (*sōma*);[74] for the consequence will be that there will be some prior entities in their case also. (968ª10–14)

This is an important passage, if we can take it to be essentially Xenocratean (as there seems no substantial reason not to do). Of course, Aristotle and his followers would not accept the necessity for there being a Form of Line, so the argument has little force against them, but for a Platonist it should be compelling enough. The problem is a general Platonist one, that of accounting for the full range of phenomena of which the universe is made up.[75] Lines and planes are features of the world, and though they can be broken down mathematically into points and lines respectively, they cannot be so broken down *ontologically*. No amount of dimensionless points, for example, can actually make up a line—and in the case of the Form of Line, there is no line prior to it into which it could be divided; there must therefore be included in the intelligible blueprint of the universe such

---

[72] It is not very clear, on the basis of Diogenes Laertius' list of his works, in what treatise Xenocrates would have put forward these arguments, but one candidate might be the treatise *On the Doctrines of Parmenides,* where he might have dealt also with arguments of Zeno—though the question might also have come up either in his work *On Forms,* or in his various works on mathematical subjects (e.g. *On Geometry,* in two books).

[73] That is, which have the same name as it (sc. particulars). Note that Xenocrates is using *synōnymos* in its Speusippan sense, not in its Aristotelian (see above, Ch. 2, p. 86).

[74] I take this to mean 'geometrical body', i.e. three-dimensional solid. There is evidence, however, as we shall see, that Xenocrates postulated atomic magnitudes in the physical realm also.

[75] We may note in this connection the assertion of Aristotle, at *De Gen. et Corr.* 316ª12, that 'some people'—presumably including Xenocrates, if not Plato himself—maintain the existence of atomic magnitudes, because 'otherwise the Form of Triangle (*autotrigōnon*) will be many', i.e. could be decomposed into lines.

a thing as the Form of Line—and, for that matter, of Plane, and of Solid—each of which is indivisible.[76]

Four more arguments of Xenocrates are presented, the latter two of which (968^b5–22) are explicitly 'mathematical', and not, it must be said, very fortunate;[77] the former two, though, are worth examining in detail. Argument (3), then, runs as follows (968^a15–18):

Again, if there are elements in a body, and there is nothing prior to the elements, *and if the parts are prior to the whole,* fire and, generally speaking, each of the elements of the body would be indivisible, so that there must be a unit without parts, not only in the intelligible realm (*en tois noētois*), but also in the perceptible.

This appears to extend the principle of atomic minima explicitly to the physical world (fire, or water, for example, would be made up of minima of fire or water, and not dissoluble into anything more basic), and this would seem to tie in with a number of other interesting snippets of information about Xenocrates' doctrine. First of all, the principle (which I have italicized) that the parts are prior to the whole seems a remarkable one for a Platonist to adopt, and requires some discussion. It was brought into the previous argument also, we may note, and that gives us a clue. There, the principle 'that the parts are by nature prior to the whole' was brought in to justify the postulation of a Form of Line prior to the whole multiplicity of lines, as though the Line were to be regarded as a 'part'.

Strange as this may seem, it finds confirmation from a rather odd source,[78] an Arabic translation of a lost treatise of Alexander of

---

[76] It might occur to one here to wonder where all this leaves the Point (*stigmē*). Interestingly, Aristotle reports, in the passage from *Metaphysics* mentioned above (n. 65) that 'Plato rejected the concept of points.' The reason that he (and Xenocrates) may have done this is precisely because a point, if it is taken as being a unit with extension, is in fact nothing other than a minimum line, and is thus a superfluous postulate. 'Point', in fact, becomes just another name for minimum line.

[77] The third (968^b5–13) seems to assume that all lines are commensurable with one another (and thus must have a common unit of measurement, which would be the minimum line), but this precisely fails to take account of the phenomenon of irrationals, as the Peripatetic author is quick to point out; and the fourth extends this argument to planes.

[78] For the discovery of which we are indebted to the Israeli scholar Pines (1961).

Aphrodisias, *On the Doctrine of Aristotle on First Principles* (= Xenocr. Fr. 121 IP):

Alexander says: Xenocrates says: If the relation between a species and a genus is like the relation between a part and a whole, and if a part is anterior and prior to the whole in virtue of a natural priority (for if a part is taken away, the whole is destroyed—this in view of the fact that no whole will remain if one of its parts is lacking), whereas a part will not necessarily be destroyed if the whole to which it belongs is dissolved, since it is possible for certain parts of a whole to be eliminated while others remain), a species is likewise undoubtedly prior to its genus.

Alexander is concerned to counter this doctrine of Xenocrates' from an Aristotelian standpoint, but it is actually strangely similar to some introductory remarks of Aristotle's at the beginning of the *Physics* (A 1, 184^{a}22 ff.), where he speaks of proceeding in our investigations from what is clearest to us to what is clearest by nature, and in that connection proceeding from 'wholes' in some sense (*ta katholou*) to 'particulars' in some sense (*ta kath'hekasta*)—by which, he goes on to explain, he means 'parts' (*merē*). This seems quite opposed to Aristotle's own position as expressed, for example, in the *Posterior Analytics* (72^{a}4 ff.), and has caused scholars some difficulty. But consistent or not, what Aristotle certainly seems to be saying here is that one must proceed from the contemplation of a general concept, loosely conceived, to the analysis of its constituent elements, whatever they may be, and it is a nice question how far removed this may be from what Xenocrates is saying.[79]

However, this notion still seems heterodox, from a Platonist point of view. Can it be that Xenocrates wished to regard species, such as dog, man, horse, as prior in their nature to the genus animal; or triangle, square, rectangle, as somehow prior to plane figure? I think that it is indeed possible, and that it throws light on a rather important aspect of Xenocrates' philosophy. It begins to look as if, in both

---

[79] For a good discussion of the doctrine of this passage, see Bolton (1991). Aristotle also seems to make use of this doctrine, with polemical intent, at *Met.* Γ 3, 3, 998^{b}30 ff., where he argues that there cannot be a genus of Number as such, nor yet of Plane Figure, over and above particular numbers or species of figures.

the intelligible and the sensible realms, Xenocrates postulated minima. At the intelligible level, these minima would be the individual Forms, which Xenocrates seems to have identified as Forms of species rather than genera (more generic Forms would then enjoy only a secondary level of reality); while at the level of the sense-world the basic realities would seem to have been elementary particles of some sort. The curious statement in the present passage that 'fire and, generally speaking, each of the elements of the body would be indivisible' can only be understood, I think, against the background of the physics of the *Timaeus,* where fire and the other elements are merely combinations of types of basic triangle.[80] Such a conclusion is supported by two bald doxographic reports of Aetius',[81] in which we learn, respectively that 'Xenocrates and Diodorus[82] defined the smallest elements [of things] as partless' (i.e. declared that there *were* minimal parts of things); and that 'Empedocles and Xenocrates compose the elements of smaller particles (*ongkoi*), which are minima (*elakhista*) and as it were elements of elements.' In either case, Xenocrates is put in rather odd company, but there was plainly a basis for thus singling him out among the Platonists. While wishing to remain faithful to Plato's teaching, it would seem that he developed the atomistic implications of the theory of basic triangles rather further than Plato himself chose to do.[83]

His atomistic proclivities come out interestingly in another context, his theory of sound and harmony, for evidence on which we are indebted to Porphyry, in his commentary on the *Harmonics* of

---

[80] I would tend to agree with Isnardi Parente (comm. ad fr. 127, p. 362) that this is probably a confused or tendentious summary by the Peripatetic author of Xenocrates' position. The relevant section of the *Timaeus* is 53C–55C.

[81] I 13, 3 p. 312b Diels (= Fr. 51 H/148 IP), and I 17, 3, p. 315b Diels (= Fr. 50 H/151 IP).

[82] This seems to refer to Diodorus Cronus, the dialectician of the Megarian school, who is reported by Sextus Empiricus (*Adv. Phys.* I 363) to have postulated as his first principles 'minimal and indivisible bodies' (*elakhista kai amerē sōmata*).

[83] Cf. the interesting criticism of Aristotle in *De Caelo* III 1, directed against 'those who construct all bodies out of planes (*epipeda*) and dissolve them into them again' (299a1), directed primarily against Plato's scheme in the *Timaeus,* but also perhaps against Xenocrates (these are arguments against indivisible lines).

Ptolemy.[84] In explaining the Pythagorean doctrine of harmonics, Xenocrates sets out, first, an analysis of types of motion (*kinēsis*), and then, when he has identified sound as a species of motion in a straight line (*eis euthy*), he presents it as consisting in fact of a sequence of sound-atoms, each occurring at a given instant, but giving the impression of a continuous flow. To illustrate this conception, he offers the interesting analogy of a spinning top with a single white or black spot on its surface, which, as the top spins, appears as a continuous line—and likewise, a single vertical line painted on the surface will appear as a solid plane of colour.

What we may presumably derive from this is the suggestion that not only sounds, but also visual data, may be analysed into atomic units, which then appear to our senses as continuous flows of auditory or visual phenomena, since our senses are not acute enough to discern the single units as they strike upon them. These observations are, admittedly, presented incidentally to an exposition of the Pythagorean theory of harmony, but there seems no reason not to take them as forming part of a serious theory of perception. Xenocrates thus begins to emerge as a kind of atomist, but not in any sense offensive to Platonism. His atomic theory is valid for the intelligible world as well as for the physical,[85] and the atomic units of the latter are essentially projections of those of the former. It was not, after all, the atomism of Democritus that appalled Plato; it was rather the randomness and purposelessness of his universe.[86]

But we must return to the realm of Forms, and address a question to which Xenocrates seems to have given the answer which remained

---

[84] *In Ptol. Harm.* p. 30, 1 ff. Düring (= Fr. 9 H/87 IP). Porphyry's primary authority is actually a certain Heraclides (possibly he of Pontus), in his *Introduction to Music,* and he is quoting Xenocrates as giving the doctrine of Pythagoras—all of which introduces complications. It is not in fact absolutely clear that Heraclides is continuing to make use of Xenocrates, but I regard it as very probable (as do Heinze and Isnardi Parente).

[85] As is attested to, after all, by the at first sight cryptic remark at the end of the third argument quoted above: 'so that there must be a unit without parts (*ti ameres*), not only in the intelligible realm, but also in the perceptible'.

[86] Indeed, Aristotle, admittedly with polemical intent, can lump them both together as atomists, in such a passage as *De Caelo* III 8, taking the basic triangles of the *Timaeus* as atoms.

definitive for later Platonism: of what things are there Forms?[87] We may take our start from the Xenocratean definition of a Form, as given by Proclus in his *Parmenides Commentary*:[88] 'the paradigmatic cause of whatever is at any time composed according to nature' (*aitia paradeigmatikē tōn kata physin aei synestōtōn*). There is actually much that is peculiar about this definition, at least in the way that it is normally interpreted,[89] that is, as excluding Forms not only of things 'contrary to nature' (*ta para physin*)—such as freaks of nature and evils—but also of products of art (*tekhnēta*). This would be a considerably narrower range of application than that fixed by Plato in his broadest definition, in Book X of the *Republic* (596A): 'We are accustomed, are we not, to posit a single Form for each of the various multiplicities to which we give the same name'—and in connection with which he then postulates the Form of Bed! Furthermore, it is not clear where Xenocrates' definition, thus interpreted, would leave Forms of abstractions, such as Justice or Moderation, which are more or less Plato's favourite types of Form. However, Harold Cherniss, in *Aristotle's Criticism of Plato and the Academy*,[90] in a valuable discussion of this question, argues that Xenocrates need only have meant by *ta kata physin synestōta* 'things properly formed', as opposed to mistakes or distortions of one sort or another, and would thus not necessarily be at variance with Plato's definition. Cherniss's interpretation is supported by Heinrich Dörrie[91] (though without reference to Cherniss). Dörrie proposes, basing himself on the evidence of the late fourth-century Sicilian Greek rhetorician Alcimus, a contemporary of Xenocrates,[92] that *physis* in Xenocrates' formulation, as in Alcimus' critique of Plato, has a broad reference to the physical realm in general, and was not intended by Xenocrates to

---

[87] Presumably he addressed this question in his treatise *peri ideōn*, listed by Diogenes Laertius.

[88] Col. 888, 18–19 Cousin (= Fr. 30 H/94 IP).

[89] Beginning with such ancient authorities as Alcinous, in the *Didaskalikos*, ch. 9, 2, and continuing with Proclus, loc. cit.

[90] (1944: 257 n. 167).

[91] Dörrie and Baltes (1987: 314).

[92] ap. DL, III 13. Alcimus' purpose in writing was to show how much of his doctrine Plato had borrowed from Epicharmus!

exclude any properly formed physical object, whether tree, dog, chair, ploughshare, or bed, nor yet physical instantiations of Forms such as Justice, Circularity, or Beauty.

I am much attracted to this point of view, but it is undeniable that, if this was Xenocrates' intention, then later Platonists lost track of it. When the question of the range of reference of Forms comes up in late times, as it does in Alcinous and later in Proclus (*In Parm.* 815, 15 ff.), artificial objects are definitely excluded, along with evils (such as Injustice or Crookedness), individuals (such as Socrates), and parts of objects (such as hands or feet). We cannot, therefore, be quite certain whether or not Xenocrates introduced this restriction into the theory, but it is very probable, at all events, that it is he who first moved to formalize the theory, if only as a defence against the attacks of Aristotle in his treatise *On Forms.*

We may turn now to consider in more detail the first element in the definition, *aitia paradeigmatikē,* 'paradigmatic cause'. This fairly plainly relates to the doctrine of the *Timaeus,* which it again formalizes. We must suppose, I think, that for Xenocrates the Forms, as mathematical formulae, each representing a 'natural' class of object in the physical world, are transmuted at the level of Soul—as implied, if not explicitly stated, in the *Timaeus*—into combinations of basic triangles, which then come to constitute physical objects, as well as instantiations of general concepts. In this way they are causes, as well as models, though the creative impulse is provided by Soul.

But we need at this point to address the other question traditionally discussed in later Platonist treatments of the topic: where are the Forms? There has always been a considerable degree of mystery made as to the ultimate origin of the prevailing Middle Platonist doctrine that the Forms are in the mind of God,[93] since our evidence does not allow us to trace it further back than the circle of Antiochus of Ascalon in the first century BC—and that only if we can associate him with the interesting essay in allegorization by Varro mentioned

---

[93] As stated without hesitation by Alcinous, *Did.* 9, and assumed already by Philo (e.g. *Opif.* 17–18). See on this the useful article of Rich (1954).

above (p. 105), where Minerva (Athena) is portrayed as Form, springing from the brow of Jupiter (Zeus).

However, once Xenocrates had declared his first principle to be an intellect, the question must arise as to the contents of this intellect: an intellect must surely think, after all, if it is to be worthy of the name. Aristotle's intellect thinks itself, but that of Xenocrates is more actively concerned with the creation of the world, as we have seen, and the obvious candidates for its contents are the form-numbers. We do in fact have some minimal evidence that Xenocrates had indeed enunciated this obvious conclusion from his doctrine, once again from the testimony of the Sicilian Alcimus mentioned above, who declares, a propos the Forms: 'Each one of the Forms is eternal, a thought (*noēma*), and moreover impervious to change.' This assertion that the Forms are thoughts has been taken as an assertion of subjectivity (thoughts in a human intellect), but in the context (sc. the Forms being eternal and impervious to change), the only intellect that they can be reasonably held to be a thought of is that of God himself. Alcimus may be a foolish and tendentious man, but he is a more or less contemporary witness, and it seems quite reasonable to suppose that he is reflecting at least Xenocratean doctrine. These Forms, then, will be projected forth from the divine intellect onto the World-Soul.

It is to this Soul and its activities that we must therefore now turn. Once again, we are vouchsafed a bald, doxographic account of Xenocrates' doctrine:[94] the Soul is 'number moving itself' (*arithmos heauton kinōn*). To grasp the true significance of this definition, we must recall Xenocrates' exegesis of the creation of the soul in *Tim.* 35A–C, as reported by Plutarch (*De Proc. An.* 1012D–E ff., quoted above, p. 100). There Xenocrates is declared to have identified the 'indivisible being' of *Tim.* 35A as the One or Monad, and the being which is 'divided about bodies' as Multiplicity or the Dyad. The 'third form of being' initially compounded from these two he identi-

---

[94] Aristotle, *De An.* I 2, 404[b]27–8, etc. (Fr. 60 H/165–87 IP). This is no doubt extracted from Xenocrates' work, *On the Soul,* in two books.

fies as Number, that is, the sum-total of the form-numbers. But at this stage, Xenocrates maintains, we do not yet have Soul; that requires the powers of mobility and motivity, and these are conferred by the addition to the mixture of Sameness and Otherness. The addition of these results in an entity which has the ontological capacity of creating individuals, of separating them off from one another, and of grouping them in genera and species, as well as the epistemological capacity of identifying them and distinguishing between them—and all this involves the intellectual motion of discursive thought.

What warrant Xenocrates may have had for interpreting the *Timaeus* account as he does we have no means of knowing, but there is at least nothing in Plato's text that makes his interpretation impossible, and he had the advantage over us of knowing how Plato intended his text to be taken. For us, the 'indivisible being' and the 'being divided among bodies' remain difficult to identify as Platonic first principles, by reason of the fact that, in the narrative, the Demiurge is manipulating them as materials ready to his hand in fabricating the soul. It is therefore necessary to adopt a non-literal interpretation of the narrative, or myth (as, of course, both Speusippus and Xenocrates did), which 'deconstructs' the Demiurge and his activities, before one can see these entities as Monad and Dyad, which are themselves responsible for uniting to produce Number and Soul.

For Xenocrates, as for his predecessors, Soul is the mediating entity *par excellence* of the universe, and it is thus necessary that it contain within itself elements which can relate both to the intelligible and the sensible realms, as well as all the ratios out of which the harmony of the cosmos is constituted. As to the relation between the World-Soul and the individual souls, which should mirror its composition, we do not learn anything explicit in our sources, except the curious report, in Damascius' *Commentary on the Phaedo*,[95] that Xenocrates (and Speusippus before him) postulated the immortality of the whole soul, including the irrational part (*alogia*). All this need mean is that

---

[95] I 177, p. 124, 13 ff. Norvin (= Fr. 73 H/211 IP). This is part of a rather summary doxography, being a student's notes of Damascius' lectures, and that must be borne in mind when evaluating it.

these Old Academicians did not make any strong distinction between the substantial status of the two parts of the soul (which they presumably recognized), despite the description of the lower part of the human soul, comprising the sense-perceptive and passionate aspects, in the *Timaeus* as 'mortal' (61C, 72D). They must have taken these references as loosely meant—'mortal' in the sense of 'concerned or involved with what is mortal', i.e. the body—but to what extent they believed the soul in its separated state to be subject to sense-perception or to the passions attendant on these is not at all clear; nor is it clear what is the relation of individual souls to soul in general. But then that is not by any means clear in Plato himself. It may indeed be[96] that this doctrinal position results simply from a concern to reconcile the account of the soul given in the *Timaeus* with that in the *Phaedrus,* where a tripartite soul is plainly immortal; but this bald doxographic report is not much to go on.

This question, at any rate, brings us to the level of the physical world. Here Xenocrates is paid the rather backhanded compliment by Theophrastus, in his *Metaphysics* (6^b6–10), that, unlike the other Platonists, who pay no attention to 'the heavens and the remaining things in the universe',[97] 'he does somehow assign everything its place in the universe, alike objects of sense (*aisthēta*), objects of intellection (*noēta*), mathematical objects, and divine things as well.' We seem to discern here, if we press the details of the text, a triadic division of reality between *aisthēta, noēta,* and *mathematika,* with 'divine things' (*ta theia*) rather tacked on. Normally, in such a context, *ta theia* might reasonably be understood as referring to the heavenly bodies, but then one might well ask why they cannot be accommodated within the compass of the previous triad of types of being. And we might wonder also what ontological status is being accorded here to the 'objects of mathematics'?

In fact, Theophrastus' rather odd list may be brought into relation

---

[96] As proposed to me, very soundly, by an anonymous reader.

[97] An extraordinary charge, surely, in view of the contents of Plato's *Timaeus,* and what we know of Speusippus' concern with the division of the physical world, but there it is. Theophrastus' *Metaphysics* is in many ways a peculiar work.

with another division of the universe attributed to Xenocrates by Sextus Empiricus (*AM* VII 147 ff.),[98] which may throw some light on it, while revealing a notable feature of Xenocrates' thought:

Xenocrates says that there are three forms of existence (*ousia*), the sensible (*aisthētē*), the intelligible (*noētē*), and that which is composite [sc. of these two] and opinable (*doxastē*); and of these the sensible is that which exists below the heaven, the intelligible is that which belongs to all things outside the heaven, and the opinable and composite is that of the heaven itself; for it is visible by sense-perception, but intelligible by means of astronomy. This, then, being the situation, he declared that the criterion of the existence which is outside the heaven and intelligible is scientific knowledge (*epistēmē*), that of what is below the heaven and sensible is sense-perception (*aisthēsis*), and the criterion of the mixed existence is opinion (*doxa*).

He then links to each of these realms one of the three Fates, Atropos to the intelligible realm, Clotho to the realm of sense, and Lachesis to the intermediate, heavenly realm—a curious adaptation of Plato's use of the Fates at *Rep.* X 617c![99]

It seems to have been one of Xenocrates' particular concerns to find a formula or formulae for linking the various levels of the universe with one another, and to employ the device of postulating an intermediate stage between the two extremes of intelligible (and unchanging) and sensible (and ever-changing) in order to facilitate this. Here we see him contrasting *epistēmē* and *aisthēsis* as two contrasting modes of cognition of two opposed modes of being. So much is Platonic enough; his interesting innovation is to borrow the Platonic concept of 'opinion' (*doxa*) for the apprehension of the intermediate, heavenly realm, on the ground that its contents, the planets and stars, are cognizable (though unreliably) by the sense of sight, but their true nature is cognizable intellectually, by means of

[98] Fr. 5 H/83 IP. This follows immediately upon the equally interesting account of Speusippus' epistemology, quoted in Ch. 2, p. 78 above.

[99] One might speculate as to the inspiration behind this 'vertical' adaptation of Plato's 'horizontal' assignment of the Fates to their tasks. As to why Atropos is assigned to the intelligible realm, and Clotho to the sensible, I have no suggestions, other than the thought that *atropos,* as meaning 'unchanging' is particularly suitable to the unchanging realm of the Forms; but the intermediary role of Lachesis *might* be influenced by Plato's portrayal of her at 617D as 'lending a hand to each' of the other two.

astronomy—that is to say, *scientific* astronomy, as outlined in Plato's *Republic* (VII 528E ff.)—and is thus to be regarded as a mixture of the other two modes of cognition.

Now of course for Plato *doxa* is not related to the knowledge of the heavenly realm, but simply to the apprehension of the physical. In the *Republic* (V 476D–478D), *doxa* is intermediate, not between scientific knowledge and sense-perception, but between knowledge and *ignorance*. Again, in the *Timaeus* (37B–C, 51D–52A), *epistēmē* or *nous* is of the intelligible realm, *doxa* of the physical. The utilization of the concept of *doxa*—viewed as a sort of *blend* of *epistēmē* and *aisthēsis*—for the intermediate realm of the heavens is thus a significant innovation of Xenocrates.

There remains the problem, however, of reconciling the report of Theophrastus, which presents an intermediate realm of *mathēmatika* between the intelligible and the sensible, with that of Sextus, which identifies the intermediate realm as that of the heavenly bodies. It is not, of course, necessary to assume that Theophrastus is intending to present a series of levels of reality, but on the other hand it is quite possible that he is, and that he is tendentiously appropriating the 'Platonic'[100] concept of 'mathematicals' as intermediate betwen Forms and particulars, and applying it to Xenocrates' concept of an intermediate realm. The fact that he seems rather to tag on 'the divine things' (meaning the heavenly bodies) at the end of the list would lend colour to this hypothesis.

We may turn now to another passage, from Plutarch's essay *On the Face in the Moon* (943E–944A),[101] describing why the moon is so well suited to serve as the linchpin holding the universe together. Here Xenocrates is presented as propounding another triadic structure, entirely within the physical world this time, with the moon, rather than the heavenly realm as a whole, holding the intermediate position:[102]

---

[100] At least according to Aristotle's interpretation.

[101] Fr. 56 H/161 IP. Plutarch, we may note, is a considerable fan of Xenocrates', and our major (sympathetic) source for his thought. This doctrine may possibly have been set out somewhere in the six books of Xenocrates' *On Nature*.

[102] I borrow here the translation of Harold Cherniss, in the Loeb edition, slightly emended.

First they [sc. the disembodied souls] behold the moon as she is in herself:
her magnitude and beauty and nature, which is not simple and unmixed, but
a blend as it were of star and earth. Just as earth has become soft by having
been mixed with breath and moisture[103] and as blood gives rise to sense-perception in the flesh with which it is commingled, so the moon, they say,[104]
because it has been permeated through and through by aether, is at once
animated and fertile (*empsychos kai gonimos*) and at the same time has the
proportion of lightness to heaviness in equipoise. In fact it is in this way too,
they say, that the universe itself has entirely escaped local motion, because it
has been constructed out of the things that naturally move upwards and
those that naturally move downwards.

This was also the concept of Xenocrates who, taking his start from Plato,
seems to have reached it by a kind of superhuman reasoning (*theiōi tini logis-
mōi*). Plato is the one who declared that each of the stars as well was constructed of earth and fire bound together in a proportion by means of the
two intermediate natures, for nothing, as he said, attains perceptibility that
does not contain an admixture of earth and light;[105] but Xenocrates says
that the stars and the sun are composed of fire and the first degree of density (*to prōton pyknon*), the moon of the second density and air that is proper to
her, and the earth of water[106] and the third kind of density; and that in general neither density all by itself nor subtility (*to manon*) is receptive of Soul.

What are we to make of this scheme?[107] Although Plutarch talks

---

[103] I take this to refer to the 'earth' that is a component of the human body, thus setting up a parallel between microcosm and macrocosm, rather than to the earth as a
whole, as Cherniss takes it; but I admit that the phraseology is obscure.

[104] The reference here is unclear, but it may most naturally, I think, be taken, along
with the similar reference in the next sentence, as referring to the Stoics. At any rate, we
know from a reference in Achilles' *Isagoge,* ch. 4 (= *SVF* II 555) that Chrysippus made
just this point about the reason for the equipoise of the earth.

[105] This seems to be a combined reference to *Tim.* 40A, where the Demiurge is said to
have composed the heavenly bodies ('the divine class', *to theion*) 'for the most part out of
fire', and 31B–32C, where the theory of proportions between solid bodies is set out, and
it is declared that 'without fire nothing could ever become visible, nor tangible without
some solidity, nor solid without earth.'

[106] There is something of a textual problem here. The MSS read either *kai aeros,* 'and
of air' (B), or *kai pyros,* 'and of fire' (E) after *hydatos.* Cherniss seems right to excise either
of them, as they break the symmetry of Xenocrates' system. One may see here, presumably, the hand (or hands) of an 'intelligent' scribe.

[107] How, for one thing, is it to be related to the earlier triadic division reported by
Sextus? The answer, perhaps, is that it is not to be related closely to it at all. The distinc-

of Xenocrates 'taking his start from Plato', there seems little enough in the dialogues to justify this triad of levels of reality, with its three degrees of *pyknon*. And yet, with a little imagination, the impulse to such a scheme might be discerned in certain hints dropped by Plato in the *Timaeus*. First of all, though, we must try to discern exactly what is being propounded by Xenocrates. To take the three elements first, I would suggest that they may best be understood in terms of the primary bodies of the *Timaeus* (53D ff.), fire, air, and water being represented respectively by pyramid, octahedron, and icosahedron (earth, it would seem, being taken as merely the ultimate density of water, instead of an element in its own right, represented by the cube[108]). Then what I take to be these three elemental forms are blended with three (presumably proportionately) increasing degrees of 'density' to form the substances proper to the three realms: first, the sun, planets, and stars; then the moon; and finally the earth and the whole sublunar realm.

But how are we to understand these 'densities', or *pykna*? It seems to me that Xenocrates is here making use of two distinct Presocratic concepts, and blending them in a rather sophisticated way. First, there is the old and rather naive doctrine of Anaximenes, according to which all other elements, or features of the world, are derived from Air, by a process of 'rarefaction' (*manotēs*) and 'compression' or 'densification' (*pyknotēs*).[109] It is this aspect of Xenocrates' theory that is probably being picked on polemically by Aristotle in *De Caelo* III 5, 303ᵇ23 ff. and 304ᵃ12 ff.;[110] but there is another aspect of *pyknon* that must not be overlooked, and that is the musical—and

tion reported by Sextus is an epistemological one; this scheme is *ontological*. Their only similarity is that both are triadic.

[108] Here, at least, Xenocrates appears to be quite un-Platonic, since Plato makes a point of the refractory nature of the cube, resulting in the difficulty with which earth can be changed into any other element (55E). This, however, would interfere with Xenocrates' triadic scheme.

[109] e.g. 13A5 D-K (= Simplicius, *In Phys.* p. 24, 26 ff. Diels).

[110] As was acutely discerned by Cherniss (1944: 143)—though I do not agree with the rest of his analysis. It is not proper, I think, to conclude that Xenocrates takes fire, air, and water to be forms of *manon*, with fire being *to prōton manon*. On the contrary, Plutarch tells us that the *manon* in itself is 'not receptive of soul'—that is to say, the purely intelligible.

thus Pythagorean—meaning of the term. As one may learn from any handbook of Greek music, the tetrachord, comprising the interval of a fourth, is divided into three intervals, bounded by four notes. When the two smaller intervals added together are smaller than the remaining interval, they are called a *pyknon*. That a *pyknon* was regarded as a definite degree of tension can be observed from a passage of Xenocrates' contemporary Aristoxenus, *On the Primary Chronos:*[111]

We must recognize that the same argument [sc. that infinity, or indefiniteness, *apeiria,* is inimical to the science of music in general] will apply to harmonic science. Here too it has become clear to us that, while the lengths of all possible intervals are an infinite number, in practice a particular scale, sung in accordance with a particular 'colour' (*chroa*), will adopt a particular *pyknon* out of the infinite number; and in the same way out of all the infinite number of intervals that might complete the tetrachord, it will choose the particular size of interval that corresponds to the *pyknon* that it has adopted.

We do not need to suppose that Xenocrates was intending to use *pyknon* in its fully technical musical sense; all he need be wishing to convey is the idea of a series of harmoniously graded and definite degrees of tension, producing, in combination with the 'formal' aspects of the relevant elemental corpuscles, three distinct, but related, levels of reality.[112]

We may note the central role played in this system by the moon. The moon also plays a significant part in Xenocrates' theory of daemons—another doctrine for knowledge of which we are indebted to

[111] Preserved in Porphyry, *In Ptol. Harm.*, pp. 79–80 Düring, and included in *Aristoxenus, Elementa Rhythmica,* ed. L. Pearson (Oxford, 1990), 32–5. I borrow Pearson's translation.

[112] It might seem to be in contravention of this triadic system that Xenocrates, as we are told by Simplicius on three occasions (= Fr. 53 H/264–6 IP), accepted Aristotle's theory of aether as the 'fifth element' and substance of the heavenly bodies, interpreting thus the fifth 'Platonic' corpuscle of the *Timaeus*, the dodecahedron, which Plato, at *Tim.* 55c, had, rather oddly, assigned to 'the universe as a whole, in his adornment of it' (*epi to pan ... ekeino diazōgraphōn*)—certainly a notable exegesis of the *Timaeus*! However, one could argue that Xenocrates in fact took the heavenly fire, combined with the first *pyknon*, as being equivalent to aether, and vulgar fire as being a by-product of the third degree of *pyknon* (which in turn might lend some credence to the variant readings in the MSS of Plutarch—but not necessarily so).

Plutarch. In his essay *On the Obsolescence of Oracles* (416C–D), we find the following testimony:[113]

In the confines, as it were, between gods and men there exist certain natures susceptible to human emotions and involuntary changes, whom it is right that we, like our fathers before us, should regard as daemons, and, calling them by that name, should reverence. As an illustration of this subject, Xenocrates, the companion of Plato, employed the order of the triangles; the equilateral he compared to the nature of the gods, the scalene to that of man, and the isosceles to that of the daemons; for the first is equal in all its lines, the second unequal in all, and the third is partly equal and partly unequal, like the nature of the daemons, which possess human emotions and divine power.

Xenocrates, then, is amplifying the suggestion given in Plato's *Symposium* (202E)—which must be regarded a basic proof text for the later Academic theory of daemons—as to the median role of daemons, by providing a mathematical model according to which it might be understood.[114] Furthermore, if we can assume that, in the passage immediately following this quotation, Plutarch is continuing to be influenced by Xenocrates, we can see that he also made a connection betwen his theory of daemons and his triadic schema for the universe (416DE):

Nature has placed within our ken perceptible images and visible likenesses, the sun and the stars for the gods, and for mortal men celestial lights, comets, and meteors . . .; but there is a body of mixed nature which actually parallels the daemons, namely the moon; and when men see that she, acting in accord with the cycles through which those beings pass, is subject to manifest waxings and wanings and transformations, some call her an 'earthlike star', others a 'heavenly earth', and others the domain of Hecate, who belongs both to the earth and to the heavens.

The daemonic level of being is thus firmly linked to the moon, in its capacity as a mixed and median entity. Both moon and daemons

---

[113] Fr. 23 H/222 IP. I borrow F. C. Babbitt's translation from the Loeb edition (*Plutarch's Moralia*, vol. 5). Xenocrates is not recorded to have composed a special treatise on daemonology, but he may have included remarks on this subject in his work *On Gods.*

[114] There is no suggestion, I think, that this is anything more than an image. There is no question of gods or daemons being made up of basic triangles of any sort.

serve to bind the extremes of the universe together, as Plutarch goes on to point out. The moon is linked in particular to the element of air, even as the heavenly realm above the moon is to that of fire, and Plutarch remarks that, even as, if the air between the earth and the moon were to be removed, the unity and community (*henotēs kai koinotēs*) of the universe would be destroyed, so 'those who refuse to recognize the race of daemons make the relations of gods and men remote and alien by doing away with the "interpretative and ministering nature", as Plato has called it.'[115]

This seems to me to be fully in accord with what we know of Xenocrates' views, though we cannot, I suppose, be sure that it is not an elaboration by Plutarch on a basic Xenocratean theme. Nevertheless, the concept of the physical as well as the spiritual, mediating position of daemons is clearly an elaboration of Plato's doctrine which we may attribute to Xenocrates.

The equation of daemons with the realm of the moon cannot, however, be complete. For one thing, there would seem to be daemons also below the moon (in the 'theological' fragment from Aetius,[116] after all, there is mention of 'sublunary daemons', *hyposelēnoi daimones*—though this should perhaps not be pressed too closely); for another, though, there are, according to Xenocrates, two types of daemon, good and evil, and the evil would seem to be lower on the cosmic scale than the good. In his essay *On Isis and Osiris*,[117] Plutarch lists Xenocrates among those[118] who identify daemons as beings

stronger than men and, in their might, greatly surpassing our nature, yet not possessing the divine quality unmixed and uncontaminated, but with a share also in the nature of the soul and the perceptive faculties of the body, and with a susceptibility to pleasure and pain, and to whatever passions (*pathē*), supervening on these changes of state, cause disturbance to them, to a greater or lesser extent. For among daemons, as among men, there are different degrees of virtue and of vice.

---

[115] A reference, of course, to *Symp.* 202E. [116] Fr. 15 H/213 IP.

[117] 360E = Fr. 24 H/225 IP.

[118] He mentions also Pythagoras, Plato, and Chrysippus! It is not clear to what text of Plato Plutarch can be referring, but what we may be seeing here is a reflection of Xenocrates' propensity to claim Pythagoras and Plato as authorities for his views.

For Xenocrates, as Plutarch explains a little lower down,[119] such phenomena as days of ill omen, and festivals which involve self-laceration, lamentation, obscenity, or such atrocities as human sacrifice can only be explained by postulating the existence of evil spirits that take delight in such things, and must be placated. It would almost seem as if *two* proportions would be required between gods and men, good and evil daemons being represented by different ratios—such as, perhaps, 4 and 6 between 2 and 8. Xenocrates' daemonology does not, in fact, seem to fit with entire neatness the logical-mathematical frame created for it. However, in its main lines, it gives further testimony to his desire to formalize all levels of the universe, and work out their mutual relations—as well as to explain the phenomena of popular religion.

The dualistic streak in Xenocrates' thought, however, manifests itself in various other ways, notably in his view of the sublunar world and of the nature of man. Let us return, first of all, to the 'theological' testimony from Aetius (Fr. 15 H/213 IP), of which we have made use earlier in connection with first principles. The passage continues:

He regards the heaven also as a god, and the stars as fiery Olympian gods, and he believes also in other beings, invisible sublunary daemons. He also holds the view that <certain divine powers> penetrate (*endiēkein*) the material elements as well.[120] Of these, <that which occupies the air> he terms <Hades>,[121] as being invisible (*aeidēs*),[122] that which occupies the water Poseidon, and that which occupies the earth Demeter the Seed-Sower. All these identifications he adapted from Plato, and passed on to the Stoics.

---

[119] 361B = Fr. 25 H/229 IP. Cf. also *De Defectu Oraculorum*, 417C-E, where the same point is made, though without adducing Xenocrates.

[120] There is a most unfortunate lacuna here. I give the suggestion of Krische, followed by Heinze and others, for filling it, which is certainly plausible, since we need an antecedent for *toutōn*, 'of these'. The interesting question here, though, is whether fire is being taken as somehow more divine than the other elements, as being the substance of the heavenly gods, and whether it is *this* that may be the divine force that is permeating the other elements. This would bring Xenocrates very close to Stoicism—as, indeed, Aetius suggests.

[121] Lacuna supplied by Heinze. The alternative, to supply 'Hera', as proposed by Heeren and Meineke, is much less plausible, for reasons discussed above, p. 104.

[122] Strictly speaking, this should mean 'formless', 'invisible' being *aidēs*, but it must be the latter that is intended, whatever the spelling.

131

In all this there is nothing on the face of it particularly dualistic, but we may focus our attention on the identification of Hades as presiding over the air (unfortunately obscured by a lacuna, but virtually certain nonetheless). This may in turn be related to certain other peculiar details of doctrine—all, alas, relayed only by late authorities, but not to be rejected for that reason alone. First of all, Plutarch tells us[123] that 'Xenocrates calls that Zeus who is in the realm of what is invariable and identical[124] "topmost" (*hypatos*), but "nethermost" (*neatos*) he who is below the moon.' We have here, on the face of it, a contrast between a higher Zeus, who should be identical with the first principle, the Monad or 'Zeus ruling in the heaven' of the Aetius passage, and a lower Zeus, who may be identified with Hades—who was often called 'subterranean Zeus' (*Zeus chthonios*)[125]—but a Hades transposed to the sublunar realm.[126] What is somewhat troublesome, though, is that this passage occurs in a context where Plutarch is comparing the *three* parts of the Platonic soul in the *Republic* to the *three* traditional pitches on the scale in Greek music, *hypatē, mesē,* and *neatē,* and in view of this—and in view of Xenocrates' otherwise attested propensity for a triadic division of the universe[127]—one would have expected also a 'median (*mesos*) Zeus', and this point has indeed been made, notably by H.-J. Krämer.[128] On the other hand, if Xenocrates had postulated a median Zeus, it is hard to see why Plutarch would not have mentioned the fact here. And yet the heavenly realm cannot be left without a pre-

---

[123] In *Platonic Questions* 9, 1007F (= Fr. 18 H/216 IP).

[124] Standard Platonist terminology for the intelligible realm—although for Xenocrates this is probably to be identified with the outer rim of the universe, rather than with any totally transcendent level of being.

[125] As by Homer, *Iliad* 9. 457, Aeschylus, *Suppl.* 156–8 and 230–1, and Euripides, *Fr.* 912 Nauck.

[126] Oddly enough, when Clement of Alexandria reports, at *Strom.* V 14, p. 405, 1–2 Stählin (= Fr. 18 H/217 IP), what is apparently the same doctrine—*Zeus hypatos* and *Zeus neatos*—he speaks as if the contrast between the two was that of father and son (i.e. he sees in the doctrine an *emphasis* of the Christian notion of God the Father and God the Son), leading one to think rather of Zeus and Dionysus than of Zeus and Hades. This may not be without significance, as we shall see presently.

[127] See above, pp. 123–9.

[128] (1964: 37 n. 58; 82 n. 209).

siding deity. A solution to the problem would be to postulate, not a median Zeus, but rather Apollo (whose identification with the sun is accepted already before Xenocrates' time), as the ruler of the heavenly realm. This would explain why Plutarch omits mention of a median deity, since Apollo would be of no relevance to his terminological point, which concerns *hypatos* and *neatos*.

The other aspect of this testimony that is interesting is, once again (as in the case of the *pykna*), the musical analogy. The cosmos is for Xenocrates held together by Pythagorean-style harmony; Hades, while in a way antithetical to Zeus, is yet a necessary component of the great musical scale which is the universe, and does his bit to hold it together.[129]

On the other hand, the dualistic aspect of Xenocrates' thought manifests itself in another intriguing snippet of doctrine, contributed this time by the late Neoplatonist Damascius, in the course of his commentary on Plato's *Phaedo* 62B,[130] where Socrates makes a reference to our being in mortal bodies 'as on a kind of guard-duty' (*en tini phrourâi*). A series of quite varied interpretations of this obscure remark are given, concluding with that of Xenocrates, that it is a reference to our 'Titanic' nature, which 'culminates in Dionysus (*eis Dionyson apokoryphoutai*)'. Behind this very compressed and obscure reference there lurks a whole complex of doctrine, which once again shows Xenocrates' fascination with Orphic mythology.[131] The relevant myth is explained more fully in other passages.[132] It concerns the rending apart and consuming of Dionysus by the Titans (at the instigation of Hera), their smiting in revenge with the thunderbolt by Zeus, and the birth of men from their ashes—this being the explanation for

---

[129] Another most interesting passage, attributed by Plutarch, oddly, to 'the Delphians' (who are most unlikely to have indulged in such sophisticated theorizing), but plainly Xenocratean in inspiration, is *Quaest. Conviv.* IX 14, 745B, where we find the cosmos divided into three regions, that of the fixed stars, that of the other heavenly bodies, and the sublunar realm, and each assigned a Muse, termed respectively *Hypatē, Mesē*, and *Neatē*, the whole being 'bound and ordered together according to harmonic ratios (*kata logous enharmonious*)'. These 'Muses' are in turn linked up, as Xenocrates did in Fr. 5 H/83 IP (discussed above, p. 124), with the three Fates of Plato, *Rep.* X 617C.

[130] *In Phd.* I p. 85 Norvin (= Fr. 20 H/219 IP).

[131] Cf. above, p. 104.

[132] Olympiodorus, *In Phd.* 1, 3; 7, 10; and cf. also Plut. *De esu carn.* 996C.

the various irrational aspects of human nature. It is the Orphic equivalent of the Judaeo-Christian doctrine of original sin. This Xenocrates would seem to have adopted in full, and to have postulated Dionysus as in some way the presiding deity of this realm of existence—that, at least, would seem to be the significance of the final obscure statement. But how, one might ask, does this fit in with his other attested divisions of the universe? The text of Damascius, it must be said, goes on (*In Phd.* I 3), to talk of a double creation, the higher presided over by Zeus, under whom are a triad of Olympian gods, the lower presided over by Dionysus, under whom are a triad of Titans. This structure of a monad presiding over a triad is no doubt Neoplatonic, but the more general division may conceivably go back to Xenocrates, because we have yet another odd snippet of doctrine, this time relayed by Tertullian,[133] in which he attributes to 'Xenocrates the Academic' a double order of gods, the Olympian and the Titanic, deriving respectively from heaven and earth.

A rather troublesome scenario seems to be building up here, much more 'dualistic' than anything that can be attributed to Plato,[134] or indeed than what we have observed of Xenocrates' own doctrine from other sources, in which the sublunary realm is given over to the administration of a subordinate divinity, whether Hades or Dionysus—these two are actually identified, albeit occasionally, in traditional religion[135]—and mortals are discerned as being condemned to serve this divinity, at least for a time, while incarcerated in a body. Can it be fitted in with what we seem to have learned so far of Xenocrates' cosmological scheme? It seems to me that it can, after all. What we have, on the one hand, is a universe held together by

---

[133] *Adv. Nat.* II 2 (= Fr. 19 H/218 IP).

[134] Although we may note, for Plato, *Laws* III 701B, where the Athenian Stranger is condemning the extreme liberty of the developed Athenian democracy for displaying and reproducing the so-called 'Titanic nature of old', by showing no respect for anything.

[135] Admittedly, the only real ancient evidence for their association is Heraclitus, Fr. 15 D-K, which states, in the course of an attack on traditional religious rites, that 'Hades and Dionysus are the same'. This may well contain a large component of Heraclitean paradoxicality, but it is fair, I think, to assume that Xenocrates could not have said it were it not for the fact of certain chthonic aspects of the cult of Dionysus.

means of a harmonious tension of opposites, but on the other, a strong contrast is established between the condition of mortals, as embodied souls, incarcerated in the sublunary realm, and the mode of existence of disembodied souls, and of the celestial divinities, established in the heavens—presided over, respectively, by Apollo (as sun-god), and Dionysus/Hades.

This may indeed seem a bizarre, almost Gnostic scenario, but it finds an echo in a treatise of Xenocrates' admirer Plutarch, *On the E at Delphi,* though, it must be admitted, without any reference to Xenocrates. At 393B–C, Plutarch makes his own revered teacher, Ammonius, extol the essential unity and simplicity of the supreme God, whom he identifies with Apollo rather than Zeus,[136] but then proceeds to exempt him from any direct involvement with the multifariousness and changeability of the physical world. Our world of change, Ammonius goes on to explain, is presided over by another, inferior divinity, whom he identifies with Pluto or Hades (393F–394A). It is impious, and indeed absurd, to suggest—here a dig at the Stoics[137]—that the supreme God produces alterations in himself (turning himself into fire, for example) or in the world as a whole, like a child building sand-castles and then knocking them down again:[138]

For on the contrary, in respect of anything whatever that has come to be in this world, for this he binds together its substance and prevails over its corporeal weakness, which tends towards dissolution. And it seems to me right to address to the god the words, 'Thou art,'[139] which are most opposed to this account, and testify against it, believing that never does any vagary or

[136] The dialogue is, admittedly, concerned with Apollo, but this is still odd; it appears to be a Neopythagorean notion, based on the etymology of *Apollon* as 'not-many', and thus to be identified with the Monad, cf. *De Is.* 354F.

[137] This picks up in an interesting way an earlier passage, 388E–389B, where Plutarch himself is speaking, which makes a similar contrast between Apollo and Dionysus, where the Stoic doctrine of *ekpyrōsis,* and in general of the concept of the supreme God as an immanent entity, is more explicitly attacked.

[138] This image from Homer (*Iliad* 15. 362–4) is particularly well chosen, since the point of comparison is in fact Apollo knocking down the wall of the Achaeans. One wonders if Plutarch is aware of a Stoic-inspired allegorization of this passage.

[139] A reference to the mysterious *E* (interpreted here as *ei*) on the portal of the temple of Apollo, which is what the dialogue is about.

transformation take place near him, but that such acts and experiences are related *to some other god, or daemon, whose office is concerned with nature in dissolution and generation.* (trans. Babbitt, emended)

Ammonius goes on to contrast this secondary deity with Apollo by means of a comparative study of their epithets: Apollo 'not-many', *Dēlios* (interpreted as 'clear'), *Phoibos* (interpreted as 'bright'), and so on; Pluto is *Ploutōn*, in the sense of 'abounding in wealth', and so in multiplicity, *Aidōneus* ('unseen'), and *Skotios*, 'dark'. A strong opposition is thus set up, but it is not, after all, a contrast between two radically opposed forces. That we get elsewhere in Plutarch, but not here. What we have here is a contrast between a primary and secondary god, and it is a most interesting one, as it seems rather to reflect what we have been observing in Xenocrates. Such an entity, however, though strongly contrasted in the present passages with the supreme God, is by no means necessarily an 'evil' or purely negative force. The figure represented in this dialogue by Dionysus or Hades/Pluto is responsible for the multiplicity, changeability, and illusoriness characteristic of the physical, sublunary world—what in Hindu thought would be termed *mâyâ*—but this is a necessary aspect of the universe as a whole, and not condemned as such. He weaves a veil of appearance around the embodied soul, from which, however, the philosopher is welcome to escape if he can—an end which he can accomplish through the practice of dialectic and an ascetic lifestyle.

Of course, there is no secure warrant for tracing this intriguing doctrine in Plutarch all the way back to Xenocrates, but, in view of the widely attested interest of Plutarch in various distinctive Xenocratean doctrines, and the tantalizing traces of such a doctrine in Xenocrates himself, it seems a pretty fair bet that some influence came to Plutarch in this instance from that source.

Ethics

That, at any rate, constitutes as much as can be discerned of Xenocrates' views on first principles and, broadly, on the area of philosophy anciently designated as 'physics'. We may turn next to consider what we can learn of his views on ethics.

This was an area of philosophy to which, plainly, Xenocrates devoted a good deal of attention, to judge from the list of his writings on ethical subjects preserved by Diogenes Laertius. We have titles *On Wealth, On Self-Control, On the Useful, On Freedom, On Friendship* (in two books), *On Decency, On Happiness* (in two books), *On Practical Wisdom (phronēsis), On Moderation, On Holiness, On Passions, On Lifestyles, On Concord, On Justice, On Virtue* (in two books), *On Pleasure* (also two books), and a number of dialogues and works addressed to individuals which may also have had ethical content. There were also, as we have seen, a number of works on political themes, and an *Oikonomikos*—presumably on household management. From all this, alas, little or nothing remains. However, we can gather that, here as elsewhere, he is concerned primarily rather to formalize what he takes to be Plato's teaching than to develop any distinctive theories of his own—though this does not in fact preclude his developing Plato's thought in interesting directions.

We may start our examination of his doctrine with a lengthy passage from Cicero's *De Finibus*,[140] where, in Book IV, Cicero himself undertakes to reply to Cato's exposition of Stoicism in Book III by taking up the point of view of Antiochus of Ascalon, for whom the Stoics are simply ungrateful and somewhat unbalanced disciples of the Old Academy, which itself forms a broad unity with the early Peripatetics. This point of view has been repeatedly dismissed as wildly tendentious, but I would maintain that, while certainly oversimplified and no doubt *somewhat* tendentious, Antiochus' position cannot have lacked *any* foundation, and that one area where his position has particular plausibility is that of ethical theory.

Cicero is expounding here the *telos,* or 'end of goods', which constituted the basic topic with which Hellenistic philosophies began their exposition of ethics. This terminology is not attested as going back to the Old Academy or Peripatos, but, on the evidence presented here, the topic itself did. Cicero begins by distinguishing three interpretations of the Stoic formulation of the *telos,* 'living in accordance with

---

[140] IV 15–18 (= Fr. 79 H/234 IP). I give the translation of H. Rackham in the Loeb edition, slightly emended.

nature': (1) 'to live in the light of a knowledge of the natural sequence of causation' (this he identifies as Zeno's own); (2) 'to live in the performance of all, or most, of one's intermediate duties (*kathēkonta, officia*)'—this, though not identified, would be the interpretation of later Stoics; and (3) 'to live in the enjoyment of all, or the greatest, of those things which are in accordance with nature'. It is this third interpretation which Cicero, wearing his Antiochian hat, approves, and which he identifies as that bequeathed to the Stoics by Xenocrates and Aristotle. As regards Aristotle, one can certainly derive such a doctrine from the *Nicomachean Ethics*; for Xenocrates we have some supporting evidence, as we shall see, that his position on this differed little from that of Aristotle. I would suggest that Antiochus is deriving his information from such a work as that *On Happiness*. Cicero's exposition is as follows:

> Again, the third interpretation of the formula is 'to live in the enjoyment of all, or of the greatest, of those things which are in accordance with nature'. This does not depend solely on our own conduct, for it involves two factors, first a mode of life enjoying virtue, secondly a supply of the things which are in accordance with nature, but which are not within our control.[141] But the chief Good (*summum bonum*) as understood in the third and last interpretation, and the way of life pursued on the basis of the chief Good, being inseparably linked with virtue, are attainable by the wise man alone; and this account of the end of goods, as we can see from the writings of the Stoics themselves,[142] was first established (*constitutus est*) by Xenocrates and Aristotle.

There now follows a most interesting exposition of a doctrine of the first principles of ethics, which, since it does not correspond to anything in Aristotle's surviving ethical writings,[143] may reasonably be attributed rather to Xenocrates. Cicero introduces it as follows:

[141] This is, of course, a significant breach with Stoic doctrine, since for the Stoics nothing which is not in our power is allowed to have any positive value towards contributing to happiness.

[142] This phrase, *ut ab ipsis Stoicis scriptum videmus,* is somewhat ambiguous, perhaps, but seems to me to imply that some Stoic authors, at least, gave credit themselves for the development of this doctrine to Xenocrates and Aristotle. This does, admittedly, seem unlikely, though, except perhaps in the context of some polemic against the New Academy.

[143] Although, I suppose, it could have appeared in one or more of his lost 'exoteric

They [sc. Xenocrates and Aristotle] therefore describe the first principles of nature (*prima naturae*),[144] which was your [sc. Cato's] starting point also, in the following terms.

Every natural organism aims at being its own preserver, so as to secure its safety and also its preservation true to its specific type. With this object, they declare, man has called in the aid of the arts also to assist nature; and chief among them is counted the art of living, which helps him to guard the gifts that nature has bestowed and to obtain those that are lacking. They further divided the nature of man into soul and body. Each of these parts they declared to be desirable for its own sake; at the same time they extolled the soul as infinitely surpassing the body in worth, and accordingly placed the virtues also of the mind above the goods of the body. But they held that wisdom is the guardian and protectress of the whole man, as being the comrade and helper of nature, and so they said that the function of wisdom, as protecting a being that consisted of a mind and a body, was to assist and preserve him in respect of both.

Another passage, independent of Cicero, but equally dependent, in all probability, on Antiochus, may be gleaned from Plutarch's polemical anti-Stoic treatise *On Common Conceptions.*[145] It comes in the context of a satirical assault on the Stoic insistence on valuing positively only what has to do with the human soul, and dismissing concerns of the body as 'indifferent':

'What, then,' says he [sc. the Stoic], 'will be my point of departure, and what shall I take as the originating principle of appropriate action (*to kathēkon*) and the raw material of virtue, once I abandon nature and what is in conformity with nature (*to kata physin*)?'

'Why, my good sir, what is the point of departure for Aristotle and for Theophrastus? And what do Xenocrates and Polemo take as principles? And has not Zeno too followed them in their assumption that nature and what is in conformity with nature are basic elements of happiness? Those former men, however, held by these things as choice-worthy (*haireta*) and

works—which, after all, would be all, so far as we know, that would have been available to Antiochus or Cicero.

[144] Presumably translating *ta prōta kata physin*—though that may well be simply the Stoic term.

[145] 1069E–F (= Fr. 78 H/233 IP). I borrow the translation of Harold Cherniss (in the Loeb edition, vol. XIII: ii), slightly emended.

good and beneficial; and having taken virtue in addition as operating among them by making proper use of each, they thought that with these constituents they were filling out and finishing off a perfect and integrated life by presenting the consistency that is truly in conformity and harmony with nature.'

The thrust of these two passages is to insist, in contradistinction to Stoic doctrine, on the role of the body and its welfare in the happiness of the whole man. It is this that Antiochus feels to be distinctive of the Old Academy (with which he links the Peripatos), while insisting that the Old Academicians, and in particular Xenocrates, first propounded the doctrine of living in accordance with *ta prōta kata physin,* 'the first things according to nature'. The question is, however, what justification Antiochus might have for such an attribution.

On this question the judgement of earlier scholars, such as Max Pohlenz,[146] was negative, but since the constructive article of C. O. Brink in *Phronesis,* 1 (1955),[147] a more positive consensus has been emerging, to the effect that Antiochus, though doubtless prone to exaggeration and oversimplification, could not have constructed his grand synthesis on no foundation whatever, and thus that there must be some substance to his claims. The problem is to discern what that might be, in the case of each of the thinkers concerned. One difficulty is that Antiochus' grand synthesis takes in not only Xenocrates, but his successor Polemo, and Aristotle and Theophrastus as well, so that, even if his broad claims are accepted, it is practically impossible to unravel what is specific to Xenocrates. On the other hand, that need not lead us to deny Xenocrates any part in the overall theory. Polemo, at least, was a devoted disciple of his, and is not likely to have done more than develop his theory in minor ways.[148]

It seems to me, therefore, that we may postulate for Xenocrates an

---

[146] (1948–9: i. 250–3).

[147] Though Brink is primarily concerned with Theophrastus' part in the development of the theory.

[148] There is, indeed, an adumbration of this theory in a passage of Plato's *Laws* (VI 782E–783A), where the Athenian Stranger identifies the desires for food, drink, and sex as three basic drives which can lead either (with proper training) to virtue, or (without it) to its opposite, but that is still some way from what we have here.

ethical theory which takes its start from something which could be described as *ta prōta kata physin,* the primary demands of nature, and these covered the needs of both soul and body, even if those of the soul were accorded much greater honour, and that virtue (*aretē*) consisted in developing each aspect of the human being to the degree and manner appropriate to it—this would seem to be the point of the phrase in the Plutarch passage (referring to virtue) 'by making proper use of each' (*oikeiōs khrōmenēn hekastōi*). Since Antiochus plainly made much of the Old Academy's paying due honour to the body and its needs as well as the soul, we can see here a clear differentiation between this position and that of the Stoics, while recognizing also how Stoic theory could be seen as a development of this, in the direction of austere self-sufficiency (which, for Antiochus, also betokened a loss of realism, and a consequent tendency to dishonest fudging!).

This, then, would be the basic ethical stance of Xenocrates. We may find confirmation of it in a testimony of Clement of Alexandria:[149]

Xenocrates of Chalcedon defines happiness (*eudaimonia*) as the acquisition of the virtue (*aretē*)[150] proper to us and of the resources with which to service it. Then as regards the proper seat (*en hōi*) of this, he plainly says the soul; as the motive causes of it (*hyph' hōn*) he identifies the virtues; as the material causes (*ex hōn*), in the sense of parts,[151] noble actions and good habits and attitudes (*hexeis te kai diatheseis*); and as indispensable accompaniments (*hōn ouk aneu*), bodily and external goods.

This, in the form relayed to us by Clement, must, I think, have passed through the alembic of late Hellenistic scholasticism,[152] but

---

[149] *Strom.* II 22, p. 186, 23 ff. Stählin (= Fr. 77 H/232 IP). Clement also subjoins Polemo's doctrine, but he does at least give that of Xenocrates separately. The testimony is presumably based, albeit remotely, on Xenocrates' treatise *Peri Eudaimonias.*

[150] In the broadest sense of 'excellence', since it comprises also bodily 'virtues'.

[151] How, we might ask, are noble actions, etc., 'parts' of virtue? Presumably in the (Aristotelian) sense that a virtuous mind-set is the product of a series of individual acts, which both arise from, and themselves reinforce, good *hexeis* and *diatheseis,* which are in turn inculcated by good training (from parents, teachers, and others). Cf. Arist. *EN* II 1; *Rhet.* I 9.

[152] It is highly unlikely, at least, that Xenocrates made use of what is termed 'the metaphysic of prepositions' to characterize his position.

it is most interesting, nonetheless, and there seems no reason to doubt its substantial accuracy. We may note in particular the recognition of the necessity of at least a modicum of bodily and external goods as indispensable for the realization of *eudaimonia* in the full sense.

The 'end' of human life is, then, for Xenocrates, 'life in accordance with nature', which implies 'life in accordance with virtue'. The only difference with later Stoic doctrine—but an important one—arose from the question as to whether or not, when once one had acquired virtue, one should abandon *ta prōta kata physin*, in the sense of the primary natural instincts of self-preservation, or at least exclude them from any part in the *telos* itself. Xenocrates, plainly, saw no need to abandon them, but simply subordinated them to the exercise of virtue, thus taking up a position in basic agreement with Aristotle and the Peripatos.

He does, however, seem to have held a theory of 'things of neutral value' (*adiaphora*), intermediate between the good and the evil, such as is not explicitly developed by Aristotle. This would accord superficially with Stoic doctrine, except that we do not know what sort of things Xenocrates would have labelled 'indifferent'. Perhaps nothing more important than trimming one's fingernails or blowing one's nose. Certainly the things which the Stoics considered 'indifferent', such as wealth or poverty, health or sickness, Xenocrates considered as goods or evils respectively, as we have seen.[153] In this connection, Sextus Empiricus, at the beginning of his treatise *Against the Ethicists*,[154] gives us a brief insight into Xenocrates' methods of argumentation (which may also help to explain why his works did not survive!). Sextus is saying that all the dogmatic philosophers make a threefold distinction between things good, bad, and indifferent, and Xenocrates is no exception:

---

[153] It is notable, as is remarked by Guthrie (1978: 481–2), that Plato himself paves the way for the Stoic doctrine of *adiaphora* by remarking at various places (*Meno* 87E–88E; *Rep.* VI 496C; *Laws* V 728D–E) that such 'goods' as health or wealth may just as well do harm as good, if not accompanied by prudence, or even if present in excess. It actually appears from Antiochus' evidence that Xenocrates regarded health and wealth as goods, but no doubt he would have agreed with Plato's reservations. For confirmation of Xenocrates' position on this, cf. Plutarch, *Comm. Not.* 1065A (= Fr. 92 H/249 IP).

[154] *Adv. Eth.* 3–6 (= Fr. 76 H/231 IP).

. . . but Xenocrates, in phrases peculiar to himself, and using the singular case, declared that 'everything which exists either is good or is evil or is neither good nor evil.' And whereas the rest of the philosophers adopted this division without a proof, he thought it right to introduce a proof as well. 'If,' he argued, 'anything exists which is apart from things good and evil and things neither good nor evil, that thing either is good or is not good. And if it is good, it will be one of the three; but if it is not good, it is either evil or neither evil nor good; and if it is evil, it will be one of the three, and if it is neither evil nor good, again it will be one of the three. Therefore everything which exists is either good or is evil or neither is good nor evil.

As Sextus remarks, this 'proof' seems to add nothing to the initial assertion, so that it hard to see the point of it.[155] It is not even clear that the first postulate makes much sense: if there exists something truly 'apart' (*kekhōrismenon*) from any of the three categories of thing, then there seems no necessity that it should itself be classed among them—unless, of course, they are taken as covering all existent things (as Xenocrates appears to be assuming); in which case, there cannot be anything 'apart' from them. However, whatever the value of the logical exercise set out here, we can at least gather that, for Xenocrates, there is a class of things indifferent.

If we can accept that from the above-quoted passage of Cicero we can derive an idea of the basic principles of Xenocrates' ethics, then from what follows it we can glean some insight into particular doctrines of his. The passage continues (*Fin.* IV 17–18):

After thus laying the first broad foundations of the theory, they went on to work it out in greater detail. The goods of the body, they held, required no particular explanation, but the goods of the soul they investigated with more elaboration, finding in the first place that in them lay the seeds of justice; and they were the first of any philosophers to teach that the love of parents for their offspring is a provision of nature; and that nature, so they pointed out,

---

[155] As is acutely noted by Isnardi Parente (1982: 419), there may be more going on here than meets the eye. She refers to Aristotle's polemical argument at *Met.* I 5, 1055ᵇ30 ff. against those who argue for the equal as intermediate between greater and smaller, and some anonymous state as intermediate between good and evil, and suggests that this may be directed against Xenocrates, as well as Speusippus. But even so, the argument as presented to us by Sextus seems to lack bite.

has ordained the union of men and women in marriage, which is prior in order of time, and is the root of all the family affections.

The line of reasoning is set out here by Cicero somewhat opaquely, but I think that we can discern an argument (perhaps derived from Xenocrates' attested treatise *On Justice*) identifying the natural affection of parents for their children as the most basic manifestation of what will later emerge as the virtue of justice, and therefore the institution of marriage as the ultimate 'seed' of that virtue, which seems here to be presented in turn as the most basic of the virtues. Something like this, after all, is laid down by Aristotle in the second chapter of Book I of his *Politics,* though without the specifically ethical conclusions stated here, so it is not improbable that Xenocrates should have been thinking along these lines.

The text continues:

Starting from these first principles, they traced out the origin and growth of all the virtues. From the same source was developed greatness of mind (*magnitudo animi = megalopsykhia*),[156] which could render us proof against the assaults of fortune, because the most important things (*maximae res*) were under the control of the wise man; whereas to the vicissitudes and blows of fortune a life directed by the precepts of the old philosophers could easily rise superior.

Since, as will become plain in a moment, we are involved in a description of a succession of four virtues, the other three of which are justice (as the basic one), wisdom, and moderation, it would seem that for Xenocrates (if it is he), 'great-souledness' is taking the place of courage (*andreia*). If that is so, we must ask ourselves why that would be. One possible answer is that courage in the vulgar sense is a somewhat problematic 'virtue' for a Platonist, as its possession is compatible with a conspicuous lack of any or all of the other three. That is what is at issue in Plato's *Laches*. One must either, therefore, radically redefine courage, or dispense with the name altogether. Xenocrates would seem to have chosen the latter option, and

---

[156] This is, of course, an Aristotelian virtue, cf. *EN* II 7, 1107^{b}21 ff.; IV 7, 1123^{a}34 ff. For Aristotle, indeed, *megalopsykhia* is 'a kind of crown of the virtues (*hoion kosmos tis tōn aretōn*), because it enhances them, and is never found without them,' 1124^{a}1–2.

selected the virtue of *megalopsykhia*.[157] This, after all, turns out to be nothing more than courage as redefined on Platonic lines as 'knowledge of what is truly to be feared and not to be feared' (cf. *Laches* 199A–B; *Prot.* 360D).[158] The statement that 'the most important things' are under the control of the wise man sounds ominously Stoic, but it is in fact presumably not something that Xenocrates would dispute; even though he recognizes the existence of bodily and external goods, he nevertheless ranks them as far inferior in importance to the goods of the soul, which are in the control of the wise man.

We pass on now to the remaining virtues of wisdom and moderation:

Again, from the elements given by nature there have arisen certain heights of excellence, springing partly from the contemplation of the secrets of nature, since the mind possesses an innate love of knowledge, whence also results the desire for argument and for discussion; and also, since man is the only animal endowed with a sense of modesty and shame,[159] with a desire for intercourse and society with his fellows, and with a scrupulous care in all his words and actions to avoid any conduct that is not honourable and seemly, from these beginnings or seeds, as I called them before, granted by nature, there were developed to perfection temperance, moderation, justice, and the whole of virtue.

This last section seems to outline the development of the virtues

---

[157] Democritus before him seems to have recognized this as a virtue (B46 D–K). The Stoics, after him, ranked it as a subdivision of *andreia* (*SVF* III 264), defining it as 'the knowledge which enables one to rise above the accidents of fortune, both good and bad'. Either, therefore, Antiochus in the present passage of Cicero is extrapolating Stoic doctrine back onto the Old Academy, or the Stoics are borrowing something from Xenocrates (and Aristotle); but there is nothing, after all, improbable about the latter supposition.

[158] We may note that Xenocrates is not recorded to have composed a treatise on courage, whereas he composed one on each of the other cardinal virtues, and this may be significant. On the other hand, it must be admitted that he is not recorded as having composed a treatise on *megalopsykhia* either.

[159] *Verecundia et pudor* here no doubt renders the Greek *aidōs*, and perhaps also *aiskhynē*. This recalls Protagoras' attribution of the virtues of 'shame' (or 'conscience', *aidōs*) and justice' (*dikē*) to men in his 'Great Speech' (*Prot.* 322c–d). There is also an interesting passage on *aidōs* in *Laws* I 647A–B. *Aidōs*, at least, was a Stoic *eupatheia*, a subdivision of *eulabeia*, the rational equivalent of *phobos*, 'fear' (*SVF* III 416, 432).

of wisdom (*sophia* or *phronēsis*—on both of which Xenocrates composed treatises, the former in six books, the latter in two) and moderation or self-control (*sōphrosynē*—on which he also composed a treatise, in one book).[160] We have here, then, somewhat obscured by Cicero's eloquence, a theory of the development of the set of four virtues, justice, great-souledness (substituting for courage), wisdom, and moderation, from a set of interconnected basic impulses, *ta prōta kata physin*, in a way which we do not find explicitly presented in either Plato or Aristotle, but which anticipates to a significant extent later Stoic doctrine. We are presented with a theory which involves a rational deduction of a system of perfected virtues from the initial impulses of affection between man and woman, leading to the establishment of the family, the natural instinct of curiosity about one's surroundings and desire to know, and a natural fellow-feeling and desire for association between members of the human race in general—all of which lead, with the application of reason, to the development of the corresponding virtues. Admittedly, the evidence available to us is open to suspicion, but I would maintain that there is at least nothing intrinsically implausible about Xenocrates having developed something like this theory. Certainly he was a man who gave a good deal of thought to ethical theory, as the many ethical titles listed among his works indicate. There is by now fairly widespread acceptance that Polemo, at least, anticipated Stoic ethical theory in various important respects, and if Polemo, why not his master Xenocrates?

The best-known utterance of Xenocrates, however, in the sphere of ethics is his dictum that a man can only be accounted 'happy' (*eudaimōn*)[161] if he has his soul in a good state (*spoudaia*); 'for the soul of each is his *daimōn*.'[162] Even from this tag, however, some useful

---

[160] Cicero's listing of both *temperantia* and *modestia* as virtues here need be no more than an instance of his characteristic verbosity. It seems fairly plain that we are dealing with a set of four virtues.

[161] Or 'flourishing', as is the currently more fashionable rendering of this troublesome word.

[162] Fr. 81 H/236–8 IP. The primary authority here is Aristotle in the *Topics* (II 6, 112ᵃ32 ff.), where he adduces Xenocrates' 'etymologizing' interpretation of *eudaimōn* as an example of the rhetorical ploy of understanding a word in its basic etymological

strands of doctrine may be derived. It seems not unreasonable to suppose, after all, that Xenocrates has in mind here (even if not exclusively) the end of Plato's *Timaeus* (90A): 'And as regards the most dominant part (*kyriōtaton eidos*) of our soul, we must think of it in this way: that God has given to each of us, as his *daimōn*, that kind of soul which we say is housed in the highest part of our body and which raises us—seeing that we are not an earthly but a heavenly plant—towards our kindred in the heaven.'

Since we cannot be quite sure what Plato meant by this statement, we cannot be sure what Xenocrates, even if he is fully endorsing it, intended by it either. However, in either case, there seems to be the implication that the highest part of the human soul, the intellect (*nous*) or reasoning part (*logistikon*), is to be regarded as partly transcendent, and a being of a higher order. That would seem also to be the sense of that notable phrase from *Republic* X (617E): 'it is not the case that a *daimōn* will be allotted to you, but you will choose your own *daimōn*.' This could, of course, mean no more than that we each of us choose our own fate, rather than having it imposed upon us, but with *daimōn* there is always some element of personification, and so it was taken in later times. At any rate, this externalizing interpretation of *eudaimōn* seems to betoken some degree of objectivization of the highest element of the soul, to which the individual must assimilate himself.

This line of argument by Xenocrates, no doubt pursued in his two books *On Happiness,* has some bearing, in turn, on the provenance of a passage of Cicero's *Tusculan Disputations* (V 38–9),[163] stemming immediately from Antiochus of Ascalon, but attributed by him to his usual pantheon of authorities, Aristotle, Speusippus, Xenocrates,

---

sense instead of its more natural, current sense. The context, therefore, while not overtly polemical, is hardly benign either. At *Topics* VII 1, 152ª5 ff. (= Fr. 82H/240 IP), he again uses Xenocrates as an example, describing him as maintaining that the happy life and the good (*spoudaios*) life are the same, since both may be characterized as 'most worthy of choice' (*hairetōtatos*), and strictly speaking only *one* thing can have that description. This sounds like an actual argument used by Xenocrates. We may note, by the way, that Plato himself indulges in word-play between *daimōn* and *eudaimōn* at *Rep.* VII 540c.

[163] The last section of this only is given as a 'fragment' of Xenocrates by Heinze and Isnardi Parente (Fr. 84 H/241 IP).

Polemo. Here, as in the passage from the *De Finibus* quoted above, while recognizing the problems, I nevertheless feel that there is something distinctively Xenocratean in the mix, particularly as regards the equation of happiness with assimilation to intellect.[164] Cicero has been discoursing on the first impulses towards perfection provided by nature to each level of living being, from plants on up:[165]

And as with other creatures nature has given to one, one distinguishing feature, to another another, which each of them preserves as its own and does not depart from, so to man she has given something far more pre-eminent—although the term 'pre-eminent' ought to be applied to things which admit of some comparison; but the soul of man, derived as it is from the divine mind (*decerptus ex mente divina*), can be compared with nothing else, if it is right to say so, save God alone. Therefore, if this soul has been so cared for that it is not blinded by error, the result is mind made perfect (*perfecta mens*), that is, complete reason (*absoluta ratio*), and this is identical with virtue. And if everything is happy which has nothing wanting, and whose measure in its own kind is heaped up and running over, and if this is the peculiar mark of virtue, assuredly all virtuous men are happy. And so far I am in agreement with Brutus,[166] that is to say with Aristotle, Xenocrates, Speusippus, Polemo.

Now there is here, admittedly, much that is compatible with Stoicism, and not with Aristotle, but I think it can be seen that what is compatible with Stoicism is also concordant with what we know of Xenocrates' metaphysics. If we cast our minds back, for example, to his interpretation of the description of the formation of the soul in *Timaeus* 35A (p. 100 above), we can see that Xenocrates identifies the 'individual essence' in the mixture with the Monad. This 'Monad' is presumably to be identified in turn with the supreme principle, the 'Zeus' or 'Intellect' of Fr. 15/213. Therefore, for Xenocrates, in his exegesis of Plato, the individual soul is in fact *decerptus ex mente divina*, even as is the World-Soul. Only in the matter of the *materiality* of

[164] This takes on also a Stoic coloration, as we shall see, but is compatible with what we know of Xenocratean metaphysics.

[165] I borrow the translation of J. E. King, in the Loeb edition, slightly emended.

[166] M. Junius Brutus, Cicero's preferred spokesman for the philosophical stance of Antiochus of Ascalon.

the first principle—in so far as 'pure fire' is to be regarded as material—do the Stoics differ from Xenocrates (and presumably from Polemo). That, indeed, is what makes it so relatively easy for Antiochus to set up his great synthesis.

Virtue, then, and happiness consist for Xenocrates in what may be described as 'assimilation to God' (*homoiōsis theōi*), which in turn means coming into full attunement with the highest (the monadic, rather than the dyadic) element of one's own soul, which can also be described as one's *daimon*. This process of getting in tune, however, does not appear to have precluded entirely (as it would for the Stoics) a moderate attention to bodily and external 'goods', far inferior though these may be to the goods of the soul. This can be seen from other passages of *Tusculans* V,[167] where Antiochus makes the consensus of Old Academy and Peripatos sound very like the Stoics (even to the extent of carrying the happiness of the sage into the Bull of Phalaris!), without, however, dismissing the lower classes of goods altogether—something that Antiochus regards as a Stoic aberration. One does not, therefore, transcend the 'primary natural instincts' (*ta prōta kata physin*), as would the Stoics; one merely sublimates them.

Before leaving the subject of ethics, it may be suitable to mention once again Xenocrates' vegetarianism. In this connection, we have the evidence of Porphyry, in his *De Abstinentia*,[168] that Xenocrates laid claim to the legendary Athenian culture hero Triptolemus as the originator of laws enjoining abstinence from the slaughter and consumption of animals:

They say that Triptolemus laid down laws for the Athenians, and of his laws the philosopher Xenocrates says that the following three still remain in force at Eleusis: 'Honour thy parents'; 'Offer first-fruits to the gods'; and 'Do no harm to animals'. The first two he considers to be precepts of patent excellence . . . but as the third one he raises the question as to what Triptolemus' intention may have been in enjoining abstinence from animal food. Did he

[167] §§ 51 and 87 (= Fr. 87 H/241, 243 IP).
[168] IV 22 (= Fr. 98 H/252 IP). This testimony is derived through the intermediacy of the Hellenistic historian Hermippus of Smyrna, a pupil of Callimachus. We unfortunately do not know what work of Xenocrates' he is drawing on.

simply consider, he says, that it was a terrible thing to kill one's kindred, or did he rather observe that it would come about that man would slaughter for his food those animals which were the most useful for him? So it would be through wishing to render life civilized that he tried to preserve those animals which were tame and the companions of men. Unless perhaps, after prescribing that we should honour the gods through the offering of first-fruits, he considered that this precept would be more likely to remain in force longer if sacrifices of animals were not offered to the gods. Xenocrates gives many other reasons for this injunction, none of them very coherent,[169] but it is sufficient for our purpose to note that this law goes back to Triptolemus.

It would seem from this report that Xenocrates was himself in favour of vegetarianism, and wished to claim Triptolemus as an authority for such a doctrine, though he was less than clear as to what motivated him to this. At any rate, his vegetarianism, which we may reasonably consider a Pythagorizing trait, is supported by the anecdote from Plutarch quoted above in n. 16: when he heard that the Athenians had prosecuted a man who had flayed a ram alive, he remarked that one who tortured a living animal was really no worse than one who deprived an animal of life through slaughtering it.

Logic

Xenocrates composed treatises *On Dialectic* (in fourteen books), *Divisions* (in eight books), *On Opposites,* and *On Genera and Species,* but we have unfortunately no idea of their contents. It seems, however, that he, like Speusippus, remained broadly faithful to Platonic logic, and that therefore the adoption of Aristotelian categorial theory and syllogistic, unless it was adopted by the Academy under Polemo's reign, was a development either of the New Academy or even of Antiochus' archaizing synthesis.

That Xenocrates employed Platonic diaeresis is evidenced by such a testimony as that of Clement of Alexandria (*Strom.* II 5),[170] to the effect that Xenocrates distinguished, in an Aristotelian manner

---

[169] I take this to be the meaning of *akribeis,* lit. 'accurate', here.

[170] Fr. 6 H/259 IP, taken from Xenocrates' treatise *On Practical Wisdom* (*Peri phronēseōs*).

(cf. *EN* VI 7), between *sophia* as the knowledge of first causes and intelligible essence, and *phronēsis,* which for Aristotle denotes practical knowledge. Xenocrates, however, makes a division of *phronēsis* into practical and theoretical, and denominates theoretical *phronēsis* as 'human *sophia*', thus implying, presumably, that true *sophia* is a form of knowledge not attainable by humans. Xenocrates will then be making the point that the knowledge that God or the heavenly beings have of themselves or of the reality around them is qualitatively different from our theoretical wisdom, and this in turn is different from our practical wisdom. Using diaeresis, then, Xenocrates distinguishes first between divine and human knowledge; and then, within human knowledge, between theoretical and practical.[171]

As regards categorial theory, he contents himself with the two Platonic 'categories' of Absolute (*kath' auto*) and Relative (*pros ti*),[172] as set out in the *Sophist* 255c–d, thus implicitly (at least) rejecting Aristotle's system of ten.[173] It is not clear from the evidence whether he adopted the more elaborate division attested for his follower Hermodorus (Fr. 7 Isnardi Parente)[174] of 'alio-relative' (*pros hetera*) into 'opposites' (*enantia*) and relatives proper. At all events, the distinction between absolutes and relatives may be taken to be valid for the realm of true being—Forms or mathematicals—as well as for that of becoming.

One further topic, already adverted to in relation to his metaphysics (above, p. 115), has a clear logical aspect also, and that is the question of the priority of the species to the genus, which Xenocrates appears to have maintained. This rather unexpected move (for a Platonist) may perhaps be seen as a reaction to the considerable attention that Aristotle had paid (with anti-Platonist polemical intent) to the problem of the unity of the subject of a definition (e.g.,

---

[171] Cf. the different, but analogous, division of knowledge made by Plato in *Statesman* 259D ff. For a quotation of Aristotle's criticism of Xenocrates on this topic in the *Topics,* see ch. 1, p. 12.

[172] Simpl. *In Cat.* p. 63, 22 Kalbfleisch (= Fr. 12 H/95 IP).

[173] Simplicius actually declares that 'Xenocrates and Andronicus' condemn the superfluousness of Aristotle's ten-category system, but this may refer only to Andronicus.

[174] See below, Ch. 5, pp. 200–4.

most comprehensively, in *Metaphysics* Z, chs. 12–14). If one accepts that the subject of a *horismos* or a *logos* must be a unified substance (*ousia*), then a genus like 'animal' or 'plane figure' simply does not qualify, as it is divided into various species with mutually exclusive differentiae. Of course, Aristotle is arguing for the priority of the physical individual (his 'primary substance'), but the trouble with individuals (as Aristotle himself recognizes, 1039^a15–23) is that, if they are incomposite, there can be no definition of them. It is not unreasonable to suppose that Xenocrates felt that the most proper subject of a definition is an *infima species,* such as 'man', 'horse', or 'right-angled triangle', and it is out of this sort of entity that 'the world', as an object of epistemology, is actually made up. Individuals need to be classified before they can be made the subject of definition; but the primary classes into which the cognizable world is divided up are species, not genera. It is 'cats', 'dogs', or 'chickens' that one sees running about, not 'animals' as such. So, if one wants to maintain the existence of separable Forms (even as quasi-mathematical formulae), it is the species rather than the genus that has the best claim. Genera are better viewed as merely secondary means of classifying the world.

Finally, it would seem from certain remarks of Aristotle in the *Posterior Analytics* (72^b5–73^a20), on the subject of how first principles may be known, if their existence cannot be established by demonstration, that Xenocrates was among those who countered the troublesome assertion of certain other thinkers (specifically Antisthenes) that the indemonstrability of first principles makes knowledge impossible by arguing that everything can be demonstrated, since one can have circular demonstration of propositions from one another. Aristotle pours scorn on this claim,[175] and in truth it does not stand up well to his analysis, but it was at least an attempt to address a serious problem.

All this serves to remind us that most of the logical questions dealt with by Aristotle in the *Organon* arose from previous and contempo-

---

[175] His own solution, of course, is that first principles are known by a kind of immediate cognition. See on this the useful discussion of Cherniss (1944: 63–8).

rary speculations, inadequate though many of them may have been, in the Academy.

Pythagorism and Allegorizing

I bring these two topics together at the end of my discussion of Xenocrates as they are at least partly interlocking, and both are of considerable significance for later philosophy. By 'Pythagorism' here I mean a more than objective interest in the thought and personality of Pythagoras, and a tendency to try to reconstruct his teachings, fathering the theories of later men, including one's own, on him in the process. This tendency begins in Platonism already with Speusippus, as we have seen, if not with Plato himself, and is observable in most later Platonists to a greater or lesser degree, the extremists in this regard being those who would actually term themselves 'Pythagoreans' rather than Platonists—such men as Moderatus of Gades, Nicomachus of Gerasa, and Numenius of Apamea, and perhaps also, before them, Eudorus of Alexandria. We have evidence, however, of a special degree of interest shown by Xenocrates in Pythagoras. We have one work of his attested, of unknown contents, entitled *Pythagoreia*, and a good deal of his work on mathematics was probably Pythagorean in outlook.[176] We have, as we have seen (above, p. 118), an extended account by Porphyry of Xenocrates' account of Pythagoras' discovery of musical harmony, and his regulation of the disorder of the sense of hearing by the application of logos. We have seen evidence also of his aversion to meat-eating, and to oath-taking.

At various points in the doxographic tradition we have a Xenocratean doctrine or formulation attributed also to Pythagoras: theory of daemons, in Plutarch, *Isis and Osiris* 360D (Fr. 24 H/225 IP); definition of the soul as self-moving number, in Stobaeus, *Ecl.* I 49, 1 (from Aetius = Fr. 60 H/169 IP); the external provenance of the

---

[176] We have evidence of a work *On Numbers,* another *On Geometry,* in two books, a work *On Dimensions (diastēmata),* and another entitled *The Theory of Numbers* (if it is not the same as the earlier one). There is also a work *On Geometers,* in five books, and a work *Peri ta mathēmata,* in six books, which could refer to mathematics, but need not.

intellect (*nous thyrathen,* Aetius again, IV 5, p. 392b Diels)—all of which seems to support the idea that Xenocrates himself was concerned to make the connection. Indeed, it is probably to Speusippus and Xenocrates that the origins of the 'Neopythagorean' tradition may be traced.

Another interesting tendency is that towards allegorization of the Olympian gods as forces of nature, such as we have seen in Fr. 15 H/213 IP. Certainly Xenocrates is not the first to practise this, but Aetius in this doxographic passage does make quite a point of his having bequeathed this type of theology to the Stoics (*tauta de khorēgēsas tois Stoikois*), so that his role was plainly seen in later times to be quite significant. As we have seen, he identified Hades with air, Poseidon with the wet element, and Demeter with the earth—not as being simply identical with the material element in question, but rather as being the 'divine power' (*theia dynamis*) which pervades it. I have suggested also that he made creative use of Orphic mythology in expounding the relationship between his two primary principles (cf. above, p. 104), and he certainly made use of the Orphic myth of Dionysus and the Titans to explain the nature of the human soul, and our 'guard-duty' here on earth (above, p. 133).

Conclusion

Unlike Speusippus, Xenocrates does seem to have had a dominant effect on the mainstream of later Platonism. The teachings of Plato seem to descend to the later Academy largely in the form in which Xenocrates presented them, although reference back to the dialogues never ceased to be made.[177] Significantly, of all his many works, only two sound from their titles like dialogues, *Arkas,* or *On the Unlimited,* and *Archedemus,* or *On Justice.* The dialogue form was not suitable to his formalizing, rather scholastic temperament. No doubt it was to this that Plato was referring when he exhorted Xenocrates to 'sacrifice to the Graces' (DL IV 6).

---

[177] Indeed, the hypothesis of Alline (1915), that we are indebted to Xenocrates for the original collected edition of Plato's works, while not provable, is still a suggestion which I find plausible.

In many respects Xenocrates seems to have conceded points to Aristotle, specifically on the nature of the supreme principle and in matters of ethics, but there is much also, as we have seen, which remains distinctive.[178] Some of his triadic formulations find a later echo only in Plutarch, but his definition of a form, and of what things there are forms, had widespread influence—even, as I have suggested above (p. 119), incorporating a certain degree of misunderstanding—and became the standard school definition, appearing in such a document as Alcinous' *Didaskalikos*.

Part of the difficulty in assessing the full extent of Xenocrates' influence on later Platonism is the fact that very little in the way of technical philosophical writing survives from the Middle Platonic period, and it is from the sort of detailed technical treatises and commentaries that we do not have that we would be able to judge the true extent of his influence. Even in the case of Plutarch, we are lacking a good many technical treatises, the titles of which we know from the so-called 'Catalogue of Lamprias', on such questions as the forms, matter, and the theory of knowledge, which would have given us a far better idea both of what Plutarch was capable of, and of how great Xenocrates' influence on him and others really was.

---

[178] We may note that after Aristotle's death relations between the Academy and the Peripatos seem to have improved somewhat. Theophrastus, as we have seen, speaks with respect of Xenocrates in his *Metaphysics,* and took the trouble to make a summary of Xenocrates' doctrines, in two books, which was not necessarily entirely polemical.

Polemo, Champion of Ethical *Praxis*

4

Life and Works

Xenocrates, as we have seen, was succeeded on his death by Polemo, son of Philostratus, a native Athenian, of the deme of Oea, notorious in his youth for riotous living. His family was plainly well-off, as his father is said to have kept race-horses (*harmatotrophesai*, DL IV 17), but no sign of the family appears, unfortunately, in the epigraphic record. Polemo appears to us primarily as a figure of anecdote, and as such constitutes a profoundly frustrating problem. He presided over the Platonic Academy for almost forty years (314–276 BC), vastly longer than either of his predecessors, and was plainly much revered by all who knew him, but he seems at first sight to have added little or nothing to the body of Platonist philosophy. As we shall see, however, appearances may be deceptive.

The edifying story of his conversion to philosophy through his chance hearing of a lecture of Xenocrates survives in many tellings, and is, indeed, the best-known feature of his life. I give here the version of Diogenes Laertius (IV 16):

In his youth he was so profligate and dissipated that he actually carried about with him money to procure the immediate gratification of his desires, and would even keep sums concealed in lanes and alleys. Even in the

Academy[1] a piece of three obols was found close to a pillar, where he had buried it for the same purpose. And one day, by agreement with his young friends, he burst into the school of Xenocrates quite drunk, with a garland on his head. Xenocrates, however, without being at all disturbed, went on with his lecture as before; and it was about self-control (*sōphrosynē*).[2] The lad, as he listened, was gradually captivated, and eventually became so industrious that he surpassed all the other students, and rose to be himself head of the school, in the 116th Olympiad.[3]

This, as I say, was a popular story, told originally—probably by the Hellenistic gossip-writer Antigonus of Carystus (*fl. c.*240 BC), who is quoted as a source just below[4]—with malicious intent, but ultimately for purposes of edification. Antigonus (who is not quite a contemporary, but knowledgeable) also tells that Polemo used to go on drunken revels (*kōmazein*) through the Cerameicus *by day,* and was an enthusiastic lover of boys and youths, behaving so badly that his wife once brought a charge of ill-treatment (*dikē kakōseōs*) against him—which latter detail seems to go against the impression given by Diogenes that he was still just a youth when converted by Xenocrates.[5] At any rate, his conversion was so complete that, 'from the time when he began to study philosophy, he acquired such strength of character as always to maintain the same unruffled calm

---

[1] That is, in the public park, not the Platonic school. Three obols was the accepted fee for the lower grade of prostitute. This concealing of bits of money is actually a rather curious detail, seeming to indicate that ancient Athenians did not normally carry loose change around with them—which, before the invention of pockets, they may not have done!

[2] On which topic, in fact, Xenocrates is recorded as having written a treatise (DL IV 12).

[3] i.e. 316–312 BC, or more precisely in 314, on the death of Xenocrates.

[4] A rather earlier version of the same story, told by Philodemus in his *History of the Academy* (IV 40–XIII 10), gives Antigonus explicitly as the source. The popularity of the story as an *exemplum* is attested by the nineteen references, from sixteen different authors, which Gigante is able to assemble in his edition (Frr. 15–33). The classic study of Antigonus is that of Wilamowitz-Möllendorf (1881).

[5] In fact, however, if we may believe Athenaeus (*Deipn.* II 44E), again on the authority of Antigonus, Polemo was fully thirty years of age when this incident occurred. Greek men did not generally get married until they were at least in their later twenties, and had their wild oats behind them. Plutarch, we may note, relates that Alcibiades' wife Hipparete walked out on him for the same sort of reason (*Life of Alcibiades* 8. 3–4), so it is not impossible that Polemo was put in a similar situation.

of demeanour; indeed, he never changed the tone of his voice' (IV 17).

I dwell on this complex of anecdotes, partly because there is little else that we know about Polemo's life, but partly also because the sphere of practical ethics seems to be that aspect of philosophy in which he particularly made his mark, as we shall see. Apart from the circumstances of his joining the Academy, we learn little enough of his long career there. Other anecdotes reinforce the tradition of his impassibility (DL IV 17–19). He was notably unaffected by the tragedies in the theatre, though he liked to attend, being especially devoted to Sophocles.[6] Readings of Homer, similarly, left him unmoved, even when performed by the noted tragic actor Nicostratus,[7] whereas his companion Crates was quite overcome. There is a story of his remaining unmoved, amid general panic, when bitten by a mad dog.[8] He seems to have taken no part in public life, spending all his time out in the Academy and the adjoining villa (*kēpos*) belonging to the school.[9] Philodemus (XIV 32 ff.) and Diogenes (IV 19), as we have seen in Chapter 1, speak of his pupils constructing huts (*kalybia*) for themselves in the grounds of the villa,[10] so as to be constantly with him. He himself is spoken of, rather mysteriously, as living, in company with his favourite pupil Crates, at the house of one Lysicles (DL IV 22). Why he should not, as head of the school, have lived in Plato's house is not clear. Perhaps it was kept as a public space. But then why should his pupils move into the

[6] Presumably in the performances of 'old' tragedies, though no doubt he read Sophocles as well. He is also recorded (by Plutarch, *De Exilio,* 603B–C) as liking to go into town for the new tragedies at the Dionysia—though in the context of specifying that this was the *only* occasion in the year when he went into town!

[7] Nicknamed 'Clytemnestra', no doubt because of his highly charged mode of delivery.

[8] This, of course, should have caused his death, very unpleasantly, from rabies. Either he was very lucky, or the dog was not, after all, rabid.

[9] Cf. Ch. 1, p. 9 above.

[10] These *kalybia* are declared to have been erected 'near to the *mouseion* and the *exedra*', which would certainly seem to imply that both were situated in the grounds of the *kēpos.* This, however, seems to conflict with Diogenes' report at the beginning of his life of Speusippus (IV 1) that a shrine of the Muses (*mouseion*) was erected by Plato *en tēi Akademiai,* which would most naturally mean 'in the Academy (park)'. Diogenes, however, may well be confused.

grounds of the *kēpos* in order to be near him? We must assume that Lysicles' establishment was itself adjacent to the Academy.

Other than this we only hear a little of his teaching methods—'he would not sit down to deal with the themes (*theseis*) of his pupils, but would conduct disputations (*epekheirei*) while walking up and down (*peripatōn*)'[11] (DL IV 19)—and of his death from *phthisis*[12] at an advanced age in 276/5,[13] which, if we take it that his initial confrontation with Xenocrates, when he was already thirty, must have taken place long enough before Xenocrates' death for Polemo to have impressed himself upon all and sundry sufficiently to be elected his successor—thus, hardly later than 320 BC—means that he must have been getting on for eighty. He was succeeded by Crates, who, however, lasted only a few years before dying himself, and being succeeded by Arcesilaus.

As regards any publications of Polemo, we have very little evidence. Diogenes speaks rather vaguely of his leaving behind him 'a fair number of works' (*hikana syngrammata*, IV 20). The only title we know of, however, is a treatise, in a number of books, *On the Life according to Nature,* mentioned by Clement of Alexandria (*Strom.* VII 6, 32, 9)—in which, Clement tells us, he condemned the eating of meat. Such a title, however, is most significant, as we shall see.[14]

Philosophy

Polemo, then, was plainly a remarkable character, but what, we may ask, does he have to show, in the way of doctrine, for his nearly forty years of headship of the Academy? As I say, the initial evidence is not promising. He is recorded as speakingly scathingly of those who theorize about ethical principles rather than just practising them (DL IV 18):

[11] It is not quite clear what the significance of this is; it is told in the context of indications of his highmindedness and austerity.

[12] Often rendered 'consumption', but probably in this case just general debilitation.

[13] The date is given in Eusebius' Chronicle under Olympiad 127, 3.

[14] If in fact the account of Academic physics given in Cicero's *Academica Posteriora* (see below, pp. 166–76) can be attributed to Polemo, then we shall have to postulate a treatise of his on physics, but no other trace of this survives.

Polemo used to say that we should exercise ourselves in real-life situations (*ta pragmata*)[15] and not with mere logical speculations (*dialektika theōrēmata*), which leave us, like a man who has got off by heart some wretched handbook on harmony and never practised an instrument, able, indeed, to win admiration for skill in fielding questions, but utterly at odds with ourselves in the ordering of our lives (*kata tēn diathesin*)'

This is the attitude of a man whom one would expect to be somewhat impatient of the development of doctrinal positions, on ethics or anything else, and indeed we cannot expect to find Polemo's name associated with any contributions to the development of logic[16] or of physics (though in this latter area he may in fact have made some contribution, as we shall see); but in the area of ethics sufficient evidence exists, I think, for crediting him with developments of some significance.

The question with which we are concerned is nothing less than the origins of the well-known Stoic doctrine of the 'purpose or end of life' (*telos tou biou*) as 'living in conformity with nature'—and/or (possibly) 'living in consistency with oneself'.[17] Now if we give due weight to the testimony of the later Platonist Antiochus of Ascalon (*fl. c.*75 BC), relayed in various contexts by Cicero, it was actually from Polemo that Zeno of Citium, who had been a student of Polemo before setting up the Stoic school, developed the main lines of his ethical theory. Antiochus, it must be said, has a definite agenda, which is to re-establish the tradition of positive dogma in the Platonist school after the almost 200-year interlude of scepticism which followed on the succession of Arcesilaus to the headship

---

[15] I take that to be the meaning of this rather flexible term in the context.

[16] Gigante, rather optimistically, includes in his collection of 'fragments' (Fr. 122), a passage from Plutarch (*Stoic. Rep.* 1045F ff.), quoting Chrysippus as remarking that 'dialectic was treated as a subject of serious concern by Plato and Aristotle and their successors down to Polemo and Strato.' Indeed, it is hardly possible that Polemo disregarded dialectic completely, but this does not tell us much. What we may reasonably attribute to him in the area of logic is summarized below, pp. 174–6.

[17] Certain scholars have tried to make something of the fact that Zeno himself is on occasion attested as defining the *telos* as *homologoumenōs zēn* (*SVF* I 179) rather than *homologoumenōs tēi physei zēn*, and this can be interpreted as meaning simply 'consistently with oneself'. No doubt he did mean that, but John Rist (1969: 2, n. 5) is surely right to insist that this does not exclude the latter meaning also.

some time in the late 270s, and to do that by appropriating a fair proportion of Stoic doctrine into an 'updated', modernized Platonism,
but nevertheless we must take his evidence seriously, as he could not
hope to have convinced even those favourably disposed to his enterprise, quite apart from his many enemies, had there not been some
basic plausibility to his reconstruction.[18]

Let us look, then, at the evidence as we have it, beginning with a
testimony of Clement of Alexandria (*Strom.* II, 22, 133, 7), which is
a continuation of passages already quoted in connection with both
Speusippus and Xenocrates:

Polemo, the associate of Xenocrates, seems to wish happiness (*eudaimonia*)
to consist in self-sufficiency (*autarkeia*) in respect of all good things, or at
least the most and greatest of them. For he lays it down that happiness can
never be achieved apart from virtue (*aretē*), while virtue is sufficient for happiness even if bereft of bodily and external goods.

It is not quite clear from Clement's form of words whether he had
first-hand access to any work of Polemo's,[19] but we may accept the
essential accuracy of his account. What this seems to betoken is a
somewhat more austere position than that of his master Xenocrates,
since Xenocrates accorded at least a subsidiary role in happiness to
bodily and external goods (cf. above, p. 138–41), while for Polemo it
would seem that *aretē* is sufficient for happiness even without them.
On the other hand, in Antiochus' eyes, there is very little between
them, as is evident from various passages quoted in the previous
chapter. What we may be witnessing is a gradual hardening of positions on this question, in contradistinction to the doctrine prevailing
in the contemporary Peripatos of Strato of Lampsacus.

Let us, however, take as evidence a few more passages. First of all,
the passage of Plutarch's anti-Stoic treatise *On Common Conceptions*

---

[18] Cicero, we may note, never accuses him of inventing his grand synthesis of
Academic doctrine out of the whole cloth, but rather of 'going over to the Stoics' on various issues of detail (e.g. *Acad. Pr.* 135; 143). This certainly implies a degree of retrojection of Stoic doctrine and formulations, but onto an already existent base.

[19] He does elsewhere in the *Stromateis*, as we have seen (above, p. 159), make reference to a work of Polemo's *On the Life according to Nature,* but it is in turn not quite clear
from *that* reference whether he had first-hand access to that.

(1069E ff.) quoted above in connection with Xenocrates (p. 139). Here no distinction is made between the positions of Xenocrates and Polemo, and Zeno is declared to follow them both 'in their assumption that nature and what is in conformity with nature are basic elements (*stoikheia*) of happiness'. This is not quite the same thing, of course, as declaring the self-sufficiency of virtue, so it leaves room for some degree of divergence on that question. Xenocrates could, and doubtless did, maintain that a modest sufficiency of the lower classes of good was 'in accordance with nature', while the Stoics classed possession of such goods as a matter of indifference (*adiaphoron*), and thus, though initially in accordance with nature, forming no part of the essence of happiness. On which side of this divide does Polemo fall?

Other passages, this time from Cicero, provide more definite pointers. Plainly, the development of the doctrine of conformity with nature as a first principle of ethics is something later seen as characteristic of Polemo, even if he was not the originator of it. If we consider two passages of Cicero's *De Finibus,* a picture begins to emerge. First, Book II, 33–4:

Every living creature, from the moment of birth, loves itself and all its parts; primarily this self-regard embraces the two main divisions of mind and body, and subsequently the parts of each of these. Both mind and body have certain excellences; of these the young animal grows vaguely conscious, and later begins to discriminate, and to seek for the primary endowments of nature and shun their opposites. Whether the list of these primary natural objects[20] includes pleasure or not is a much-debated question; but to hold that it includes nothing else but pleasure, neither the limbs, nor the senses, nor mental activity, nor bodily integrity, nor health, seems to me to be the height of stupidity. And this is the fountain-head from which one's whole theory of goods and evils must necessarily flow. Polemo, and also before him Aristotle,[21] held that the primary objects were the ones I have just mentioned. Thus arose the doctrine of the Old Academy and of the Peripatetics, maintaining that the end of goods is to live in accordance with nature, that

---

[20] *Prima naturalia* presumably translating *prōta kata physin.*

[21] It is not clear what Cicero can be thinking of, but we must reflect that in any case his Aristotle is not the Aristotle of the esoteric works that are available to us.

is, to enjoy the primary things granted by nature (*prima a natura data*) with the accompaniment of virtue.

There emerges here a distinct doctrine of Polemo, which owes much to that of Xenocrates (as one would expect), while stopping short of the absolutism of the Stoics. Polemo, we can gather, while insisting on the absolute centrality of virtue to happiness, does not reject *ta prōta kata physin* as an accompaniment—that is, such things as the bodily integrity and health mentioned above. This is confirmed a little further down (35), where a distinction is made between those who hold that the *telos* consists of a combination of virtue with some additional element (*cum aliqua accessione*), such as Polemo, and those who make it consist in virtue alone, such as Zeno.

The distinction between Polemo and Zeno is developed further in Book IV, 14–15, a passage which, with its continuation, I have dwelt upon in the last chapter (p. 138), since it seems to me to constitute an important exposition of the ethics of Xenocrates, as well as of Polemo. There Cicero is concerned to tease out where precisely Zeno feels himself to be parting from his predecessors. In this connection he says (14): 'Previous thinkers, and among them most explicitly Polemo, had explained the highest good (*summum bonum*) as being "to live in accordance with nature" '; this formula is then taken up by the Stoics in three senses, the third of which, as we have seen in Chapter 3, was 'to live in the enjoyment of all, or the greatest, of those things which are in accordance with nature'. This formulation, however, which leaves a place for a modicum of bodily and external goods, is then attributed to Xenocrates and Aristotle, and Polemo is left out of the reckoning. He must surely, however, be still there, as the essential link in the chain connecting Old Academic ethical theory with that of the Stoa.

Later in the book (IV 50–1), where Cicero is becoming more heated in his remonstrations with Cato, Polemo makes a significant reappearance (Cicero has been criticizing Cato for indulging in various fallacious Stoic arguments):

As for your other argument, it is by no means 'consequential', but actually dull-witted to a degree—though, of course, the Stoics, and not you yourself, are responsible for that: 'Happiness is a thing to be proud of, whereas it cannot be the case that anyone should have good reason to be proud without virtue (*honestas*).' The former proposition Polemo will concede to Zeno, and so will his master [sc. Xenocrates] and the whole of their clan, as well as all the other philosophers who, while ranking virtue far above all else, yet couple some other thing with it in defining the highest good; since if virtue is a thing to be proud of, as it is, and excels everything else to a degree hardly to be expressed in words, Polemo will be able to be happy if endowed solely with virtue, and destitute of all besides, and yet he will not grant you that nothing except virtue is to be reckoned as a good.

The situation should now be clear enough, I think, and the adducing of further passages[22] would be redundant. The doctrinal positions of Xenocrates and Polemo cannot be disentangled on the basis of the evidence available to us, but Polemo should take the credit for providing the stimulus to Zeno for the development of the distinctive Stoic doctrine—a development which, in the eyes of Antiochus, is no development at all, but a deviation in the direction of unreality. It is slightly uncomfortable to reflect that we are very largely (though not entirely) dependent on Antiochus for our information, since he was certainly, as I say, pursuing an agenda of his own, but there is really little danger that he invented the position of his spiritual ancestors out of the whole cloth.

The further question might be raised as to whether Polemo did not also to some extent prefigure the Stoic doctrine of 'self-conciliation' (*oikeiōsis*). Antiochus, at *Fin.* II 33–4 and V 24 ff., is quite firm about ascribing to 'the ancients' (*veteres*)—his normal term for the Old Academy—the doctrine that 'every living creature loves itself, and from the moment of birth strives to secure its own preservation'. This basic principle is then pursued, in the latter passage, in all its ramifications, up to the rational purpose of human life, 'concordance with nature' (*Fin.* V 27). The Stoics are described as simply 'taking over' this theory.[23] This, together with Antiochus' defiant claim that 'Stoic theory should be considered a correction of the Old Academy rather than actually a new system' (Cic. *Acad. Post.* I 43),

---

[22] e.g. *Fin.* IV 61; *Acad. Pr.* II 131–2; *Tusc.* V 30.

[23] *Institutio veterum, quo etiam Stoici utuntur* (*Fin.* V 23).

may be taken, I think, as prima facie evidence that Polemo had uttered sentiments that could be construed as equivalent to Zeno's later formulation of the *oikeiōsis* doctrine.[24]

Apart from the question of first principles of ethics, we seem to have a slight indication of Polemo's views on one particular area of practical ethics, and that is his theory of philosophical love. In what sense, and to what extent, the philosopher may indulge in amatory activity was an issue much discussed in the Hellenistic and Roman periods of Greek philosophy.[25] The parameters of later discussion were set by Plato, not only in the *Symposium* and *Phaedrus*, but also in the *First Alcibiades*,[26] where Socrates is shown approaching his beloved in a properly philosophical and benevolent manner. The main components of the *topos,* as they emerge in later Platonism (but already also, it would seem, in the Stoicism of Chrysippus), are (1) selecting a proper object of love (*axierastos*); (2) making his acquaintance; and (3) benefiting the beloved by exhorting him to, and training him, in virtue.[27] We do not know of any views which Speusippus or Xenocrates may have had on this important topic, but one obscure dictum of Polemo (reported by Plutarch in his essay *To an Uneducated Ruler,* 780D) may constitute a significant scrap of evidence: 'Love is the service of the gods for the care and preservation of the young.'[28] This at first sight rather baffling utterance, if pressed, could be seen as anticipating most of the later Platonist doctrine, and deriving its inspiration in turn from an interpretation of the *First Alcibiades.* Socrates' kind of loving could be viewed as a service of the gods in the form of conferring benefits on the youth.[29] If

[24] Theophrastus' doctrine of *oikeiotēs* probably had some part to play also in the development of the doctrine. See Brink (1955).

[25] I have discussed this more fully in Dillon (1994).

[26] Regarded as genuine, of course, by all later Platonists.

[27] Heterosexual philosophic liaisons, we may note, are not envisaged. The doctrine is presented in summary form in Alcinous' *Didaskalikos,* ch. 33.

[28] *Theōn hypēresia eis neōn epimeleian kai sōtērian.* This might, of course, merely refer to the love of man for woman, with a view to the production and care of children, but the word *neōn,* rather than *paidōn,* would seem to belie that.

[29] Polemo, we may recall, had been a notorious lover of boys and lads in his youth, and, even in his philosophic period, his affection for Crates was very close. They lived together, and were actually buried in the same tomb (DL IV 21).

so, we have here the bare bones of the later Stoic/Platonist 'art of love', and our appreciation of Polemo's contribution to the development of Hellenistic philosophy may move up another notch.

The chief contribution of Polemo to ethical theory, however, would seem to be an increase in austerity of Academic doctrine which anticipates, to a significant extent, that of Zeno and his successors. It is a much more controversial question, on the other hand, whether he in any way anticipated the main features of the Stoics' metaphysical system, their so-called 'materialism', or their theory of the *Logos* and Fate. The ideal of conformity with nature in itself, after all, does not necessarily involve the Stoic doctrine of Fate in its strong form, or in general the Stoic concept of the nature of the universe. On the other hand, it may be that Polemo was not entirely without influence on Zeno in the area of physics also. There is not much to go on here, in truth, but there is one straw in the wind, in the shape of a bald doxographic report of Aetius, which comes in Stobaeus just prior to his exposition of the theology of Xenocrates (Fr. 15 H/213 IP): 'Polemo declared that the cosmos is God.'[30]

It might be thought that the sentence in itself need only mean that Polemo regarded the cosmos as *a* god. However, the context in which it occurs excludes that. The whole section in Stobaeus is concerned with the nature and functions of the supreme God, so this must give Polemo's view on that subject. In fact, however, Polemo's doctrine here could be seen as being in line with certain other views that had been manifesting themselves in the Old Academy (particularly those of Philippus of Opus, which will be examined in the next chapter). There is a tendency discernible, within the Academy, even if not within the thinking of Plato himself, to identify the supreme divinity as no more nor less than a rational World-Soul. This World-Soul, while not being a *material* entity—that is to say, one composed of the purest sort of fire, as would be the first principle of the Stoics—was nevertheless not transcendent over the physical universe, but immanent within it, residing most particularly at the outer rim of the

---

[30] *Polemōn ton kosmon theon apephēnato.*

heavens, in the sphere of the fixed stars. I have even ventured to suggest (Ch. 3, p. 102 above), on the basis of the troublesome doxographic summary of Aetius (which, as I say, follows immediately upon this report of Polemo's doctrine), that Xenocrates himself is operating with such a scenario, though one cannot be sure.[31] In that case, however, Polemo would once again simply be following his master's lead. It may seem surpassingly odd to us that any follower of Plato's should think in this way, but in fact there are many parts of Plato's works (not least the *Phaedrus* myth, which seems to be what Xenocrates is evoking in the Aetius passage mentioned above) which lend themselves to such an interpretation. Plainly, Philippus of Opus thought that this was the doctrine to be derived from Book X of the *Laws.* What Aetius would be telling us, then, in bald doxographic terms, is that Polemo believed in an immanent deity of some sort, which could in its broadest sense be identified with the cosmos.

Now of course that is what could be said of the god of Zeno and the Stoics. Indeed, the same Aetius, in reporting their doctrine, gives it as follows (*SVF* II 1027):[32]

The Stoics declare God to be intelligent (*noeron*), a designing fire (*pyr tekhnikon*) methodically proceeding towards the generation of the world, and encompassing all the seminal principles (*spermatikoi logoi*) according to which everything comes about according to fate, and a breath (*pneuma*) pervading the whole world, which takes on different names corresponding to the alteration of the matter through which it passes.

If one subtracts from this the description of God as fire or *pneuma*, and the reference to *spermatikoi logoi* and fate, I would suggest that there is nothing here that would not accord with the views of Polemo, or even of Xenocrates. Even the important move of Zeno, to characterize God as a sort of fire, by virtue of which the Stoics are generally denominated 'materialists', is not really so radical as it seems. The *pyr tekhnikon* is a very particular kind of 'matter', owing

---

[31] He speaks, we may recall, of God as a monad and an intellect, 'ruling in the heavens' (*en ouranōi basileuousa*).

[32] I borrow here the translation of Long and Sedley, *The Hellenistic Philosophers* (1987: §46A), slightly altered.

much to the *logos* of Heraclitus (and to that extent constituting a dim prefiguration of the modern concept of 'energy'), having very little in common with all other types of matter—the four sublunary elements—and a good deal in common with the active, demiurgic first principle of the Platonists. Indeed, the Stoics could be seen as taking to heart a dictum of the Eleatic Stranger's at *Sophist* 248C: 'We proposed as a sufficient mark of real things the presence in a thing of the power of being acted upon or of acting in relation to however insignificant a thing', and concluding that, in order to qualify, a first principle must be composed of some kind of substance that has these qualities.

That, indeed, seems to be the position of Antiochus, to judge by such a passage as Cicero, *Academica* I 24–9, a passage which, approached with proper care, may be pressed to yield insights into the state of Platonist metaphysics at the latter end of the Old Academic period.[33] M. Terentius Varro, who is the spokesman for Antiochus here, is in the midst of expounding the 'Academic' system, in Antiochus' interpretation of it, and has moved on from ethics to the topic of physics. This passage is deserving, I think, of extended examination:[34]

The topic of Nature, which they treated next, they approached by dividing it into two principles, the one the creative (*efficiens* = *poiētikē*), the other at this one's disposal, as it were, out of which something might be created. In the creative one they deemed that there inhered power (*vis* = *dynamis*), in the one acted upon, a sort of 'matter' (*materia* = *hylē*);[35] yet they held that each of the two inhered in the other, for neither would matter have been able to cohere if it were not held together by any power, nor yet would power with-

---

[33] When dealing with this passage in Dillon (1977: 82–3), I hesitated to claim its contents as authentic Old Academic doctrine, but Sedley (2002) has effectively disposed of my inhibitions. Sedley's essay should change the way we think about the Old Academy—that of Polemo in particular—and its relation to Stoicism.

[34] I am indebted at various points to Sedley's excellent translation of the passage, though I base myself generally on the Loeb translation of Rackham.

[35] Cicero's use of a form of the indefinite adjective here (*materia quadam*)—as in the case of his introduction of the neologism *qualitas* just below to translate the Greek *poiotēs*—need not indicate any corresponding hesitation about the use of the term *hylē* in his source, whatever that may be; he is simply being apologetic about introducing new technical terminology into Latin.

out some matter (for nothing exists without it being necessarily some-where).[36] But that which was the product of both they called 'body' (*corpus* = *sōma*), and, so to speak, a sort of 'quality'.[37]

We may pause to consider what we have here. It is a two-principle system very similar to that of the Stoics, certainly, but also to that which we have seen Theophrastus attributing to Plato himself in Chapter 1 (above, p. 21), and what has emerged as the logical result of a non-literal exegesis of the *Timaeus,* such as we may attribute to Xenocrates. The active, demiurgic principle, which emerges as a rational World-Soul, having as its contents the Forms, acts on a pas-sive, infinitely malleable 'material' principle[38] to create a world of physical bodies. Notable here, besides the influence of the *Timaeus,* is what seems to be a certain degree of influence from a scholastic exegesis of the *Theaetetus,* both in the matter of denominating the forms as 'qualities' (*poiotētes*), and, I think, in describing the active principle as a 'power' (*dynamis*). It may be that the passage at 156A, where Socrates, with his usual irony, is describing the position of 'the initiated', those sophisticated persons who believe also in unseen realities, is an influence here:[39]

Their first principle, on which all that we said just now depends, is that the universe really is motion and nothing else. And there are two kinds of motion. Of each kind there are any number of instances, but they differ in

[36] This is a most interesting reference back to the authority of a passage of the *Timaeus,* 52B: 'everything that exists must necessarily be in some place (*en tini topōi*)', equating *topos* here, and by implication the Receptacle in general, with matter.

[37] The term *poiotēs* really seems to be have been coined by Plato at *Theaet.*182A, to describe what it is that an active principle (*poioun*) brings about in a passive, or receptive, one—in this case a sense-organ. However, it would seem that, in the later Academy, helped by a perceived etymological connection between *poioun* and *poios* or *poiotēs,* this term became generalized as a description of forms in matter; and that is how it is being used here.

[38] Sedley makes the interesting point that, as this principle is described below (27) as infinitely divisible, this should imply that it in effect offers no resistance to the demiurgic principle, in contradistinction (possibly) to the system of Xenocrates, who postulated indivisible lines (cf. above, pp. 111–18), which would imply some measure of resistance on the part of the basic triangles to the creative endeavours of the Demiurge. I am not sure, though, that that was Xenocrates' intention in making this postulation.

[39] I borrow here the translation of Cornford (1935: 46).

that the one kind has the power of acting, the other of being acted upon (*dynamin to men poiein ekhon, to de paskhein*).

This is really only, of course, intended to make a distinction between perceiving agents and things perceived, but it seems to me that a scholastic mind (which was already operating with a two-principle universe) might be tempted to make it into a principle of quite general application. Such a development, at any rate, would provide us with a good Platonic origin for all the technical terms in this passage.

Varro now passes on (after a little interlude (25) in which Cicero in effect apologizes gracefully for introducing the neologism *qualitas* to translate *poiotēs*) to distinguish between two levels of 'quality' in the world (26):

Of those 'qualities', some are primary,[40] others derivative from these. The primary ones are each of a single kind and simple, while the ones derivative from them are various and, so to speak, multiform.[41] Thus air, fire, water, and earth are primary, while derivative from them are the forms of animals and of the things which grow out of the earth. Hence the former are called 'principles' (*initia = arkhai*) and—to give a translation from the Greek—'elements' (*elementa = stoikheia*). Of those, air and fire have the power to move and act (*vis movendi et efficiendi*),[42] while the other parts—I mean water and earth—have the capacity to receive and, as it were, to be acted on (*vis accipiendi et quasi patiendi*).[43]

---

[40] Cicero uses the word *principes,* which may translate either *arkhai* or *arkhikai.* As Sedley notes, the Stoics did not refer to the four elements as *arkhai,* but only *stoikheia,* 'elements', reserving the former term for God and Matter (cf. DL VII 134); whereas Plato in the *Timaeus* (48B) uses both terms to describe the elements.

[41] The adjective *multiformis* probably translates *polyeidēs,* a respectably Platonic adjective (contrasted with *haplous* at *Phdr.* 270D).

[42] This presumably translates something like *dynamis kinētikē kai poiētikē.* Zeno, we may note, is attested (*SVF* I 27, 5, from Aetius) to have described Fate (*heimarmenē*) as a *dynamis kinētikē tēs hylēs*—necessarily as the agency of the supreme divinity.

[43] Here again we seem to have a Greek technical term lurking—a *dynamis pathētikē,* and perhaps also *dektikē.* I have chosen to render this 'passive' sense of *dynamis* as 'capacity'. The Stoics do not seem to have attributed a passive *dynamis* to matter, but that does not preclude Old Academics from having done so. We may recall that Aetius attests of Xenocrates, in the notable Fr. 15 H/213 IP (above, p. 131)—though there is unfortunately a lacuna at the vital point, as we have seen—that Xenocrates declared that earth, water, and air are pervaded by 'divine powers', with the implication that fire is the active

What we find here is certainly a remarkable employment of the term *poiotēs*. In the case of the 'primary' qualities, it is less odd, because one could perhaps take the four elements as cold', 'hot', 'dry', and 'wet' respectively—though that is not the most natural way of understanding them here—but when we get to the 'derivative qualities' we seem to be faced with, not what any Aristotelian logician would describe as a quality, but rather a Platonic embodied form. If we accept, however, that *poiotēs* has acquired this meaning in the Old Academy before Polemo, the strangeness is dissipated somewhat. We can see it, rather, perhaps, as an anticipation of the Stoic doctrine of the *idiōs poion,* as a description of the unique bundle of qualities that make up a sensible individual.

Varro then goes on, slightly curiously, to mention the 'fifth element' of Aristotle (though without terming it 'aether'), as the substance of which the heavenly bodies and minds (*astra mentesque*) are made.[44] This he neither commends nor condemns, but passes on directly (27) to describe 'matter':[45]

But they hold that underlying all things is a substance called 'matter' (*materia quaedam*), entirely formless and devoid of all 'quality', and that out of it all things have been formed and produced, so that this matter can in its totality receive all things and undergo every sort of transformation throughout every part of it, and in fact even suffer dissolution—not into nothing, but into its own parts, which are capable of infinite section and division, since

agent behind these 'powers'. The difference here is that air as well as fire is regarded as *active,* according to normal Stoic doctrine—but even this could just as well be a Polemonian innovation as a Stoic one.

[44] Of course, the concept of aether had already been accepted by Xenocrates, who even read it into the *Timaeus* as the dodecahedron, as we have seen (above, p. 128, n. 112); and by Philippus of Opus, though in a rather peculiar form, as we shall see in Ch. 5 (below, p. 193).

[45] As Sedley points out (2002: 66), no fuss need be made about the use of the term *hylē,* 'matter', since Polemo would be composing long after Aristotle had developed this technical usage—if, indeed, it was not already in use in Academic circles in Speusippus' time, as I would suggest (cf. above, p. 44, n. 34). Sedley further suggests, however (p. 70), that *materia* here may in fact be being used by Cicero to translate *ousia,* as it is in his translation of the *Timaeus,* which he was composing at around the same time. That is an interesting possibility, as it would suggest that the Stoic use of *ousia* might derive from Academic exegesis of the 'divisible substance' (*ousia meristē*) which is one component of soul in *Tim.* 35A.

there exists nothing whatever in the nature of things that is an absolute minimum, so as to be incapable of division; but that all things that are in motion move by means of 'interspaces' (*intervalla* = *diakena*), these likewise being infinitely divisible; (28) and since the force that we have called 'quality' moves in this manner and since it thus travels back and forth (*ultro citroque versetur*),[46] they think that the whole of matter also undergoes complete change throughout, and that thus those things are produced which they call *qualia* (*poia*)—from which latter, in a nature which as a whole coheres and forms a continuum with itself, there has been produced a single world (*mundus, kosmos*), outside of which there is no portion of matter and no body, while all the things in the world are parts of it, held together by a sentient nature (*natura sentiens*),[47] in which inheres perfect reason (*ratio perfecta* = *logos teleios*), and which is also eternal, since nothing stronger exists to cause it to perish; (29) and this force they say is the soul of the world (*animus mundi*),[48] and is also perfect intelligence and wisdom (*mens sapientiaque perfecta*),[49] which they call 'god', and is a sort of providence (*prudentia quaedam* = *pronoia*), presiding over all the things that fall under its control, governing especially the heavenly bodies, and then those things on earth that concern mankind. This force they also sometimes call 'necessity' (*necessitas* = *anangkē*), because nothing can happen otherwise than has been ordained by it under, as it were, a 'fated and unchangeable concatenation of everlasting order'—although they sometimes also call it 'fortune' (*fortuna* = *tykhē*), because many of its operations are unforeseen and unexpected by us on account of their obscurity and our ignorance of causes.

There are various interesting problems to be addressed here. First of all, the active principle is now identified as a rational World-Soul, residing primarily in the heavens, but pervading all parts of the universe. This, as has been remarked before, while being thoroughly Stoic in appearance, is not in conflict with the doctrine of the later

[46] This does sound very like the Stoic doctrine of *tonos*, but it is also a possible description of what is envisaged in Xenocrates, Fr. 15/213, where 'powers' are described as 'pervading' (*endiēkein*) the passive elements.

[47] This, I would suggest, probably translates *noera*, rather than *aisthētikē physis*, though one cannot be sure. It could be seen as a reminiscence of the *emphrōn physis* mentioned at *Tim.* 46D, as I propose below.

[48] For Cicero, *animus* as well as *anima* can translate *psykhe*.

[49] This may actually be a reminiscence of Plato, *Phil.* 30c, where the 'cause of the mixture', the supreme principle in the system there adumbrated, is described as 'wisdom and intellect' (*sophia kai nous*).

Academy, nor is it incompatible with the *Timaeus* itself, at least as it was read by the later Academy. After all, if the Demiurge is conflated with the World-Soul, as seems to follow from a demythologizing interpretation, we find ample confirmation from the text of an active principle answering to the description presented here. One remarkably apt passage occurs at *Timaeus* 46D, where Soul is presented as the only thing that can possess Intellect, and there is talk of 'the causes which pertain to the intelligent nature (*emphrōn physis*)', which are 'artificers (*dēmiourgoi*) of things fair and good', as opposed to those connected with the four elements, which are essentially passive.

It may be noted that there is no assertion in the *Academica* passage that the first principle is composed of pure fire; nor is there any mention of the distinctive Stoic doctrine of periodic cosmic conflagration (*ekpyrōsis*). On the other hand, the doctrine of fate propounded here does seem distinctively Stoic. David Sedley[50] is rather more disturbed by this than seems to me necessary, suggesting that, if we fail to find warrant for such a doctrine within the Academic tradition, 'those who believe this text to represent a retrojection of Stoicism will find their case much strengthened, and doubt will be cast on the entire reconstruction' that he has proposed.

That Antiochus is indulging in a certain amount of 'retrojection' is not a proposition that I would be concerned to deny—though, for the present purpose, the less would certainly be the better. And in fact Sedley presents a most persuasive argument for the derivability of this doctrine from an interpretation of the account of 'necessity' (*anangkē*) in *Timaeus* 47E–48A. There, in the context of the myth, 'necessity', as 'the wandering cause', is represented as presenting a degree of resistance to the benevolent will of the Demiurge. But if one deconstructs the Demiurge, and asserts, as is done in that passage, that 'matter', as the passive principle, is infinitely divisible and malleable by the active principle, then *anangkē* could be interpreted, by such thinkers as Xenocrates and Polemo, not as a force which provides resistance to the will of the active principle, but rather as representing the necessary mode of its operation in the material world.

[50] (2002: 73–4).

Causal necessity, or 'fate', thus, as Sedley remarks, becomes 'in itself a positive aspect of divine benevolence'. We do not need to assume that the Academics had already worked out the full implications of Stoic determinism, as developed by Chrysippus, though this may be the logical consequence of their position. All they need to be maintaining is that the providence of the World-Soul guides all things inexorably to the best conclusion of which they are capable.[51]

Even in the area of logic, if we are prepared to accept Antiochus as a reasonably reliable witness, we need not despair entirely of uncovering the main lines of Polemo's position. Once again, it will not be much different from that of Xenocrates, and indeed Varro presents it as the basic consensus of both Academics and Peripatetics, but there seems little reason to doubt that it broadly reflects Polemo's position. At *Acad.* I 30–2, we find the following:

Then the third part of philosophy, which comprises reasoning and discourse,[52] was treated by both of them [sc. Academics and Peripatetics] as follows. The criterion of truth,[53] although having its basis in the senses, does not reside in the senses; the judge of things they wish to be the mind (*mens* = *nous*). They consider that it alone deserves credence, because it alone perceives that which is eternally simple and uniform and identical with itself.[54] This thing they call the *idea,* a name already given to it by Plato; we [sc. Latin-speakers] can correctly term it 'form' (*species*).

This presents a position which is certainly not Stoic (except, perhaps, for the actual term 'criterion of truth'), and which goes even beyond Antiochus (who, from other evidence, seems to have viewed

---

[51] Xenocrates is recorded, indeed, as having composed a treatise *On Fate* (DL IV 12), though we have no idea what he said in it. The very occurrence of the word *heimarmenē,* however, does seem to betoken some concern with the concept—and, after all, the *nomoi heimarmenoi* which the Demiurge is described at *Tim.* 41E as expounding to the souls prior to their embodiment needs some explanation.

[52] *Quae erat in ratione et in disserendo:* probably translating *logikē* and *dialektikē*—or just a doublet for *dialektikē* alone.

[53] This term itself may well not go back to the Old Academy, but that does not affect the basic doctrine.

[54] A rendering into Latin of the standard formula for the nature of the Forms in the *Phaedo* (78D).

the Platonic Forms in a way compatible with Stoicism, as *logoi* immanent in the human mind)[55] in postulating a set of transcendent Forms—though here we may note that Varro uses the singular *idea,* in line with the later doxographic tradition, perhaps referring to the Paradigm of the *Timaeus* as the sum-total of the Forms. In any case, there is nothing here incompatible with an Old Academic provenance.[56] We may continue:

All the senses, on the other hand, they consider to be dull and sluggish, nor are they at all capable of perceiving any of the things which are supposed to come within the scope of the senses, because they are either so small as to be imperceptible by sense,[57] or subject to such violent motion that no single thing is ever stationary, nor even remains the same thing, because all things are in continual ebb and flow;[58] accordingly this whole level of reality they call 'opinable' (*opinabilis = doxastē*). Knowledge (*scientia = epistēmē*), on the other hand, they consider to exist nowhere except in the notions and reasonings[59] of the mind. Consequently, they adopt the method of definitions (*definitiones = horoi*) of things, and they apply this to all subjects that they discuss. They also approve the analysis of words, that is, the statement of the reason why each class of things bears the name that it does—a subject they term *etymologia.*[60] They then use these [sc. definitions and etymologies] as 'tokens' or, so to speak, 'marks' of things,[61] as guides for arriving at proofs

[55] Cf. e.g. *Acad. Pr.* II 30, where a much more Stoic scenario is presented.

[56] We must not, of course, assume that we are back with what is regarded as the 'classical' Theory of Forms (of the *Phaedo*). If anything, we must imagine a thoroughly mathematized model, based on a non-literal exegesis of the *Timaeus,* and refined by the critiques of Speusippus and Xenocrates, among others.

[57] This really only makes sense if what are being referred to are the basic molecules of matter, out of which sensible objects are composed; but if so, Varro is hardly making himself clear.

[58] Here we have a thoroughly 'Heraclitean' picture of the physical world, based on the description of sense-perception given in *Theaet.* 155D–157C.

[59] *Notiones atque rationes* probably represent *ennoiai te kai logismoi.*

[60] The actual term does not occur in extant sources before Strabo and Dionysius of Halicarnassus in the late 1 cent. BC, more or less contemporary with the present text, but the method envisaged is doubtless that of the *Cratylus.* We find a nice example in Philo (*Plant.* 165), about half a century later, where *methē,* 'drunkenness', is etymologized as deriving from *meta thysias,* 'accompanying sacrifice', and *methesis,* 'relaxation' (of the soul)—very much in the spirit of the *Cratylus.*

[61] *Argumenta et quasi rerum nota* are probably, as Rackham suggests, being used here as a translation of *symbola.*

175

or conclusions as to anything of which they desire an explanation. Under this heading is imparted their whole system of dialectic, that is, speech couched in logical form (*oratio ratione conclusa*); as a 'counterpart'[62] to this is added the faculty of rhetoric, which presents continuous speech adapted to the purpose of persuasion.

We have here, then, what may reasonably be taken to be the whole range of Old Academic logical theory in its final form, comprising definition, etymology, the construction of logical proofs (or dialectic), and rhetoric—a rational form of which is recognized, after all, even in the *Phaedrus* (269B–272C). We have no indication, unfortunately, as to whether the Academy under Polemo to any extent adopted the Aristotelian syllogistic. All one can say is that Varro gives no indication that there was any longer much distinction between the two schools in the area of the construction of logical proof during the last stage of the Old Academy. None of this, of course, is explicitly attributed to Polemo himself, but we must assume, I think, that even a man contemptuous of 'logical speculations', as he is attested to have been,[63] cannot have dispensed entirely with the various tools of logic, even if he was not concerned to develop them to any significant extent.

With some difficulty, then, and a good deal of speculation, our exiguous information on Polemo's philosophical position can be fleshed out somewhat. If the exposition of Academic doctrine in Cicero's *Academica Posteriora* can be essentially claimed for Polemo, as I believe, with Sedley, that it can, we are in possession of a conspectus of his physical and logical theory, as well as the basic lines of his ethics. He still remains, however, a rather shadowy figure—much revered for his personal integrity, and head of his school for almost forty years, but with very little to show for it in terms of distinctive doctrines. Even such doctrines as we have unearthed probably dif-

---

[62] Rackham is doubtless right to see in *ex altera parte* an effort to render the Greek *antistrophos*, as used by Plato e.g. at *Gorg.* 464B or *Rep.* VII 522A.

[63] Cf. above, p. 160. We should note that Polemo is only, strictly speaking, contemptuous of those who resort to logical speculations as a substitute for involvement with 'real life' (*ta pragmata*).

fered little from those of his master Xenocrates, though we seem to discern some signs of increased austerity in the sphere of ethics. All we can say is that they sufficiently impressed Zeno of Citium, and, much later, Antiochus of Ascalon, to make Polemo an important bridge figure between Platonism and Stoicism, and a key element in the revival of dogmatic Platonism in the first century BC.

Minor Figures 5

In this chapter, I gather together a number of other members of the Academy who contributed something to the development of Platonism, and try to provide some evaluation of their work. A full list of all known members of the Old Academy after Plato is given in Chapter 1,[1] so that I will confine myself here to those members of whose works or opinions something is known.

First, I will consider the contribution of Plato's 'secretary', Philippus of Opus, whom I accept, following what is now virtually the consensus of scholars, as being the true author of the pseudo-Platonic *Epinomis;* then the slightly mysterious Hermodorus of Syracuse, author of a book on Plato's life and doctrines; then the flamboyant and volatile Heraclides of Pontus (at least for that portion of his career which relates to the Academy). These personages all belong to the generation immediately following on Plato himself, but there are a number of others who belong rather to the generation of Polemo, to wit, Crantor of Soli and Crates (though about the latter, in truth, there is very little to be said). Lastly, some note must be taken of the radical change of direction adopted by Arcesilaus, on his assumption of the headship, which inaugurated almost two centuries of the New, or 'Sceptical', Academy. I recognise that all this involves a certain degree of chronological distortion (we turn back almost half a century from Polemo to Philippus), but as long as that is borne in mind it should not occasion too much confusion.

---

[1] pp. 13–14 above.

Philippus of Opus

It is by now, I think, a reasonably uncontroversial postulate—in the wake of the researches of Leonardo Tarán,[2] among others—that the author of the Platonic *Epinomis* is in fact Plato's faithful amanuensis, Philippus of Opus, who had spent some years of his life before composing it in putting his master's last work, *The Laws,* in reasonable order for publication.[3] On this assumption, Philippus will have composed this appendix to the *Laws* as a pseudepigraphon, not really with the intention of deceiving his fellow-Academics (which he could hardly hope to do—though he was somewhat more successful with later generations), but rather as a way of advancing his own view of what Plato's final position was on the nature of the first principle and supreme reality (which therefore would be his own position as well).

Before focusing on the *Epinomis,* however, we must review what is known of Philippus' life and other works. He is described in the sources as a Locrian, stemming either from Opus in Central Greece, or from Medma, a colony of the Epizephyrian, or western Locrians, on the western side of the toe of Italy. The latter is far more likely, but interesting patterns of provenance are hereby revealed. If this is

---

[2] In his definitive edition of the *Epinomis* (1975). The modern campaign against Platonic authorship may be seen as commencing with the monograph of F. Müller (*Stilistische Untersuchungen der Epinomis des Philippus von Opus,* Berlin, 1927), which, despite some excessive claims that it makes, has won general acceptance. The attempt at rebuttal by Taylor (1929), while scoring some effective points of detail, fails in its overall claim: the *Epinomis* simply does not come across as the final effort of an old man whose powers are deserting him; it is redolent far more of the attempt of a rather woolly-minded and over-enthusiastic disciple to emulate the more extreme stylistic quirks of his master, while putting his own doctrinal gloss on his master's work. Tarán's treatment of the whole question is most judicious.

[3] Two considerations in particular I find persuasive: one, that, unlike such works as the *Alcibiades I* or the *Hippias Major,* whose authenticity had been doubted in modern times, but which were never doubted in antiquity, there was a persistent—although minority—tradition as regards the *Epinomis* in antiquity that it was not by Plato—and indeed that it was, specifically, by Philippus of Opus (DL III 37; Proclus, *ap. Anon. Proleg.* 25; Suda, s.v. *Philosophos*); and secondly, that there was a firm tradition (DL, ibid.) that the *Laws* was Plato's last work, and left unfinished, or at least in need of editing ('in the wax'), at his death—so that there is no room for another work from his hand to serve as an appendix to it.

correct (and it is hard to see how the rather obscure town of Medma could have got into the story, were it not in fact his place of origin), Philippus would be the only disciple of Plato (apart, of course, from Dion of Syracuse, and perhaps Hermodorus, on whom see below) coming from Magna Graecia. If we allow our fancy to play about his origins, we may conjecture that he was scion of a prominent family of Medma—possibly even the founders of the colony—got to know, or at least hear of, Plato, on one of Plato's trips to the west, and followed him back to Athens. It is theoretically possible that he was an Opuntian Locrian who later emigrated to Medma, but this is so unlikely as to be hardly worth mentioning. Much more probable is that, once Philippus returned to mainland Greece, he 'rediscovered his roots' in Opus, and perhaps reclaimed the citizenship to which he was entitled. The *Suda* lists among his works a treatise *On the Opuntian Locrians,* which would have been a celebration of his ultimate homeland.

As for his chronology, we have really no clues as to his dates of birth or death. The *Suda* declares him to have been a pupil, not only of Plato, but of Socrates, but we do not have to take the latter assertion seriously.[4] We may reasonably imagine him to have been born shortly after the beginning of the century, and to have joined the Academy some time in the later 360s. He is grouped by Proclus[5] among the 'mathematicians' in the Academy, though as the last of a trio of younger scholars who developed the insights of their predecessors (such as Eudoxus), the former two of these being Hermotimus of Colophon and Theaetetus. Proclus tells us that Plato encouraged him to study mathematics, and that 'he carried on his investigations according to Plato's instructions, and set himself to study all the problems that he thought would contribute to Plato's

---

[4] Although Tarán (1975: 127) toys with it as a possibility, suggesting that he might have been ten years or so younger than Plato, and so could have met Socrates before his death, while still living until 340 or so; but he wisely rejects this in favour of the probability (advanced by Kurt von Fritz), based on Proclus' mode of reference to him in his *Commentary on Euclid*, that Philippus wrote on mathematics somewhat later than Eudoxus, who is agreed to have been born *c.*400 BC, and so should be somewhat younger than him. This seems quite reasonable.

[5] *Comm. in Eucl.* 67, 23 ff. Friedlein.

philosophy.' This certainly accords with the impression one receives from the *Epinomis*, as we shall see.

However, although mathematics, and in particular astronomy, is plainly central to Philippus' interests, he did not confine himself to those topics. We find mention in the *Suda* biography of works also *On the Gods* (in two books), *On Time*, *On Myths*, *On Freedom*, *On Anger*, *On Pleasure*, *On Love*, *On Friends and Friendship*, and *On Writing*, as well as a work on Plato himself (presumably a biography),[6] and that on the Opuntian Locrians mentioned earlier.[7] On the other hand, we also have a significant number of titles on astronomical and mathematical topics: *On the Distances of the Sun and Moon*, *On the Eclipse of the Moon*,[8] *On the Size of the Sun and the Moon and the Earth*,[9] *On Lightning*, *On Planets*, *Arithmetical Investigations*, *On Polygonal Numbers*,[10] *Optics* (2 books), *On Mirror Vision* (2 books),[11] *On Circular Motions*,[12] *Means* (*mesotētes*).[13] It is these latter that no doubt represent the main thrust of his interests, but it is plain from the *Epinomis* that Philippus was a man of profound religious convictions as well.

---

[6] As in the case of Hermodorus (cf. below, p. 199), he may have given an account of Plato's doctrines as well as of his life. At any rate, we have a reference in Philodemus' *History of the Academy* (III–V) to Philippus' relating, presumably in his *Life*, that, in his old age, Plato received in the Academy a 'visitor from Chaldaea (*xenos Chaldaios*)'—who no doubt gave him an account of Babylonian astrology.

[7] The work *Peri antapodoseōs* is something of mystery, since *antapodosis* can mean a variety of things, from the return of favours and repayment of loans, to alternation and reciprocal reactions of bodies, to the rhetorical balancing of clauses. However, the subject was probably ethical. We may note that virtually all of these titles coincide with those of works of Speusippus and/or Xenocrates, indicating a wide range of common interests, such as one would expect. Both Speusippus and Xenocrates wrote works on the gods, for instance, and both of them, as well as Eudoxus, wrote on pleasure.

[8] We learn from a snippet of doxography preserved by Stobaeus (*Ecl.* I 26, 3) that Philippus mentioned the doctrine of the Pythagoreans that eclipses of the moon were caused sometimes by the interposition of the earth, and sometimes by that of the anti-earth; so he discussed the views of predecessors, as one would expect.

[9] In the *Epinomis* (983A), Philippus asserts that the sun is actually larger than the earth, and that the other planets are very large also. No doubt he elaborated on that in this work.

[10] This subject was also dealt with by Speusippus in his treatise *On Pythagorean Numbers* (Fr.28 Tarán). The concept was in fact first developed by the Pythagoreans.

[11] If we may thus render *Enopt(r)ika*. We seem to have a reference to this work in Alexander of Aphrodisias, *In Meteor.* 151, 32 ff., where he mentions Philippus' discussion of the rainbow, in connection with mirror vision.

Astronomy for him, as we shall see, was above all a means of penetrating the nature of God, and its study should make one not only wise but morally good.

Philippus' main claim to fame, however, has always been that, as Plato's 'secretary' (*anagrapheus*) in his last years, he took on the task, on Plato's death in 347, of editing his last work, *The Laws,* which Plato had left in an unfinished state ('in the wax', *en kērōi*).[14] Much ingenuity was expended by nineteenth-century German scholars, in particular, in trying to work out how much Philippus contributed to the *Laws* in its finished form—some, like Ast and Zeller, and more recently G. Müller,[15] seeking to deny that it is a work of Plato's at all. The modern consensus, however, it is fair to say, is that the work as we have it is Plato's, and that, despite some passages in the middle books that plainly need further editing, it is both coherent and compatible with the rest of his œuvre. The question of the degree of Philippus' tampering with his master's work is of some importance for my thesis, since what I would wish to maintain is that, in the *Epinomis,* Philippus is presenting his own distinctive 'take' on Plato's doctrine, primarily in the *Laws* (though also in the *Timaeus,* and even in the *Republic*), and moreover that he has some justification for his position—a thesis that would be somewhat undermined if it were to be assumed that he had largely rewritten the *Laws*.

It is reasonable to assume, however, that Philippus devoted some years of his life, both before and after Plato's death, to, first, helping the old man put the work together, and then to transcribing it and tidying up loose ends. In the process, he immersed himself in Plato's late, 'hieratic' style, to the extent that, when he came to compose his

[12] If that is the meaning of *kukliaka*—the word is unique, and may be corrupt, but some work on either circles or circular motion seems to be indicated.

[13] The study of mean proportionals is made an important part of higher education in the *Epinomis,* 991A–B.

[14] What is to be made of this expression? Doubtless one did compose first onto wax tablets, in order to save valuable papyrus, but it is difficult to conceive of the whole of the *Laws* piled up on a series of wax tablets. Far more probably, the expression is (wholly or largely) metaphorical.

[15] (1951).

own afterpiece, he could give a very fair imitation of the more extravagant aspects of that style—even to the point of virtual incomprehensibility on occasion.[16]

That said, we may turn to an examination of the work itself. The *raison d'être* of the *Epinomis*,[17] set out at the beginning of it (by the Cretan Cleinias, as it happens, not by the Athenian Visitor), is to give a more specific account of 'what it is that mortal man should learn in order to be wise', on the grounds that that was not dealt with in the previous conversation.[18] In fact, Plato himself seems to be deliberately refraining from giving any details about this; he doubtless felt that it was better transmitted orally. This, however, gives Philippus the opportunity to provide his own view of what the members of the Nocturnal Council of *Laws* XII (and indeed every man who desires to be wise) should be studying, and to lead up to that by providing the theological underpinning to justify that. It is this theological underpinning that I wish to dwell on in particular, as it reveals most clearly Philippus' distinctive philosophical position.[19]

Now it is clear, I think, from the *Epinomis* that the supreme active principle in the universe favoured by the author is in fact a rational World-Soul, not transcending the physical world, but presiding in the celestial realm, of very much the type proposed in the previous chapter as being favoured by Polemo—though, of course, preceding that of

[16] There is a useful discussion of the question of style (which can hardly be illustrated in a work of this sort) in Tarán (1975: 14–19).

[17] Whose title for the work this is (*Epinomis* =something like 'Appendix to the *Laws*') is not clear—hardly that of Philippus himself. The other title of the work in the manuscripts, 'The Philosopher' (*Philosophos*), on the other hand, is even less likely to be his, being presumably an optimistic guess that this might be the lost third member of the 'trilogy' *Sophist-Statesman-Philosopher*, which Plato seems to promise at the outset of the *Sophist*, but never delivered on.

[18] This is more or less true; only rather obscure hints were dropped in Book XII of the *Laws* as to what would be the subject-matter of the higher studies of the members of the Nocturnal Council. As far as we can gather from the sketch of their education given at 965A–966B, this was intended to consist of dialectical exercises, leading to a clearer view of the nature, unity, and distinction of the virtues.

[19] One can also, I think, derive something of an ethical theory from the text of the *Epinomis*, a matter to which I will turn presently.

Polemo, perhaps by half a century. This assertion, so boldly made, requires comprehensive support, and to do that we must turn to a series of significant passages of text. There are four in particular that I should like to examine, 976D–977B, 982A–983C, 984B–C, and 988A–E, all from the preamble, as it were, to the exposition of that science which Philippus declares to be the supreme and most divine one—not dialectic, as one might expect, but rather astronomy, understood in its Platonic sense (that is, as expounded in Book VII of the *Republic*).[20]

First, then, let us consider 976D ff. Here the Athenian Visitor begins his search for the single most basic science, without the possession of which, as he says, 'mankind would be the most mindless and senseless of creatures'. This science he declares to be that of number—a gift to us from God himself. He then proceeds to explain to us what he means by 'God'—a move interesting in itself, since Plato, in using the indefinite term *ho theos,* would never bother to provide any gloss of it.[21]

And I must explain who it is that I believe to be God, though he be a strange one (*atopos*)[22]—and somehow not strange either: for why should we not believe the cause of all the good things that are ours[23] to have been the cause also of what is far the greatest, understanding (*phronēsis*)? And who is it that I magnify with the name of God, Megillus and Cleinias? It must be Heaven (*Ouranos*) which has full claim, no less than all the other daemons and gods also, to our honour and especially to our prayers. That it has been the cause of all the other good things we have, we shall all admit; that it really gave us

---

[20] Dialectic does indeed appear, briefly, in 991c—Philippus, as a good Platonist, could hardly dispense with it altogether—but, most interestingly, simply as a tool for pursuing astronomy.

[21] I borrow the Loeb translation of W. R. M. Lamb, with minor emendations.

[22] There may indeed be an element of word-play being indulged in here, since Ouranos (for it is he) is indeed 'out of place' (the etymological meaning of *atopos*) in being elevated to the rank of supreme deity, since in Greek mythology he had been stripped of all power at an early stage of cosmogony—but again, etymologized as 'heaven', he is very much in place, as we shall see.

[23] Again, how can Ouranos, in his traditional role, be spoken of as 'cause of all the good things that are ours'? Only, I would suggest, as being the ruling principle of the heavens—not the sun, but rather the 'Good' of the *Republic,* taken here, not as a transcendent, immaterial first principle, but rather as the immanent ruling principle of the universe. But this is to anticipate.

number also, we assert, and that it will give us more gifts yet, if we will but follow its lead. For if one enters on the right theory about it, whether one be pleased to call it World-Order (*kosmos*) or Olympos or Ouranos—let one call it this or that,[24] but follow where, in bespangling itself and turning the stars that it contains in all their courses, it produces the seasons and food for all. And thence, accordingly, we have understanding in general, we may say, together with all number, and all other good things: but the greatest of these is when, after receiving its gift of numbers, one explores the whole circuit (*periodos*).

This is surely a remarkable passage. The old god Ouranos is pressed into service in quite a new role, as the immanent guiding principle of the universe, and assigned a demiurgic function (though one proper also to the Good of the *Republic*), that of the ultimate provider of all good things to mortals, but in particular—by reason of the alternation of day and night, and the movements of sun and moon, and the other planets—of number and reasoning in general.

There is not yet here, admittedly, any mention of a World-Soul; but for that we do not have to wait very long. Let us turn next to 982A ff. Here Philippus has just finished (981B–E) setting out his five-element universe (fire, water, air, earth—and aether[25]), each with its proper inhabitants, ending with a distinction between two basic types of creature in the universe, immortal and mortal. He now goes on to expand on this:

Let us therefore first observe that, as we state it, such creatures are of two sorts—for let us state it again—both visible, one of fire, as it would appear, entirely,[26] and the other of earth; and the earthy one moves in disorder, whereas that of fire has its motion in perfect order. Now that which has

[24] This is very probably, as Tarán suggests (1975: 236), a reminiscence of *Tim.* 28b2–4; and if so, a further example of Philippus' manipulation of his sources, as *ouranos* in the *Timaeus* simply refers to the heavens, not to any deity.

[25] The remarkable introduction of aether, as *second*-highest element in a five-element universe, will be discussed below.

[26] This might seem to suggest that the heavenly bodies (for it is those to which he is referring) are composed not only of fire, but also of immaterial souls, but, as Tarán points out (1975: 267), what Philippus seems rather to have in mind (cf. 981 D–E) is that they have slight portions of all the other elements also—a thoroughly materialist scenario, therefore.

motion in disorder we should regard as unintelligent, acting like the animal creatures about us for the most part; but that which has an orderly and heavenly progress must be taken as providing strong evidence of its intelligent life. *The necessity (anangkē) of a soul that has acquired intellect* will prove itself by far the greatest of all necessities; for it makes laws as ruler, not as ruled; and this inalterable state, when the soul has taken the best counsel in accord with the best intellect, comes out as the perfect thing in truth and in accord with intellect, and not even adamant could ever prove stronger than it or more inalterable, but in fact the three Fates (*Moirai*) have taken hold, and keep watch that what has been decided by each of the gods with the best counsel shall be perfect.

There is a good proportion of obscurantist guff in all this, but nevertheless it can be seen, I think, that Philippus is touching certain significant bases. Specifically, he is making reference to the myth of *Republic* X. The mention of the *anangkē* of soul here would seem to be a reference, above all, to the passage 616C–617C, which presents us with the image of the great cosmic Spindle, consisting of the outer circle, or 'whorl', of the fixed stars, and seven inner ones, representing the planetary circuits, which rests on the knees of Necessity, who turns it—that would be the point of the remark that it acts 'as ruler, not ruled' (by contrast to the *anangkē* of the *Timaeus,* for instance, which is controlled by the Demiurge, *qua* Intellect, cf. *Tim.* 48A). The suspicion that Philippus has the *Republic* in mind here is strengthened by the references to 'adamant' (cf. 616^{c}8: the staff and the hook of the Spindle are made of adamant) and to the Fates (cf. the 'Moirai, daughters of Necessity', who sit around the Spindle at equal intervals (617C), and help their mother to turn it).

Does this, one might ask, imply a commitment by Philippus to what may be termed 'astral determinism'? Much later, Plotinus, in *Enn.* II 3 ('On Whether the Stars are Causes'), chapter 9, identifies the Necessity who turns the Spindle as precisely that, the principle of cosmic determinism which rules the lower levels of life of the human soul, but which can be transcended by the higher, rational soul. The truth probably is that Philippus was not much concerned with the problem of determinism, since, before Chrysippus, it had not been stated in its starkest form;[27] for him, but not for Plotinus, the hand that turns the Spindle is the supreme principle, not anything that can be transcended. The fact that its determinations are ineluctable was not yet seen as a serious problem for human autonomy.

At any rate, it should be clear that in the above passage Philippus is presenting Soul as the supreme active principle in the universe. This is confirmed a little further on, at 983c ff., where Soul is presented as creating all the various classes of being, from the heavenly gods on down, through the aetherial and aerial daemons, to the denizens of water and finally men. And yet, in the middle of this, we suddenly find a reference to 'God', being differentiated from the various levels of daemon, as not being subject to passions (985A): 'For we know that God, who has the privilege of the divine portion, transcends these affections of pleasure and pain, but has a share of intelligence and knowledge in every sphere.' There is nothing else for 'God' to be here, however, than the World-Soul.

This is confirmed a little later on, at the end of what is Philippus' elaborate preamble to his proposing of astronomy (which he manages to identify with the dialectic of *Republic* VII) as the highest science. He is criticizing the primitive conceptions of divinity held by men of former times, in contrast with the best thinking of the present day (988c–E):

And indeed there is much good reason to suppose that formerly, when men had their first conceptions of how the gods came to exist and with what qualities, and whence, and to what kind of actions they proceeded, they were spoken of in a manner not approved or welcomed by the prudent, nor were even the views of those who came later,[28] among whom the greatest dignity was given to fire and water and the other bodies, while the wonderful soul was accounted inferior; and higher and more honoured with them was a motion assigned to the body for moving itself by heat and coolings and everything of that kind, instead of that which the soul had for moving both

[27] But see the remarks made in the previous chapter, à propos Polemo and the controversial passage from Cicero's *Academica Posteriora* (above, pp. 173–4).

[28] This would seem to refer to the early 'physicists', from Thales on down—the first group being therefore those at a mythological level of thought, represented by Homer and Hesiod.

the body and itself. But now that we account it no marvel that the soul, once it is in the body, should stir and revolve this and itself, neither does soul, on our reckoning,[29] doubt her power of revolving any weight. And therefore, since we now claim that, *as the soul is the cause of the whole,* and all good things are causes of like things, while on the other hand evil things are the causes of other things like them,[30] it is no marvel that the soul should be cause of all motion and stirring—that the motion and stirring towards the good are the work of the best soul, while those tending to the opposite are the opposite— it must be that good things have conquered and conquer things that are not their like.

Once again, Soul emerges as the cause of all things, here in con- trast to earlier theories which wished to derive *the gods* from material principles, indicating that, for Philippus, questions as to the true identity and composition of 'the gods', or of 'God', can be answered in this way. The reasoning may leave something to be desired (how valid is it to deduce, from the fact that *our* souls can move our bodies, the conclusion that the World-Soul is the sole mover of the whole universe?), but the doctrine is not in doubt.

Enough evidence has by now, I think, been presented to make clear Philippus' position on the nature of God, or the supreme principle. The next question to which we must address ourselves is how he can have believed that this doctrine was in agreement with that of his master, Plato—since this, after all, would seem to be the justification for his exercise in pseudepigraphy. If we turn back to Book X of the *Laws,* what we find, I think, is interesting. If one resolves to screen out the rest of Plato's works in which he touches on the nature of the first principle—such dialogues as the *Phaedo, Republic, Symposium, Phaedrus, Timaeus,* or *Philebus*—and looks solely to the *Laws,* one observes, I think, a strange thing: despite periodic mentions of 'God', 'gods', and even at one point (902E–903B) a demiurgic figure,

---

[29] I would agree with Taylor, in his translation (ad loc.), in taking *hēmin* as a sort of ethical dative. Certainly what is being spoken of in this clause is not 'our' soul, but soul in general, or the World-Soul.

[30] Philippus here seems to be picking up on certain remarks of Plato in *Laws* X 896E about the soul 'of opposite capacity' to the good, as being responsible for evil, but he only succeeds in obscuring his main point.

who cares for every detail of the world and its human inhabitants,[31] when it comes down to it, there is nothing higher than the World-Soul.

Let us look at a few key passages. First, 891E–892B, where the central theme of the theodicy of Book X is introduced. The Visitor from Athens (of course) is speaking:[32]

> So it looks as if I must now produce a rather unfamilar argument (*ouk eiōthota logon*).[33] Well then, the doctrine which produces an impious soul also 'produces', in a sense, the soul itself, in that it denies the priority of what was in fact the first cause of the birth and destruction of all things and regards it as a later creation. Conversely, it asserts that what actually came later, came first. That's the source of the mistake these people have made about the real nature of the gods.[34]

CLEINIAS: So far, the point escapes me.

ATHENIAN: It's the *soul*, my good friend, that nearly everybody seems to have misunderstood, not realizing its nature and power. Quite apart from other points about it, people are particularly ignorant about its birth (*genesis*). It is one of the *first* creations, born long before all physical things, and is more than anything else the cause of all their alterations and transformations. Now if that's true, anything closely related to soul will necessarily have been created before material things, won't it, since soul itself is older than matter?

Now this is something, but it does not get us all the way. Soul is simply asserted to be superior to body, and to material elements, and to be cause of their existence, rather than the other way about, as materialist philosophers (we may think particularly of the Atomists) assert. But on the other hand we find talk of the soul being 'generated' (*geneseōs, genomenē*), which, if taken literally, implies a higher power again, superior to Soul, which would do the generating.

---

[31] And cf. also *hēmōn ho basileus* at 904A.

[32] I borrow the translation of Trevor Saunders, with minor alterations.

[33] This turn of phrase may in fact be picked up by Philippus at *Epin.* 986D (quoted above, p. 184). If so, this would be significant, since Philippus is here introducing his supreme deity.

[34] Philippus, again, seems to pick up on this attack on materialists at 988C–E (quoted above, p. 187)

As the exposition proceeds, however, it becomes much less clear that there is anything in the universe superior to Soul.[35] Let us turn now to the core of the argument, at 896A ff.:

ATHENIAN: So what's the definition of the thing we call the soul? Surely we can do nothing but use our formula of a moment ago: 'motion capable of moving itself'.

CLEINIAS: Do you mean that the entity which we all call 'soul' is precisely that which is defined by the expression 'self-generating motion'?

ATHENIAN: I do. And if that is true, are we still dissatisfied? Haven't we got a satisfactory proof that soul is identical with the original source of the generation and motion of all past, present, and future things and their contraries, since it has been shown to be the cause of all change and motion in everything?

CLEINIAS: Dissatisfied? No! On the contrary, it has been proved most adequately that soul, being the source of motion, is the most ancient thing there is.'

We have now advanced to the position where Soul, being endowed with self-motion (and thus, in effect, ungenerated and eternal), is presented as prior to all other things, and as the *cause* of all other things. One could still, perhaps, argue for a supreme deity which would be a sort of 'unmoved mover' (like the Good of the *Republic*), but we must reflect at this point that this whole argument is directed towards establishing the nature of *God,* so that, if the soul is *not* God, we are wasting our time establishing the existence and superiority of soul—unless we are then going to proceed to an investigation of whatever the *real* supreme principle might be. But in fact we never move beyond this demonstration of the nature and power of soul; on the contrary, the role of Soul becomes ever more central and more exalted.

If we move on, for instance, to 896E, we learn that 'Soul, by virtue

[35] There is an excellent discussion of this question in a (very characteristic) footnote in Cherniss (1944: 429, n. 365). The fact that the soul is not explicitly stated in *Laws* X to be eternal and ungenerated need not, as he says, imply any more than that Plato thought it was obvious—he had stated it in *Phdr.* 245C–246A. Cf. also Cherniss (1944: Appendix XI, pp. 603–10).

of its own motions, stirs into movement everything in the heavens and on earth and in the sea.' A long list of psychic states and functions then follows, which govern a long list of physical conditions, at the conclusion of which (897B) we are told that soul 'governs all things rightly and happily, *when it takes intellect to itself*.[36]

Finally, at 898B ff., it is made clear both that the driving force of the universe is a World-Soul, and that each of the heavenly bodies, which are in fact the 'gods' that we have been in search of, is a (fiery) body guided by a soul of its own (898D–E). At 899C–D, the whole course of the argument is summed up, in most significant terms:

ATHENIAN: Now then, Megillus and Cleinias, let's lay down limiting conditions for anyone who has so far refused to believe in gods, and so dispose of them.

CLEINIAS: What conditions do you mean?

ATHENIAN: Either he must demonstrate to us that we're wrong to posit Soul as the first cause to which everything owes its birth, and that our subsequent deductions were equally mistaken, or, if he can't put up a better case than ours, he should let himself be persuaded by us and live the rest of his life a believer in gods.

We may note here how much the status of Soul has been enhanced from its first introduction at 892A. There, it was spoken of as itself having a *genesis,* albeit one antecedent to all other things; here, however, it itself *is* the *prōtē genesis* of all things, and so, inevitably, the supreme deity. As for the other gods, whose existence and providential care for mankind the Athenian Visitor wants to establish, they are revealed as celestial deities subordinate to Soul, though each ruled by their own soul. All other references throughout the book of a more traditional nature to 'God' or 'the gods' must, I would argue, be interpreted in the light of these facts.

---

[36] If only we could be sure what followed this in the MSS, we might be even clearer as to the divine status of Soul, but the text is sadly disturbed, and it is unsafe to base any conclusions on it. I leave aside, by the way, the element of dualism that enters in here, as being not central to our concerns at the moment. As we have seen, Philippus makes a nod in the direction of dualism in an attempt to explain evils (988D–E), but he does not care to dwell on the concept of an 'evil' soul.

So then, if Philippus in the *Epinomis* is seeking to foist a purely astral theology onto Plato, may he not be said to have some excuse for this? We may seek to maintain that the theology of *Laws* X can be explained by the circumstance that the Athenian does not want to confuse his essentially unphilosophical immediate audience of Cleinias and Megillus, nor yet his notional ultimate public, consisting of the good citizens of Magnesia, by the imposition of the full complexity of Platonic theology, but that will not do, I think. After all, the concept of a universe ruled by a rational World-Soul, with, as its subordinates, a group of astral deities resident in the heavens, is quite bizarre enough, one would think, to give grave offence to such traditionally minded men as Megillus and Cleinias, but in the event they take it like lambs—just occasionally expressing some confusion, which they are then glad to have cleared up by even more remarkable revelations. No, it is more reasonable to postulate that, if Plato puts this view of divinity across at this stage of his life, it is because he has come round to believing it himself. And Philippus, who lived closely with him, and with the composition of his last work, over a considerable number of years, was in an excellent position to know this.

He did plainly feel, however, that this interpretation of Plato's theology would prove controversial—after all, what about the Good? What about the Beautiful Itself? What about the Demiurge and his Paradigm? And what about the Cause of the Mixture in the *Philebus*?—and this led him, I would submit, to the composition of the *Epinomis* (whatever he called it himself). And indeed he was right to doubt that his interpretation of Platonism would meet with anything like a consensus. Certainly, Speusippus was not impressed by the claims of a World-Soul to be the supreme principle; he went rather for a One above Being, and a second principle of Multiplicity. Xenocrates, in turn, as we have seen, favours a Monad (which is probably also an Intellect) and a Dyad, the product of which is Soul. Only Polemo, in the next generation, may perhaps have been influenced to some extent, in the development of his theology, by the version of Platonism propounded by Philippus—and, of course, the Stoics, following on from Polemo, though with the modification that for them the World-Soul is composed of 'intellectual fire' (*pyr noeron*).

Another significant aspect of the doctrine of the *Epinomis* is its theory of daemons, and, tied in with that, its system of five cosmic elements, as opposed to the more traditional system of four utilized by Plato in the *Timaeus*.[37] The theory of daemons proposed (981C–D, 984C–E) relates interestingly to that of Xenocrates, without being identical to it, as it also establishes daemons in a median position in the universe, as well as granting them the mediating role laid down in the *Symposium*.

At 981B, the author sets out a five-tiered structure of the universe, making use of the four traditional (and Platonic) elements, fire, air, water, and earth, and adding to them as a fifth aether, which, however, he puts to a use very different from that to which it was put (perhaps contemporaneously) by Aristotle, and by Xenocrates. Philippus presents us with a scheme in which the cosmos is ordered in five zones, each composed predominantly of one element, though with admixtures of all the others in small quantities (this postulate introduced to bind the cosmos together). Highest is the zone of fire, in which dwell the heavenly gods—and indeed the gods in general, since Philippus, as we have seen, does not acknowledge any supramundane reality; second to this is the zone of aether (represented as the purest sort of air, rather than as the purest fire, 984B–C): 'For let us consider aether as coming next after fire, and let us hold that Soul fashions from it live creatures with their faculties—as in the creatures of the other kinds—, belonging for the most part to that one substance, but in the lesser parts derived from the other elements for the sake of combination'[38] (trans. W. R. M. Lamb).

[37] Xenocrates, of course, had also wished a five-element system onto the *Timaeus*, as we have seen (above, p. 128), but the system propounded by Philippus differs interestingly from his—which was a straightforward adoption of Aristotle's doctrine of aether.

[38] This remarkable insertion of aether in *second* place, rather than the highest, in the universe is probably stimulated by such passages as *Tim.* 58D, where aether is described as 'the most translucent part of air', and *Phd.* 109B and 111B, where, again, aether is presented as a purer form of air. Philippus thus must have felt that he was cleaving closer to Plato, but in doing so he lays himself open to serious difficulties of a mathematical nature, as we shall see below—a strange situation for such a devotee of mathematics to find himself in.

Below these again is the zone of air, inhabited by an aery race of beings (not explicitly described as daemons, though it is hard to see what else they can be described as), and below that again that of water, again inhabited by its proper beings, which will be nymphs and water-sprites (*not* fish, we may note). Indeed, this whole scheme can be seen as a misinterpretation—or perhaps rather a deliberate alteration—of the scheme presented in the *Timaeus* 41B, where the 'three mortal kinds' still uncreated, which are to inhabit the realms of air, water, and earth, are plainly intended to be birds, fish, and land animals, not varieties of superior being (cf. 40A).[39] Philippus' view was, plainly, that each zone of the universe should be endowed by Soul with beings proper to it, in descending order of dignity, from gods to men, and that birds and fish are therefore really earthy denizens, and not the proper inhabitants of the zones of air and water. This position was destined to have considerable influence on later Platonism.

There follows next a passage which, if it is not corrupt (and even, I think, if it is), exhibits a certain muddleheadedness on the part of our author—explicable, as Tarán suggests in his commentary ad loc. (1981: 283), as a result of superimposing his own more elaborate theory on the simpler one of Plato, according to which daemons are median between men and gods and inhabit the air:[40] 'and after these [sc. the heavenly gods], and next below these, come the daemons, and the aery race, holding the third and middle situation, source of interpretation, which we must specially honour with our prayers for the sake of an auspicious conveyance across.' Philippus here seems to combine, with a slightly ungrammatical sleight of hand, the daemons proper and the aery race, and grant them both equally the median and mediating role of daemons in the *Symposium*—their roles of *hermēneia* and *diaporeia* clearly alluding to the terminology of

---

[39] The *Epinomis* did, however, have its influence on the interpretation of this passage, as we can see from Proclus' commentary ad loc. (*In Tim.* III 104,26–112,19 Diehl), but already from the brief allusion to it by Alcinous in his *Didaskalikos*, ch. 15.

[40] In the *Symposium,* it must be admitted, there is no mention of the physical place of daemons, but they must have been seen as inhabiting the space between earth and heaven.

Symp. 202ᵉ3.[41] It is only true of the aery race that they hold the 'third and middle' situation, but plainly the aetherial daemons are being assigned the same role as they are (while the role of the watery nymphs is deliberately obscured).

Philippus certainly does seem to have involved himself in conceptual difficulties by his introduction of aether between the heavenly fire and air—as opposed to his colleague Xenocrates, who seems to have simply adopted Aristotle's postulation of aether as the celestial element, and then fathered it upon Plato in the *Timaeus*—and it is worth while asking ourselves why he should have done this. As Tarán points out, in his most useful discussion of the problem,[42] Philippus seems to be adapting Plato's scheme of the four elements and the five regular solids in the *Timaeus,* and is trying to give a place in a system of elements to the dodecahedron, which Plato (being somewhat embarrassed, perhaps, by its peculiar properties[43]) assigns to the construction of the universe as a whole (*Tim.* 55ᶜ4–6). This solution, however, must have seemed to Xenocrates unnecessarily vague, especially after Aristotle had postulated the aether as a fifth, celestial element, and, as we have seen, he boldly claimed the dodecahedron as a Platonic anticipation of Aristotle—presumably glossing Plato's phrase 'God utilized it for the construction of the universe (*to pan*) in his decoration of it' as a reference to the *heavens* rather than to the universe as whole.[44]

---

[41] Again, though, one may discern a slight alteration of sense: *diaporeia*—a rare word (in the genuine Platonic corpus, used only, in a metaphorical sense, at *Critias* 106ᵃ3)—refers here, it seems, to the safe conveyance of the soul, presumably to the heavenly regions, after death, whereas *diaporthmeuon* in the *Symposium* seems only to be amplifying *hermēneuon*, and to refer to the conveyance of petitions and responses between gods and men.   [42] Tarán (1975: 36–42).

[43] The dodecahedron is actually constructed from twelve pentagons, which are in turn constructed from 'an isosceles triangle in which each of its base angles is double of the vertical one, so that it cannot be constructed out of either of the two elementary triangles used for the construction of the other four regular polyhedra' (Tarán 1975: 38, quoting Sir Malcolm Heath). It would thus constitute a serious obstacle to Plato's scheme for the interchangeability of the elements other than earth.

[44] This, of course, is to disregard the possibility of a lengthy period of discussion of these questions within the Academy subsequent to the publication of the *Timaeus,* in which Aristotle himself would have participated, which is something we cannot reasonably do.

Xenocrates' innovation, however, has at least the advantage of utilizing the incompatibility of the dodecahedron with the other elements to set up a contrast between the celestial and the sublunar realms. Philippus, on the other hand, by situating it between fire (as tetrahedron) and air (as octahedron), leaves Plato's scheme of interchangeability of elements in total disarray. It is significant, therefore, that no mention is made in the *Epinomis* of the five regular solids, despite its author's strongly asserted devotion to mathematics as the supreme science (cf. 976D ff.).[45]

Finally, can we derive anything by way of an ethical theory from the pages of the *Epinomis*? It seems to me that we can, though it differs little enough in substance from that which can be derived from the *Laws*. It is plain, after all, that the overall thrust of the work is an ethical one. Right at the outset (973C), the Athenian Visitor makes clear that his enquiry into the nature of wisdom involves a search for goodness, which in turn will lead to happiness (*eudaimonia*), though that, in truth, is attainable by very few—in this life, at least. Then, towards the end of the work (989A ff.), having expounded his doctrine of the motions of the planets, the Visitor turns again to enquire into the true nature of wisdom (*sophia*). This, of course, he equates with virtue, and virtue in turn with piety (*eusebeia*);[46] and this, in its turn, will result from the proper study of astronomy (990A). In most of what he says, he hews fairly close to the *Laws*, but in his description of 'the best sort of natures', he also makes interesting use of a doctrine advanced by Plato in the *Statesman* (306F–309E), according to which these will result from a proper tempering or blending of the 'slow' or cautious, and the 'hasty' or

---

[45] On the same theme, it is peculiar that Philippus, in the course of his encomium of the gift of number as the condition of rationality, makes no reference to the problem of incommensurability, which is dwelt on by Plato in Book VII of the *Laws* (819E–820B). It almost looks as if this great devotee of the virtues of mathematics was not too comfortable himself with the finer points of the discipline.

[46] This, at least, as Tarán points out (1975: 33) is at variance with Plato, who never ranks *eusebeia* as the highest of the virtues, or identifies it with wisdom. Rather, piety for Plato is a part, or counterpart, of justice, e.g. *Euthy.* 5B ff., *Gorg.* 507B, *Prot.* 330B.

impetuous natures, such as it is the job of a good lawgiver to bring about:[47]

> For let no one ever persuade us that there is a greater part of virtue, for the race of mortals, than piety; and I must say it is owing to the greatest stupidity that this has not appeared in the best natures. And the best are they which can only become so with the greatest difficulty, but the benefit is greatest if they do become so: for a soul that admits of slowness and the opposite inclination moderately and gently will be good-tempered; and if it gives due respect to courage, and yet is easily persuaded to temperance, and, most important of all, has the strength to learn and a good memory,[48] it will be able to rejoice most fully in these very things, so as to be a lover of learning (*philomathēs*).   (989B–C, trans. Lamb, slightly emended)

This all leads up, after some further elaboration of the theme, to the revelation that the highest form of both wisdom and piety is *astronomia* (990A), under which are included the mathematical sciences of arithmetic, geometry, and stereometry. This course is for the few, but for Philippus it is the only road to virtue; the truly ethical course for the mass of mankind is to follow the guidance of the few enlightened astronomers.

That is more or less the sum of the doctrine to be derived from the *Epinomis*. As can be seen, it embodies various interesting developments on the thought of Plato. The only area, however, in which the doctrines of the *Epinomis* had much influence on later Platonism is in that of daemonology. Philippus' elevating of a rational World-Soul to the level of the supreme principle, and his lauding of astronomy as the true path to virtue and the knowledge of God, though having some influence, perhaps, within the Old Academy, on Polemo, and later, through him, on the Stoics, were substantially ignored by later generations of Platonists. Even his authorship of the *Epinomis* was only dimly remembered as a rumour, of which not much account was taken.

---

[47] Indeed, Philippus may be taking particular note of the 'divine bond' mentioned at 309C, which for him would be instruction in astronomy.

[48] For quickness to learn and good memory as advantages, cf. *Rep.* VI 487A.

Hermodorus of Syracuse

Hermodorus of Syracuse[49] has two claims to fame: one, that he composed a book about Plato, covering both his life and his doctrines; the second, more dubious, one is that he brought 'the books of Plato' (presumably a collection of the dialogues) to Sicily, and sold them.[50] This latter piece of information has a number of oddities attendant upon it, so let us start with that. First of all, we may note that this story would seem to indicate the existence of something like a collected edition of the dialogues, such as we presume to have been put together by the Old Academy after Plato's death, but of which we have really no other hard evidence. Secondly, what, one might ask, was so disgraceful about bringing a collection of Plato's works to Sicily, and marketing them? By Cicero's time, the story, which had become proverbial,[51] has taken on Pythagorean overtones, as if the sin was the publicizing of Plato's doctrines at all, instead of keeping them a secret within the school.[52] But originally Hermodorus' offence must have been just the unauthorized marketing of the texts, and the unphilosophical degree of venality associated with that.

As to who Hermodorus was, or how he came to be a student of Plato's, we have no information, but, since he was a Syracusan, it is a ready conjecture that he first met Plato on one of his ill-fated Sicilian expeditions, perhaps the last one, in 361, and followed him back to Athens. He would in that case have remained in association with the Academy for some fourteen years, up to Plato's death in 347, after which he will have written his book.

Of the contents we know only a little, but that little is quite signif-

---

[49] A useful collection of testimonia is published by Margherita Isnardi Parente as a sort of appendix to her edition of the fragments of Xenocrates (Isnardi Parente 1982).

[50] Philod. *Hist. Acad.* VI 6–10; Cicero, *Ad Att.* XIII 21, 4; *Suda*, s.v. *logoisin.*

[51] The proverb seems to have been *logoisin Hermodōros emporeuetai,* which may be rendered 'Hermodorus is travelling in *logoi*'—in the sense of being a commercial traveller, and thus reducing philosophy to a vulgar commodity.

[52] The reference to Hermodorus occurs in the context of Cicero's scolding Atticus, *semi*-humorously, for allowing L. Cornelius Balbus to make a copy of Book V of his *De Finibus,* before he (Cicero) has had a chance to give a copy to Brutus, to whom it is dedicated.

icant. The book seems to have contained an account of Plato's life as well as of his doctrines. Of the former section we have just one detail, given twice by Diogenes Laertius (II 106, III 6). Hermodorus told how, after the execution of Socrates, Plato and 'the other philosophers' (i.e. philosophical companions of Socrates) left town, 'fearing the savagery of the tyrants' (a rather tendentious way to describe the Athenian *dēmos*), and retired to Megara, to consort with the philosopher Eucleides.[53]

A second item, from Diogenes' Prologue (I 2), is somewhat odder. As Diogenes presents it, it does not even seem to come from Hermodorus' *Life of Plato,* but from something called *Peri Mathēmatōn*—perhaps 'On the (Mathematical) Sciences'—though this could, possibly, refer to a section of the doxographic portion of the *Life.* At any rate, what Hermodorus is reported as asserting is 'that from Zoroaster the Persian, the founder of the Magi, to the Fall of Troy, is five thousand years'.[54]

Now why, one might ask, would Hermodorus be concerned with the dating of Zoroaster? One possibility, though it is only a possibility, is that Zoroaster was already by Hermodorus' time beginning to be seen as a remote antecedent of Plato. This might, after all, be connected with a report of Eudoxus, relayed by Pliny in his *Natural History* (XXX 3), that he claimed that 'Zoroaster lived six thousand years before Plato's death'. This in turn has been connected by some—rather optimistically, I think—with the idea of the 'Great Year', if we could assume a tradition according to which this was 5,900 years long,[55] which would then allow for the possibility of Plato being a reincarnation of Zoroaster! All we can safely derive

[53] Eucleides (c. 450–380 BC) had himself been a follower of Socrates (though how far he had been able to consort with him, because of the Peloponnesian War, is a nice question), who founded a philosophical school of his own in Megara. Plato pays him the graceful compliment of working him into the prologue of the *Theaetetus.*

[54] Diogenes reports another snippet a little later (*Prol.* 8), not noted by Isnardi Parente, giving a (false) etymology of Zoroaster's name as signifying 'he who sacrifices to the stars.'

[55] That is to say, 100×59 (the length of so-called 'Saros' cycle); but in fact the length of the Great Year, as alluded to by Plato at *Rep.* VIII 546B and *Tim.* 39D, is quite uncertain (it may after all be 36,000 years).

from this reference, in my view, is that there was a certain degree of interest, among members the Old Academy, in Persian religion and 'philosophy'. With this may be connected the story, reported in Philodemus' *History of the Academy* (II 35–41), and referred by him back to Philippus of Opus, that 'in his old age Plato received a visitor from Chaldaea'. Plato himself, of course, makes respectful mention of Zoroaster, 'son of Oromazes', in the *First Alcibiades* (122A), but this indicates only a basic knowledge. Nevertheless, there is a persistent tradition in later strata of the Academy of a 'Persian connection',[56] and Hermodorus may have had something to do with propagating this.

However, of much greater importance is his evidence on Plato's doctrine of first principles. This comes down to us in a curious and troublesome form, but it should not be dismissed for all that. In his *Commentary on Aristotle's Physics*,[57] Simplicius, à propos Aristotle's report (at *Phys.* IV 209^{b}33 ff.) that Plato's term for what *he* called 'matter' was 'the great-and-small', relays the information that Porphyry said that (the early Middle Platonist) Dercyllides quoted Hermodorus, in his work on Plato, as specifying that Plato identified matter (*hylē*) with 'the unbounded and indefinite' (*to apeiron kai aoriston*), a characteristic of this being 'the more and less' (*to mallon kai to hētton*)—that is to say, an indefinite capacity for moreness and lessness—and that 'the great-and-small' is merely an aspect of this.

Dercyllides then goes on to quote Hermodorus verbatim, to very interesting effect. What Hermodorus sets out, in fact, is a division of reality similar to that which we have already seen expounded by Xenocrates,[58] but rather more elaborate, in the interests of placing his characterization of matter in a broader context.

---

[56] Favorinus of Arles, for example, in his *Apomnēmoneumata* (ap. DL III 25), reported that a certain Persian Mithridates, son of Orontobates, set up a statue of Plato in the Academy, commissioned by the sculptor Silanion, who flourished in the late fourth century, and would thus be contemporary with the first generation after Plato's death. Also, as we shall see below, Heraclides of Pontus composed a *Zoroastres* (probably a dialogue), but it did not necessarily have anything directly to do with Plato.

[57] p. 247, 30 ff. Diels = Hermodorus, Fr. 7 Isnardi Parente (quoted in part again a little further on, at 256, 31 ff. (Fr. 8 IP).

[58] Above, Ch. 3, p. 151 (also relayed to us by Simplicius).

Of the things that are (*ta onta*), some are said to be absolute (*kath' hauta*), such as 'man' or 'horse', others alio-relative (*kath' hetera*), and of these, some have relation to opposites (*enantia*), as for instance 'good' and 'bad', others to correlatives (*pros ti*); and of these, some to definite correlatives, others to indefinite ones.

—and a little further down he continues:[59]

and those things which are described as being 'great' as opposed to 'small' are all characterized by more and less; for it is possible to be greater and smaller to infinity; and in like manner what is broader and narrower, and heavier and lighter, and all that can be described in similar terms, will extend to infinity. Those things, on the other hand, which are described as 'equal' and 'stable' and 'harmonious' are not characterized by more and less, whereas the opposites to these have this character. For it is possible for something to be more unequal than something else unequal, and more mobile than something else mobile, and more unharmonious than something else unharmonious, so that, in the case of each of these pairs, all except the unitary element (in the middle)[60] possess moreness and lessness. So such an entity[61] may be described as unstable and shapeless and unbounded and non-existent, by virtue of negation of existence. Such a thing should not be credited with any originating principle (*arkhē*) or essence (*ousia*), but should be left suspended in a kind of indistinctness (*akrisia*);[62] for he shows[63] that even as the creative principle (*to poioun*) is the cause (*aition*) in the strict and distinctive sense, so it is also a first principle (*arkhē*). Matter (*hylē*), on the other hand, is not a principle. And this is why it is said by Plato and his followers (*hoi peri Platōna*) that there is only a single first principle.

If this remarkable passage is pressed, as it should be, quite a deal of significant material may be seen to emerge. First of all, we have the problem of the term 'matter'. Notoriously, this is not a technical

---

[59] This may represent editorializing by Dercyllides, or Porphyry, or Simplicius himself, but it matters little for our purpose.

[60] The phrase *panta plēn tou henos stoikheiou* is somewhat obscure, but I think that this must be what is meant. Hermodorus must be thinking of e.g. 'the equal' as *hen stoikheion* in the middle of an indefinite spectrum of inequality stretching away to either side of it.

[61] Sc. any given pair of such opposites.

[62] This last section of the quotation is given by Simplicius only on the second occasion on which he quotes it (p. 256, 31 ff.).

[63] Since this appears to be still a verbatim quotation of Hermodorus, the 'he' in question here will presumably be Plato.

term for Plato himself,[64] but, as I have argued in the case of Speusippus,[65] Aristotle did not have copyright on the term, and in any case, it would seem from the context here that Hermodorus is actually responding to Aristotle's identification of Plato's 'great-and-small' with his own concept of matter, so that there is no reason why he should not have used the term himself.

As we can see, Hermodorus is not here disputing Aristotle's identification; he is merely amplifying it by putting it properly in context. Plato may indeed have termed his material principle 'the great-and-small', but what he meant was something a good deal broader: the whole range of the unbounded and indefinite in the universe, however manifested. Thus expanded, the concept can be seen to relate closely to the metaphysical scheme outlined in the *Philebus* (esp. 16C–D and 26E–31B), where 'the Unlimited' represents all those aspects of the universe which admit of infinite variation in one or other direction or dimension, and which therefore require limiting by the active cause[66]—a process which produces the full range of definite entities in the universe.

We thus have here, attested by Hermodorus, independently of Aristotle, in the first generation after Plato's death, confirmation of the two supreme principles of Plato's so-called 'unwritten doctrines' (though indeed they are fairly plainly written about in the *Philebus*), and the unhesitating identification of the 'unlimited', passive principle as 'matter'.[67]

We may also note that Hermodorus declares matter *not* to be a principle, just because it is not itself active or creative, and thus asserts a certain degree of metaphysical monism for Plato. This is

[64] Though such interesting usages as *Tim.* 69A6 and *Phlb.* 54C1 should not be ignored; in neither case is the use of *hylē* fully 'technical', but it is not far off.

[65] Above, Ch. 2, p. 44.

[66] We may note, in this connection, Plato's association at 26E of the creative principle (*to poioun*) with the cause (*to aition*), which Hermodorus seems to be echoing in the last section of the passage quoted above. I would argue that, despite Plato's distinction in the *Philebus* between Limit itself and 'the cause of the mixture', that the creative principle may reasonably be held to do its own 'mixing'.

[67] Aristotle had of course already done this, both in the *Physics* passage mentioned above, and in *Met.* A 6, but he has always been thought, at least by Harold Cherniss and his followers, simply to be misunderstanding Plato.

interestingly at odds with what we have seen Speusippus asserting,[68] in the fragment preserved by Proclus in his *Parmenides Commentary,* to wit, that, without the accession of the Indefinite Dyad, the One would not even count as a principle, since it could not have created anything by itself. There may indeed be an element of intra-Academic polemic going on here, but the contradiction could be viewed rather as a difference of emphasis. After all, Speusippus would not really wish to deny the One the title of 'principle', *provided* one has assumed the existence of the Indefinite Dyad, or, in his own teminology, Multiplicity; nor in turn, I think, would Hermodorus wish to deny that matter has an essential role to play in the creation of the universe, even if, for technical reasons, he would deny it the title of *arkhē.*

On the level of logic there is much of interest in this passage as well. For one thing, it bears an intriguing resemblance to an account of 'Pythagorean' logic presented by Sextus Empiricus in *Adversus Mathematicos* X 262–84,[69] where we find a diaeretic division of things into 'absolutes' (*kata diaphoran* or *kath' heauta*), such as 'man', 'horse', and so on; 'opposites' (*kat' enantiōsin*), such as 'good' and 'evil', 'just' and 'unjust'; and 'relatives' (*pros ti*), such as 'right' and 'left', 'above' and 'below' (§§262–5). Opposites are said to differ from relatives in that, in the case of the former, the destruction of the one is the generation of the other (e.g. health and disease), and that there is no intermediate state (*meson*) between the two, whereas relatives have the property of co-existence and co-destruction one with the other (e.g. there can be no right without a left, nor greater without a smaller), and they admit of a middle state between them (e.g. the equal between the greater and the smaller) (§§266–9).

As can be seen, while there is a certain similarity between these two schemata, there are also differences. For one thing, Sextus presents a trichotomy, not a proper diaeresis; and for another,

---

[68] Above, Ch. 2, pp. 56–7.

[69] This passage, and its relation to Hermodorus and Academic doctrine in general, has been discussed illuminatingly, though from opposite points of view, by such authorities as Cherniss (1944: 286–7), and Hans-Joachim Krämer (1959: 284–7). See also Isnardi Parente's discussion of Frr. 7–8 (1982: 439–44).

Hermodorus, in the cause of defining matter, wishes to make a further distinction between definite and indefinite relatives. However, it may be that there is some confusion in Sextus' source,[70] which omitted the general class of 'alio-relative' (*kath' hetera*), because Sextus gets into some difficulty just below, when he seeks to relate back these three categories of thing to just two first principles, the One and the Indefinite Dyad. However this may be, the two schemes are sufficiently similar to provide evidence, especially when one also takes into account such Platonic passages as *Soph.* 255B, *Polit.* 283C–286C, or *Phlb.* 24A–C, of an Old Academic diaeretic division of reality which constituted a formalization of suggestions put out by Plato himself, and which may also, as I suggest in n. 70 above, have been projected back onto Pythagoras by one or other of the founders of Neopythagoreanism, Speusippus, or Xenocrates.

Heraclides of Pontus

Hermodorus, then, whatever offences against the Platonist fraternity he may have been accused of in later times, does contribute something to our knowledge of Academic logic and metaphysics, as well as some intimations of the growth of a biographical tradition relating to Plato himself. We turn next to a notorious maverick, a quondam member of the Academy who is said in some sources to have abandoned it for the Peripatos,[71] but who may nevertheless be considered to have contributed something to the development of the Platonist tradition, Heraclides of Pontus.[72]

---

[70] Which may be, immediately, some later Pythagorean, such as Nicomachus of Gerasa, Moderatus of Gades, or even Eudorus of Alexandria, but ultimately an Old Academic source, such as Xenocrates, who may have sought to father such a logical scheme on Pythagoras on the strength of a sympathetic interpretation of the Pythagorean table of Opposites.

[71] Diogenes Laertius, in his *Life* (V 86) makes the troublesome assertion that 'at Athens he first attached himself to Speusippus, . . . and later became a follower of (*ēkousen*) Aristotle', quoting the 2nd-cent. BC Peripatetic biographer Sotion, in his *Successions of Philosophers,* as his authority for this; but this evidence must be addressed with great caution, as we shall see.

[72] There is an excellent study of Heraclides and his philosophy by Gottschalk (1980), to which I am much indebted in what follows.

Heraclides was born in Heracleia Pontica, on the Black Sea coast of Asia Minor, son of one Euthyphro, and a member of one of the most distinguished families in the state, tracing his descent from one of the founders of the colony, Damis. Chronologically, all we know, or think we know, of him is that he came to study in the Academy early enough to be entrusted with the supervision of the school during an absence of Plato which is universally agreed to be his third visit to Sicily, in 361/0; and that having stayed on in the school during the scholarchate of Speusippus, he went back to Heracleia in 339 (perhaps in dudgeon), after having put himself forward as a candidate to succeed Speusippus, and having lost to Xenocrates in the election which followed.[73]

In order to attain this position of responsibility, it is pretty generally agreed that he must have arrived in the Academy, at the latest, at some time in the early 360s, and therefore was probably born no later than the mid-380s. Diogenes quotes Sotion (cf. n. 71 above) as declaring that, when Heraclides came to Athens, he attached himself first to Speusippus, and later became a pupil of Aristotle.'[74] This has misled some interpreters into assuming that Heraclides must have arrived in the Academy only in the scholarchate of Speusippus, and subsquently defected to the Peripatos; but this is quite at variance with our other information on him. It is more reasonable to suppose that Sotion is talking about factions within the Academy under Plato himself (such as we see some trace of in the anecdote told by Antigonus of Carystus about Aristotle),[75] and that what is being

---

[73] Various malicious stories are relayed by Diogenes (V 89–91), on the authority of such gossip-mongers as Demetrius of Magnesia, Hippobotus, and the Peripatetic Hermippus of Smyrna, about Heraclides' attempts to have himself divinized in later life. Such tales, while they should be taken with many grains of salt, may at least reflect a tendency by Heraclides to play the grand panjandrum at home in Heraclea. He is described as cutting an elegant, if portly, figure even in Athens (DL V 86), where the citizens nicknamed him *pompikos,* as a play upon *Pontikos.*

[74] A phrase in the middle of this sentence, 'he also attended the lectures of the Pythagoreans and admired the writings of Plato', comes in so ineptly as to lead Gottschalk (1980: 3) to conclude that it is an interpolation by Diogenes himself, a conclusion with which I concur. Diogenes himself will have been somewhat baffled as are many modern scholars, by Sotion's way of describing the situation.

[75] See above, Ch. 1, pp. 3–4.

described is rather a shift in Heraclides' interests from the more Pythagoreanizing, mathematicizing wing of the Academy, represented by Speusippus, to the more 'physicist' wing led by Aristotle[76]—though this plainly did not involve anything like an overt break with Speusippus, under whom Heraclides seems to have been happy enough to serve in the years after 347.

Certainly this combination of loyalties would seem to be reflected in the records that we have of his published works.[77] We find works in all three categories of logic, physics (including psychology), and ethics, as well as treatises on rhetorical, literary, and historical or antiquarian subjects, and a number of polemical or exegetical works. Some of his best-known works were dialogues, such as that *On the Woman Who Stopped Breathing (Peri tēs apnou)*,[78] *On the Things in Hades*, or the *Abaris*—but also a number of works which would have been assumed to be treatises, did we not know otherwise, such as *On Pleasure* and *On Moderation*,[79] which are characterized by Diogenes (V 88) as being composed 'in a comic mode', while certain others, such as *On Piety* and *On the Exercise of Authority (peri exousias)*[80]—as well as *On the Things in Hades* above-mentioned—are described as 'in a tragic mode', which implies that they too were dialogues. How many more titles may be in this category we do not know, but titles such as *Kleinias* (presumably featuring either the father or the brother of Alcibiades,[81] and possibly identical with another title, the *Erōtikos*), and *Protagoras, or On the Practice of*

---

[76] This would, of course, be the Aristotle of the dialogues and the *De Philosophia*, not the fully-fledged Aristotle of the bulk of the esoteric works. Heraclides' doctrine of the soul concords, as we shall see, with the author of such a work as the *Eudemus*, not with the author of the *De Anima*.

[77] A useful list of these, supplementing the copious, though chaotic and incomplete, list provided by Diogenes Laertius (V 86–8), is given in Schneider (2000).

[78] Well discussed by Gottschalk (1980: ch. 2).

[79] Topics, we may note, also dealt with by Speusippus and/or Xenocrates

[80] Probably 'authority' is the meaning of *exousia*; it would therefore be a political dialogue. The word can, however, mean simply 'abundance of means', or 'excessive wealth', in which case it would be an ethical dialogue.

[81] Or possibly even his cousin, son of his uncle Axiochus, who figures in the pseudo-Platonic *Axiochus*. One is even tempted to wonder whether there might be some connection between the surviving *Axiochus* and this work—though as it stands, the *Axiochus* must be a later work.

Rhetoric, are fairly obviously dialogues, as may also be the *Zoroastres* (this last being, perhaps, a further contribution to the topic of Plato's links to eastern wisdom).

Heraclides' contribution to the development of the philosophical dialogue was in fact of some importance. Cicero, when composing his own dialogues in the mid-first century BC, gives evidence in various passages[82] of making a distinction between the 'Heraclidean' and the 'Aristotelian' mode of composing dialogues (Plato himself being entirely left out of account!), depending on whether one made use of characters and a setting from a former age, or used contemporary ones, including oneself—Heraclides being noted for the former alternative, Aristotle for the latter.[83] The *Peri tēs apnou,* for example, featured a discourse by Empedocles on the last day of his life, and the *Abaris* presumably involved a dialogue between Abaris and Pythagoras. Various colourful stories about Pythagoras are suspected of having their origin in dialogues or other works of Heraclides, but the evidence is unfortunately less than compelling.

Other works of some importance will have been *On Intellect, On Forms (Peri eidōn),*[84] *On Nature, On the Soul, On Celestial Phenomena (peri tōn en ouranōi)* and essays (or dialogues?) in the ethical realm, *On Virtue* and *On Happiness,* as well as on the individual virtues of justice and courage (the dialogues on moderation and piety have been mentioned already). He also composed a work *On the Pythagoreans,* critiques of Zeno of Elea and of Democritus, and (intriguingly) *four* books of *Exegeses of Heraclitus.* His works of literary criticism and antiquarianism, in a distinctly Aristotelian mode, we may leave aside in the present context, but they testify to the wide range of his interests and his rather Herodotean liking for a good story.

---

[82] e.g. *Ep. Ad Att.* XV 27, 2; XVI 11, 3 (= Fr. 27 Wehrli).

[83] A Ciceronian example of the Heraclidean mode would be the *De Republica* or the *De Natura Deorum,* of the Aristotelian the *De Finibus* or the *Tusculan Disputations.* Plutarch too, indulged in both modes, though without acknowledging the distinction (e.g. the *De Genio Socratis,* as opposed to the *De E apud Delphos*).

[84] If this indeed concerns 'forms' in the Platonic sense; it could have concerned 'kinds' or 'species' of a purely logical sort. Theophrastus, after all, composed two books *Peri eidōn.*

From the philosophical perspective, there are four items of doctrine in particular which are distinctive to Heraclides, and which serve to remind us what a range of doctrines were acceptable in the school. They all concern the sphere of physics in the broader sense—including under this heading the question of the nature and destiny of the human soul. Of his views on matters of ethics or logic, though he undoubtedly had some (to judge from his list of titles), we unfortunately know nothing. One feature of Heraclides' thinking which we note at the outset is his degree of independence from any sort of Platonic orthodoxy—in so far as there was such a thing in the Old Academy. Plutarch, in an admittedly polemical context (attacking the Epicurean Colotes[85]), lists Heraclides, along with Aristotle, Theophrastus, and other Peripatetics (and also, admittedly, Xenocrates, though without mentioning specific works of his), as disagreeing on important questions with Plato:

> And first let us consider the diligence and learning of our philosopher [sc. Colotes], who says that these doctrines of Plato [sc. the theory of Forms] were followed by Aristotle, Xenocrates, Theophrastus, and all the Peripatetics. In what wilderness did you write your books, that when you framed these charges you failed to look at their writings, or take into your hands Aristotle's works *On the Heavens* and *On the Soul*, Theophrastus' *Reply to the Natural Philosophers*, Heraclides' *Zoroaster, On the Things in Hades*, and *Disputed Questions in Natural Philosophy*, and Dicaearchus' *On the Soul*, in which they constantly differ with Plato, contradicting him about the most fundamental and far-reaching questions of natural philosophy? (tran. Einarson/De Lacy)

This certainly puts Heraclides in interesting company, and indicates at least that he had important modifications or objections to the theory of Forms, but also to other cornerstones of Platonic doctrine. As we shall see, these include at least the immateriality of the soul, and the movement of the earth. On the other hand, though, none of Heraclides' innovations are entirely out of line with what we have seen already emanating from other figures within the Academy.

---

[85] *Adv. Col.* 1114F–1115A. Colotes, it would seem, had lumped Academics and Peripatetics together for the purposes of his polemic.

We may begin with his remarkable version of atomism, which may not in fact be as much of a deviation from Plato's doctrine as it appears.[86] There is a well-founded report in the doxographic tradition, deriving, in its present form at least, probably from Aetius,[87] but possibly going back originally to Theophrastus, that Heraclides (perhaps in his work *On Nature,* but no doubt also in his polemical treatise *Against Democritus*) propounded a theory of 'unarticulated particles' (*anarmoi ongkoi*), as the basis on which all sense-perceptible entities were compounded. The most circumstantial of our reports, that from Bishop Dionysius of Alexandria (as relayed by Eusebius) is worth quoting, as it serves to put Heraclides in context (Fr. 118 Wehrli):

But others changed the name of the [sc. Democritean] atoms and said that the basic constituents (*merē*) of all things are partless bodies (*amerē sōmata*), which are indivisible, of which all other things are composed and into which they are dissolved. And, they say, it was Diodorus [sc. Cronus] who gave the indivisible bodies this name. But Heraclides, they say, gave them a different name, and called them 'particles' (*ongkoi*), and Asclepiades the physician inherited this name from him.

Dionysius does not give us the characterizing epithet *anarmoi* (this is supplied by Galen and Sextus), but he seems to set out a plausible context for the exposition of Heraclides' theory. As we have seen in connection with Xenocrates (cf. above, p. 111), there is nothing intrinsically un-Platonic about postulating indivisible *minima* as basic building blocks of the universe: that, after all, is the role performed by the molecular bodies and the basic triangles of the *Timaeus*. Indeed, both Xenocrates and Heraclides can be seen as carrying on the

---

[86] This is dealt with very fully, and soundly, by Gottschalk (1980: ch. 3, 'The Theory of *anarmoi ongkoi*').

[87] In its present form, Heraclides is linked with the 1st-cent. BC physician Asclepiades of Bithynia, who seems to have adopted his theory, though probably giving it a more materialist twist. Asclepiades was primarily concerned with explaining the origins of diseases, by relating the atomic particles to 'pores' in the body, which receive them (cf. e.g. Sextus Empiricus, *AM* III. 5; Caelius Aurelianus, *Morb. Acut.* I 14, 105–6). The Aetian report is represented by Galen, *Hist. Phil.* 18, two passages of Sextus Empiricus (*PH* III 32 and *AM* X 318), and Bishop Dionysius of Alexandria (ap. Eusebius, *PE* XIV 23).

implied polemic of Plato in the *Timaeus* against Democritus. What Plato objected to in Democritus, we must remember, was not his atomic theory as such, but the total lack of divine purposefulness in his construction of the universe. Nevertheless, he and his followers would not pass up the opportunity to attack the details of Democritus' atomic theory as well, and that is probably what Heraclides may be seen as doing here.

A peculiarity of Democritus' atoms, after all, was that, although theoretically 'unsplittable', as their name implies, they were of various shapes and sizes, and in some cases had protuberances and 'hooks', which made some atoms more prone to combine than others. Now Democritus may have had adequate theoretical justification for this rather curious doctrine, but it left him open to criticism, and it is in this connection that Heraclides' epithet *anarmos,* to characterize his basic entities, takes on significance.[88] *Anarmos* can, admittedly, have a variety of meanings,[89] but the only relevant one, really, is 'without joints, or external fastenings'. The point of this might then be that, unlike the atoms of Democritus, Heraclides' basic elements would be smooth and free from 'joints' on the outside.

On the other hand, that cannot be the whole story. Heraclides has still to explain how the variety of entities in the physical universe comes to be at all, which is what Democritus was trying to provide an adequate account of in the first place. To do that, he has to postulate something like the four (or five)[90] Platonic bodies, composed as they are of basic triangles, and capable of both constituting composite bodies, and changing into each other (save, of course, for the triangles that constitute earth-molecules). This capacity to change into one another may lie behind the curious specification given by Sextus in his reference to Heraclides' theory at *AM* X 318, where he describes the *anarmoi ongkoi* as 'unlike [sc. the things formed out of

---

[88] What line was taken by Diodorus Cronus on this is quite mysterious. He was primarily, after all, a dialectician. But he may in fact have made the same criticism of Democritus' theory which I am imputing to Heraclides.

[89] The matter is well discussed by Gottschalk (1980: 38–40).

[90] Heraclides does seem to have accepted the Aristotelian doctrine of aether as a fifth element, as we shall see in a moment, and would no doubt have identified this, as did Xenocrates (cf. above, p. 128, n. 112) with the dodecahedron.

them], but subject to being affected (*anomoioi, pathētoi de*)'—as opposed to the atoms of Democritus, which are *anomoioi te kai apatheis.* The point of this would presumably be that, unlike the Democritean atoms, which never change their configuration, Heraclides' *ongkoi* can change into one another. This brings them very close to the molecular bodies of the *Timaeus,* and that in turn may lend point to a somewhat troublesome alternative characterization of Heraclides' minimal bodies in another part of the doxographic tradition[91] as 'fragments' (*thrausmata*). Gottschalk (1980: 54) suggests that these 'fragments' may correspond to the basic triangles out of which the Platonic bodies are formed, and that thus Heraclides, like his master Plato, would be postulating two levels of basic entity.[92]

Heraclides' theory, then, if inserted into its historical context, can be seen as little more than a further development of the doctrine presented in the *Timaeus,* with the addition of a more explicit polemic against the atomism of Democritus. If we ask to what further use this doctrine of *anarmoi ongkoi* was put, the answer would seem to be, based on a further doxographic snippet from Stobaeus (= Fr. 122 Wehrli) and upon the evidence of the later theory of Asclepiades of Bithynia, that he wished to explain how the sense-organs receive impressions from outside: 'the perceptions of the particular senses are due to the symmetry of the pores, when the appropriate [emanation] from a given sensible object fits into [the pores of] each of the sense-organs.' This is confirmed by a testimony from Clement of Alexandria (*Protr.* V 66. 4 = Fr. 123 Wehrli), which suggests that Heraclides effectively adopted the atomist theory of a stream of 'images' (*eidōla*) emanating from objects and impressing themselves upon the sense-organs; and that is precisely the use to which Asclepiades put the doctrine later (though with a specifically medical slant).

---

[91] Stob. *Ecl.* I 14, 4 = Fr.121 Wehrli.

[92] As Gottschalk notes (1980: 54), Plato does use compounds of *thrauein* to denote the process by which particles of fire, and so on, are resolved into triangles (*Tim.* 56E4–5; 57B1), and this may have been a stimulus to Heraclides in coining this term, as he seems to have done.

It would seem, then, that Heraclides took considerable interest in the mechanics of sense-perception, though without necessarily deviating far from Platonic principles. Rather more deviant, however, is his view of the soul.

Heraclides, as a Platonist (and indeed to a large degree a Pythagoreanizing Platonist), accepted the doctrine of an immortal soul, and of reincarnation (Fr. 97 Wehrli), but he seems to have been distinctive in declaring the soul to be composed of at least a quasi-material substance, 'light' (Fr. 98), or 'aether' (Fr. 99),[93] and to have its home, when not enclosed in a body, in the Milky Way. One problem with interpreting testimonies about Heraclides, it must be said, is that, as suggested above, he composed works of varied levels of literary and imaginative elaboration. On the question of the soul, its nature and fate, we have evidence, on the one hand, of a presumably fairly sober-sided treatise *On the Soul*, but on the other, of a rather more imaginative production, *On the Things in Hades*, which seems to have featured, among other things, the report of a character called Empedotimus of Syracuse,[94] who had an out-of-body experience while resting in the noonday from a hunt, which involved an interview with Hades and Persephone themselves,[95] and, by their courtesy, a vision of 'the whole truth about the souls (in Hades) in a series of direct visions (*en autoptois theamasin*)'. These different sources need to be borne in mind when interpreting the data.

---

[93] This testimony, from the proem of John Philoponus' commentary on Aristotle's *De Anima* (p. 9 Hayduck), runs as follows: 'Of those who have declared the soul to be a simple body (*haploun sōma*), some have declared it to be an aetherial body, which is the same as to say 'heavenly' (*ouranion*), as for instance Heraclides of Pontus.' This leaves it a little vague as to whether Heraclides himself used the term *aitherios* or *ouranios*, but for Philoponus it plainly means the same thing.

It is an attractive suggestion of Pierre Boyancé's (*per litteris* to Fritz Wehrli, 1969: 93) that the anonymous philosopher at Plutarch, *De E* 390A, who terms the substance of the heavens 'light' (*phōs*) rather than aether is none other than Heraclides. This would certainly accord best with the evidence that we have, making the substance of the soul the same as that of the heavens.

[94] As suggested by Wehrli (1969: 91), this name may be an evocative conflation of those of Empedocles and of Hermotimus of Clazomenae, both notable shamanistic figures.

[95] This we learn from Proclus, *In Remp.* II 119, 18 ff. Kroll = Fr. 93 Wehrli.

That said, then, what we have evidence of, for Heraclides, is a tri-partite division of the cosmos (Fr. 95 Wehrli), not dissimilar to that attested for Xenocrates, into a highest realm, that of the fixed stars, ruled over by Zeus, an intermediate realm, that of the heavens,[96] ruled over by Poseidon, and a lower realm, ruled over by Pluto/Hades. We also hear, from the testimony of Varro (Fr. 94 Wehrli), that Empedotimus saw three roads, starting from three gates corresponding to points on the circle of the Zodiac, the first, adjacent to the sign of Scorpio, being 'the road by which Heracles ascended to the gods', while about the roles of the other two (between Leo and Cancer, and between Aquarius and Pisces) noth-ing is specified. If we make the supposition, however, as does Gottschalk (1980: 99), that Heraclides is playing variations on the Myth of Er in the *Republic* (X 614C), we might conclude that the other two gates lead, respectively, sinners to the realm of Hades, and those deserving neither of punishment nor of deification to the inter-mediate realm of Poseidon.[97]

All this is most intriguing, and testifies to the literary and myth-making talents of Heraclides. His most philosophically significant contribution, however, is the doctrine that the substance of the soul is light (which he would seem to have equated with the Aristotelian aether). This may well seem far from Platonic, but against the back-ground of at least one strand of Old Academic interpretation of

[96] In fact, Damascius (who is the source of Fr. 95), in his *Commentary on the Phaedo*, §131, describes the realm of Poseidon as extending to 'the spheres as far as the Sun', and Pluto (Hades) 'the remaining (spheres)', but this seems an odd place to make the cut, and leaves the sublunary realm unaccounted for. Normally, in philosophical circles (for Xenocrates, cf. p. 132 above), the realm of Hades was the air between Moon and Earth, and it seems probable that it is such here too, whatever Damascius' transcribing student (for that is who we are dealing with) has to say. We do have, however, it must be said, a report from Proclus (*In Tim.* II 15 ff.) that 'the Pythagoreans' made a distinction between the heavenly realms above and below the sun, denominating the former *ouran-ios*, and the latter *aitherios*—so there is a possibility that after all there is some such dis-tinction being made here by Heraclides. It does not, however, seem to me to fit the context in Damascius, where divisions of the *world as the whole* are being discussed.

[97] As Gottschalk also points out (1980: 99), we find a distinction in the *Phaedrus* (249A–B) between those who have lived a truly philosophic life and return to the suprace-lestial realm, and those who have lived merely righteously, who are in consequence 'raised by their justice to some place in heaven.'

Plato's doctrine, I think that it can be seen as fitting not too badly. After all, as we have seen in the case both of Philippus of Opus and of Polemo (if the Ciceronian account of Academic doctrine can be attributed to him, as I believe it can), the notion of a first principle which is soul, or mind, and yet composed of 'pure fire'—on the understanding that that is a very different sort of substance, and indeed in important ways an antithetical sort of substance, from any of the four sublunary elements—is an acceptable option within the spectrum of Academic thinking. Once Aristotle had propounded the idea of a special sort of substance which was proper to the heavenly realm, he removed one of the chief objections to the idea that the soul might be composed of some *material*, since this new material was not subject to the strictures of alterability, and perishability, that were characteristic of sublunary substances. Against such a background, Heraclides' identification of the substance of the soul becomes, I think, much less revolutionary, and more reasonable. The gain, after all, is that the problem that Plato never really addresses, to wit, what interaction there can be between the material and the totally immaterial, becomes distinctly less troublesome: pure fire, or aether, can be regarded as a very special sort of *active* and intelligent substance, but still a substance.[98] Indeed, the Stoics are largely anticipated—but that, after all, is the impression that is being borne in upon us from other angles as well.

However that may be, the last aspect of Heraclides' thought that merits discussion can also be seen to arise from a problem left unsolved, or at least obscure, by Plato in the *Timaeus*: that is the question of the rotation of the earth on its axis. The problem centres on what Plato really meant, at *Tim.* 40^{b}8–^{c}1, by the term *illomenēn/eillomenēn* (the reading is disputed) in relation to the phrase 'about the axis stretching throughout all'. Either he is declaring that the earth is

---

[98] In this connection, we may note a remarkable passage of *Laws* X, 898E–899A, where the Athenian Stranger actually addresses—for the only time in the Platonic corpus—the problem of how the soul might be supposed to interact with the body (in this case, that of the sun), and comes up with three possibilities, of which the middle one is that it might take to itself a body 'of fire, or air of some sort'. It sounds here as if Plato is (rather grumpily) taking account of problems about soul–body interaction being raised by such troublesome younger colleagues as Aristotle and Heraclides.

revolving on its axis, or that is *compressed about* its axis—the verb *illō/eillō/eileō* can mean either 'press' (as of olives or grapes) or 'wind, turn around.' The former alternative has been thought to involve Plato in incoherence, since he has already stated, in 39c, that the universe as a whole revolves in a day and a night, and if the earth had a revolution of its own, this would seem to cancel out the cosmic circuit.[99] Loyal Platonists, therefore, such as Plutarch (*Quaest. Plat.* 8, 1006c), Alcinous (*Didasc.* ch. 15), and, most copiously, Proclus (*In Tim.* III 136, 29–138, 11), maintained that Plato can only have meant that the earth is 'compressed about' its axis. However, we have the awkward fact that Aristotle (who should have known), in the *De Caelo,* 2. 13 and 14 (293^{b}30–2 and 296^{a}26–7), presents Plato as postulating the *rotation* of the earth on its axis in the *Timaeus,* glossing *illesthai* by *kineisthai.* It is probably in the context of this controversy that Heraclides' solution is to be viewed. A series of authorities (Frr. 104–110 Wehrli) testify that he declared that the earth revolved about its axis, while the heavens remained fixed. The doxographic report of Aetius (preserved by Pseudo-Plutarch and Eusebius) is the clearest: 'Heraclides of Pontus and Ecphantus the Pythagorean postulate that the earth moves, not from place to place (*metabatikōs*), but turning on the spot (*treptikōs*), spinning like a wheel on its axis, from west to east about its own centre.' The introduction of the Pythagorean figure of Ecphantus has been thought by some authorities to imply that Heraclides subscribed to the Pythagorean doctrine, advanced in particular by Philolaus, that the earth, like the other planets, revolves round a central fire, but there is really no call for this presumption; nor yet is it prudent to assume that Heraclides had anticipated the full sophistication of the later astronomical theories of Aristarchus. The evidence points simply to the conclusion that Heraclides proposed the rotation of the earth and the fixity of the sphere of the 'fixed' stars as an elucidation, or possibly a tactful correction, of Plato's position in the *Timaeus.*

---

[99] Actually, as is pointed out by Cornford (1937: 120–34), Plato could have taken the earth's rotation into account in calculating the movement of the whole universe, so that it is precisely if the earth did *not* rotate on its axis that there would be no day and night. But no one seems to have thought of that.

We see, then, in Heraclides an example of the sort of original mind produced by the milieu of Plato's Academy. Something of a maverick he may be, but there is no need to regard him as turning his back on the overall doctrinal position of the Academy, or being untrue to the spirit of speculation which prevailed there.[100] That he should have been entrusted by Plato with the management of the school (whatever that really involved) during his last visit to Sicily is a notable accolade, and there is no reason to suppose that Plato's confidence was misplaced.

Crantor of Soli

We turn next to a figure of the next generation, Crantor of Soli. Crantor,[101] we are told by Diogenes Laertius (IV 24),[102] had gained the admiration of his fellow-citizens in his home town of Soli[103] in Cilicia before he came to Athens to join the Academy under Xenocrates. We are not told why he gained this admiration, though some have suggested that he had already acquired distinction as a poet. He may simply have been of prominent family.[104] We have no exact dates for either his birth or his death, but he is generally granted a lifespan of approximately 345 to 290 BC, assuming his arrival in Athens around 320.[105] He is generally agreed to have been somewhat junior to Polemo, though he predeceased him, since he is

---

[100] We do not, after all, as we must recognize, know anything about his views on most central issues of physics or ethics—what, for instance, his stance was on first principles, or on the status and nature of Forms.

[101] There is a collection of his fragments by Mette (1984: 7–94), and a much older one by Kayser (1841).

[102] Dependent here, as so often, on Antigonus of Carystus, as becomes plain from the parallel passage in Philodemus, *Acad. Hist.* XVI 1 ff.

[103] This town, an old (8th-cent.) Rhodian foundation, superseding a previous Phoenician settlement, gave to the world the term 'solecism', by reason of the bizarre nature of the Greek dialect that arose there; no such irregularities, however, are imputed to Crantor.

[104] He was able, at any rate, on his death to leave his favourite pupil Arcesilaus property to the value of twelve talents—a very considerable sum, which he hardly accumulated through philosophizing at the Academy (DL IV 25).

[105] That he did not survive to what generally passed for old age is attested by a

described (by Philodemus, in his *History of the Academy,* XVI 6–8) as being a pupil of Polemo's as well. Diogenes (no doubt still following Antigonus) relays an odd story of his falling ill and retiring for a while to the temple of Asclepius, where he 'walked about' (*periepatei*), leading some people (including Arcesilaus, the future founder of the 'New' Academy) to assume that he was proposing to found a new school, so that they went to join him. However, when he recovered, he returned to Polemo and the Academy—for which action, Diogenes tells us, he was much admired! There may be somewhat more to this story than meets the eye—*peripatein* certainly can be taken to betoken some form of philosophical activity. The 'illness' may therefore have been of the diplomatic variety; but if there was an intra-Academic row at the back of this, it was plainly patched up, or patched over.

However, in later times there does seem to have been something of a pairing off within the Academy, as between Polemo and Crates, and Crantor and Arcesilaus, though there is no suggestion of any serious tensions, or of disagreement on philosophical issues. Crantor, indeed (like Heraclides before him), seems to have been as concerned with literature as with philosophy. He is reported by Diogenes (IV 26) to have been a great lover of poetry, favouring in particular Homer and Euripides (hardly revolutionary tastes!), and was even reputed to have composed poetry himself. He left a considerable œuvre, it would seem, amounting to 30,000 lines—though some critics, it seems, attributed some of his works to Arcesilaus.[106] Whatever the truth of that, it serves to underline the perceived connection between them. To some degree, Crantor may be seen as constituting a bridge to the scepticism of the New Academy (even as Polemo forms a bridge to Stoicism), though there is nothing in the

---

funerary epigram on him by the poet Theaetetus (DL IV 25), which also praises him as 'pleasing to the Muses'.

[106] The reason for this may lie in the fact that Arcesilaus is said to have edited his works after his death (DL IV 32). As for his poems, Crantor is said to have deposited them under seal in the temple of Athena in his home town of Soli—a curious move, perhaps, but by no means an unexampled one (cf. Heraclitus' depositing of his book in the temple of Artemis at Ephesus).

exiguous remains of his thought to lend credence to that possibility. Of all these works, the only one of which we know the name is a short protreptic discourse in epistolary form *On Grief,* which enjoyed considerable popularity in later times (serving Cicero, for example, as a model for his *consolatio* for his daughter Tullia). As we shall see, he is credited with comments on various aspects of Plato's *Timaeus,* and is described by Proclus (*In Tim.* I 76, 1–2 Diehl), remarkably, as 'the first commentator' (*ho prōtos exegētēs*) on that work; but Diogenes provides no list of works, other than mentioning the *On Grief,* nor does he convey, in his admittedly feeble notice of him, that he made any contributions to philosophy whatever.

Nevertheless, it is to these contributions that we may now turn. They mainly concern the interpretation of the *Timaeus,* and it is here that Crantor perhaps makes his most distinctive contribution to the development of Platonism, *the idea of a commentary.* We have very little idea of the nature or degree of detail of this commentary, but Proclus is quite definite that Crantor was 'the first exegete of Plato' (loc. cit.), and he must mean something by that— even if his information is second-hand. Certainly by this time people had developed the tradition of writing *exegēseis* of earlier poets and philosophers, from Homer and Hesiod on down. Xenocrates, for instance, had composed a treatise *On the Writings of Parmenides,* and something on the Pythagoreans (*Pythagoreia*), while Heraclides had composed *Exegeses of Heraclitus,* and a presumably polemical work on Democritus (*Pros ton Dēmokriton Exegēseis*), as well another work *On the Pythagoreans*—and the exegetical work of Aristotle and Theophrastus is too well known to need dwelling on.[107] But the idea of taking a particular dialogue of Plato and expounding the philosophical positions set out—or latent—there seems a new development, not picked up on again before the first century BC.

At any rate, we find comments by Crantor on a number of key

[107] There is also the remarkable phenomenon of the Derveni papyrus—an exegetical commentary, by a philosophically sophisticated partisan, on a body of Orphic poetry. It is not clear how generally available such a document was, but the main thing is that it existed.

issues, or passages, in the dialogue. First of all, he gives an intriguing account, relayed by Proclus in his *Timaeus Commentary* (I 75. 30 ff.), of the reason why Plato attributed to the Egyptians the story of the War with Atlantis:

(Crantor) says that Plato found himself mocked (*skōptesthai*) by contemporary critics, with the allegation that he was not the inventor of his constitution (*politeia*),[108] but had based it on that of the Egyptians. He was so stung by this mockery that [in the *Timaeus*] he attributed to the Egyptians this story about the Athenians and the Atlantians, which indicated that the Athenians once lived under such a constitution: the prophets of the Egyptians, after all, he declares, say that these events are inscribed on stelae that are still preserved.

There is much that is peculiar about this anecdote, interesting as it is. First of all, who were the mockers, and why should Plato be stung by their mockery? As to the first question, one would think most naturally of contemporary sophists, such as Isocrates, but we have no evidence to go on. As to the second question, it is surely odd that Plato should be offended by the suggestion that he had borrowed an idea from the Egyptians, in view of his well-attested admiration of all things Egyptian; but an allegation of plagiarism is always annoying, no doubt, and it is conceivable that Plato should have been concerned in the *Timaeus* to deliver a literary counterblow.

There are broader implications, however, in this story, if we were to accept it. What we have here is a piece of intra-Academic gossip, passed down to a second generation of Platonists. Can it reflect any modicum of truth? As regards the possible origins of Plato's ideal state in the *Republic,* many critics have thought, plausibly enough, of the Pythagorean regimes of South Italy, which seem to have involved a ruling council of Pythagorean sages, and inevitably also a corps of armed auxiliaries, with which to control the possibly ungrateful or unappreciative masses—and in particular the regime which Archytas may have run in Tarentum in Plato's own day; but no one, to my knowledge, in modern times, has proposed the view that Egypt, with its priestly elite and strict hierarchies of class and occupation, might

---

[108] i.e. the ideal state of the *Republic.*

have been Plato's main inspiration. And yet this does not seem by any means improbable. Nor does it seem beyond the realm of plausibility that Plato, admirer though he was of many aspects of Egyptian culture, should nevertheless be provoked into this ingenious piece of Hellenic oneupmanship, which involves an Egyptian priest, while chiding the Athenian Solon (*Tim.* 22B) for the 'childishness' of his countrymen (including, no doubt, Plato's own critics!), acknowledging that it was actually the constitution of antediluvian Athens that was the archetype for that of Egypt.

This, then, is one contribution of Crantor to the exegesis of the *Timaeus.* It is slightly disturbing that Proclus, in introducing his view, ranks him as among those who take the Atlantid War to be 'history plain and simple' (*historia psilē,* 76, 1), since that would not at first sight seem to have been Crantor's point. But in fact, since Crantor seems to maintain that the stelae on which the tale was told were still in existence, it may well be that he accepted the historicity of the tale himself. This, however, would seem to involve accepting the historicity of Plato's story about Solon's visit to the priests of Naucratis, and of the epic poem which he began on the subject of the Atlantid War, but never published, which seems quite a lot to swallow. Proclus may actually be imputing too much credulity to Crantor here, and missing the point of his tale.

At any rate, on the general question of whether the account of the generation of the world in the dialogue is to be taken literally, Crantor is firmly of the view of Speusippus and Xenocrates that it is not. His particular contribution, it would seem, is to begin the long scholastic discussion (brought to a kind of culmination many centuries later, in the mid-second century AD, by Calvenus Taurus in his *Timaeus Commentary*),[109] as to what precise sense can be accorded to the apparently unequivocal statement of Timaeus himself at 28B about the physical cosmos: 'it came into being (*gegonen*)'—that is, if one does not wish to take it in its literal sense. Crantor's contribution to the debate, begun by Aristotle in *De Caelo* I 11, is relayed to us,

---

[109] See on this my discussion in Dillon (1977: 242–4). I should have specified there, however, that Aristotle already, in *De Caelo* I 11, 280ᵇ15 ff., in the context of a critique of Plato's doctrine in the *Timaeus,* makes a distinction between various possible meanings of *genētos.*

once again, by Proclus (*In Tim.* I 277, 8–10 Diehl): 'The commentators on Plato of the school of Crantor[110] declare that the cosmos is "generated" in the sense of being produced by a cause other than itself (*hōs ap' aitias allēs paragomenon*), and not self-generating nor self-substantiating.' This implies already a notable degree of sophistication in the interpretation of Plato's text. It is interesting that neither Speusippus nor Xenocrates is credited in the later tradition with attempting to put an exegetical gloss on particular words of Plato's text, and it may be that Crantor is responding specifically to Aristotle's distinction of three meanings of *genētos* in *De Caelo* 280[b]15 ff., by supplying a fourth one more in accord with what he saw as the overall thrust of the work; what is important, after all, is to emphasize the cosmos' permanent dependence on an external and superior creative cause.

It is Plutarch who gives us our only further evidence on Crantor's exegetical position, in his treatise *On the Generation of Soul in the Timaeus* (1012D–1013B), in conjunction with his critique of the position of Xenocrates (which we have examined above, pp. 121–3). Plutarch, as we have seen, is opposed to what he presents as the established Academic interpretation of the *Timaeus,* which denies that the description of the generation of the cosmos is to be taken literally (*Proc. An.* 1013B). Here, however, at 1012D–1013A, he is merely giving a non-polemical account of Crantor's analysis of the meaning of blending of the soul out of various elements in *Tim.* 35A–B, as he has done for Xenocrates just above. Plutarch begins his critique as follows (1012D):

Since, however, of those most highly esteemed [sc. within the Platonist tradition] some were won over by Xenocrates, who declared the soul's essence to be number being moved by itself, while others adhered to Crantor of Soli, who makes the soul a mixture of the intelligible nature (*noētē physis*) and of the opinable nature of perceptible things (*hē peri ta aisthēta doxastē*), I think that the clarification of these two when exposed will afford us something like a keynote (*endosimon*).[111]

[110] Proclus uses here the *hoi peri X* formulation, which may or may not signify any more than X himself.

[111] That is, a basis for discussion. Plutarch employs a musical metaphor.

He then sets out Xenocrates' doctrine (quoted above, p. 121), deriving the soul from the mixture of the Monad and the Dyad, which produces primarily Number, to which is then added Sameness and Otherness, to generate the mobility and motivity which is the proper characteristic of Soul, and continues (1012F):

> Crantor and his followers,[112] on the other hand, supposing that the soul's peculiar function is above all to form judgements of intelligible and perceptible objects and the differences and similarities occurring among these objects both within their own kind and in relation of either kind to the other, say that the soul, in order that it may know all [sc. classes of thing], has been blended together out of all; and that these are four: the intelligible nature, which is ever invariable and identical, the passible and mutable nature present in bodies, and furthermore the natures of Sameness and Otherness, because each of the former two also partakes of diversity and identity.

Crantor, we may note, is here presented by Plutarch as giving an alternative explanation to that of Xenocrates, emphasizing the epistemological function of the soul rather than its ontological status [sc. as a self-moving numerical entity], but it is not necessary, I think, that he in fact differed radically from him in his metaphysics. Crantor may well have accepted the Monad and Dyad as the two ultimate creative principles in the universe, but, taking account also of Plato's description of the soul's modes of cognition in 37A–B, he is more concerned with how the soul comes to know the various levels of entity in the universe, and to make proper distinctions between them. This leads him to postulate, on lines rather closer to the text of the *Timaeus* than Xenocrates, what he calls the intelligible and sense-perceptible natures as the primary ingredients of the soul—to which are added Sameness and Otherness, though for reasons somewhat different from those given by Xenocrates, that is, the discernment of identity and difference at and between all levels of reality, rather than as a principles of motion and rest.

However, if one asks oneself what exactly Crantor might have

---

[112] The *hoi peri X* formula again, though who may have composed Crantor's 'school' is quite obscure to us—unless Arcesilaus interested himself in the exegesis of the *Timaeus!*

had in mind by the *noētē physis* and the *pathētikē kai metablētē physis*, one is, I think, driven back to something very like the Xenocratean Monad and Dyad; a deconstructed Demiurge inevitably becomes nothing other than a cosmic Intellect (such as was Xenocrates' Monad, as we have seen), while the passive and changeable element which is 'about bodies' (*peri ta sōmata*) can hardly be anything else than the Unlimited Dyad, or, in Aristotelian terms (accepted by now freely in the Academy), Matter. Crantor may well have expressed himself differently, but it is hard to see that he is at serious odds with Xenocrates, despite the antithesis that Plutarch wishes to set up.

In any case, as regards the main issue, both are in the same boat as far as Plutarch is concerned. He concludes:

All these interpreters are alike in their opinion that the soul did not come to be in time and is not subject to generation, but that it has a multiplicity of faculties (*dynameis*), and that Plato, in analysing its essence into these for theoretical reasons (*theōrias heneka*), represents it verbally as coming to be and being blended together. And it is their view that he had the same thing in mind concerning the cosmos as well: he knew that it was eternal and ungenerated, but, seeing that the manner of its management and organization would not be easy to discern unless one presupposed its generation and a conjunction of generative factors at its beginning, he had recourse to this procedure.[113]

Crantor was, then, plainly at one with his immediate predecessors on the broad question of how the *Timaeus* was to be understood, whatever minor differences of emphasis he might exhibit on the particular problem of the composition of the soul. For one more detail of Crantor's exegesis we are also indebted to Plutarch (*Proc. An.* 1027D, 1022C–E), and that is the information that Crantor chose to arrange the numbers, or rather numerical ratios, out of which the soul is described at *Tim.* 36A–B as being composed, that is to say, 1, 2, 3, 4, 8, 9, 27, and the double and triple intervals between them, in the form of a lambda-shaped figure (with 1 at the top, and the double and triple ratios, 2–4–8 and 3–9–27, arranged down either of the legs). In this, says Plutarch, he was followed by his compatriot

---

[113] That is, a narrative involving creation in time by a demiurgic divinity.

Clearchus of Soli, but opposed by another compatriot, Theodorus, who preferred to arrange the numbers in a straight line. It was this latter arrangement, we may add, which found favour in later times, with the Middle Platonist Severus, and Neoplatonists from Porphyry on; but Crantor's lambda-shaped figure is still to be found in Calcidius, who seems to be following here the second century AD Peripatetic Adrastus; so Crantor's scheme was not entirely forgotten.

We further learn from Plutarch (ibid. 1020c) that, in order to avoid the introduction of awkward fractions arising from the filling in of the intervals between the basic numbers, Crantor picked as his first number, not 1, but 384, this being $64 \times 6 - 64$ itself being the cube of the first square (4^3) and the square of the first cube (8^2). This may seem enormously cumbersome, but in fact it is based on good mathematical calculations, if one wants to avoid fractions.[114]

What all this evidence reveals is an impressive degree of detail in the exegesis of, in particular, *Tim.* 35A–37B, but of the proem and of 28B as well. Whether or not Crantor's 'commentary' covered anything like the whole work we have no means of knowing, but the argument from silence would indicate that it did not. One would expect, however, some comment on all major issues in the first part of the work, at least, for Crantor to qualify as the *prōtos exēgētēs* of Plato.

At any rate, we may now turn to the work for which Crantor was best known in later antiquity, his essay *On Grief.* For this, our two main sources are Cicero, in *Tusculan Disputations* I and III,[115] and Plutarch (or, more probably, Pseudo-Plutarch), in the *Consolation to Apollonius.*[116] Both Cicero and the author of the *Consolation* are

---

[114] Plutarch himself plumps for half of this number, 192, but, as he should have observed, this does not in fact avoid all fractions.

[115] *Tusc.* I has as its topic 'contempt for death', and III 'the alleviation of grief, or distress', both topics addressed by Crantor. Cicero also refers, most warmly, to the *On Grief* at *Acad.* II 135 (quoted below).

[116] I am inclined to regard the *Consolatio ad Apollonium* as not worthy of Plutarch, by reason of the clumsiness of its structure—unless we can suppose that we have it in an unfinished state (i.e. still needing pruning). However, for the present purpose, it matters very little whether it is genuine or not.

plainly making extensive use of Crantor (as they do not mind letting us know), but just how extensive the use is we cannot be sure. If one screens out patently later material, however, from either work, a coherent outline does seem to emerge, which is certainly in line with what we know of Old Academic ethics. Cicero's reference to the work at *Academica Priora* II 135 gives a good impression of both its influence and its general tone:

That school [sc. the Old Academy] were upholders of the mean in things, and held that in all emotion there was a certain measure that was natural. We have all read the Old Academician Crantor's *On Grief,* for it is not a large, but a golden little volume (*non magnus verum aureolus libellus*), and one to be thoroughly studied word by word, as Panaetius recommends to Tubero. And the Old Academy indeed used to maintain that the emotions in question were bestowed by nature upon our minds for actually useful purposes— fear for the sake of exercising caution, pity and sorrow for the sake of mercy; anger itself they used to say was a sort of whetstone of courage—whether this was right or not let us consider on another occasion.'[117]

We seem to have here a digest of Polemonian doctrine on the emotions, which will have formed the underpinning for Crantor's work. The emotions (*pathē*) are in accordance with nature (*kata physin*); they are inherent in us for good reason, and do not require extirpation, but merely control. In the context of the grieving associated with bereavement, Crantor seems to have maintained that grief as such was perfectly proper, but enough was enough. As means of helping the reader to control excessive grief, he seems to have mixed exhortation with the adducing of *exempla* from Greek history, both ancient and recent, and relevant quotations from the poets. In the *Consolatio,* by far the most popular poetic sources are Homer and Euripides, and we may recall that these are attested to have been Crantor's two favourite poets. On the other hand, such a preference can hardly be accounted exotic, so that we cannot confidently assume that all of Pseudo-Plutarch's quotations go back to Crantor.

Attempts have been made to reconstruct in some detail the contents

---

[117] This appears actually to be a reference to the *Tusculan Disputations.*

of the treatise,[118] but, tempting though this is, it seems safer to stick to attested references. At Ps.-Plut. *Consol.* 104B–C, we learn that the work was composed to comfort a certain Hippocles on the death of his children. There Crantor is quoted as follows (Fr. 4 Mette):

All our ancient philosophy states this and urges it upon us;[119] and though there may be in it other things which we do not accept, yet the statement that life is often toilsome and hard is only too true. For even if it is not so by nature, yet through our own selves it has reached this state of corruption. From way back, and indeed from the beginning, this uncertain fortune has attended us and to no good end, and even at our birth there is conjoined with us a portion of evil in everything. For the very seeds of our life, since they are mortal, participate in this causation, and from this there steals upon us barrenness of soul (*aphyia psykhēs*),[120] bodily diseases, bereavements, and the common portion of mortals.

None of this is very deep philosophy, but it is of interest as one of the few verbatim quotations surviving from any of the members of the Old Academy. Another passage, somewhat earlier in the work (102C–D), contains a briefer quotation, embedded in a context which, though explicitly anti-Stoic (and which thus might seem hardly attributable to Crantor on chronological grounds),[121] seems to reflect the essence of his position:

The pain and pang felt at the death of a son has in itself good cause to awaken grief, which is only natural, and which is not in our power to control. For

---

[118] As by Pohlenz (1909: Appendix, pp. 15–19), and, more recently, Johann (1968: 28–35 and 127–64).

[119] The immediately previous context (which must therefore reflect Crantor's own text) indicates that the reference is to the transitoriness and mutability of human life. We may note that Homer, Pindar, and Euripides have just been quoted in support of this point. By *arkhaia philosophia,* Crantor may in fact mean the philosophical lessons to be extracted from the early poets, but we cannot be sure.

[120] This does indeed seem to be a reference back to a passage of Euripides' *Ino* (Fr. 419 N²), which has just been quoted.

[121] On the other hand, we must reflect that, since Zeno is stated to have studied with Polemo for ten years (DL VII 2), there would be ample opportunity for an exchange of views with Crantor, if we may assume Zeno to have hammered out the main lines of his own philosophy before the turn of the century. In any case, a parallel passage from Cicero, *Tusc.*, III 12, shows this sentiment to have part of Crantor's own text.

I,[122] for my part, cannot concur with those who extol that harsh and callous impassiveness (*apatheia*), which is both impossible and unprofitable. For this will rob us of the kindly feeling which comes from mutual affection and which above all else we must preserve. But to be carried beyond all bounds and to help in exaggerating our griefs I say is contrary to nature, and results from our depraved ideas. Therefore this also must be dismissed as injurious and depraved and most unbecoming to right-minded men, but a moderate indulgence (*metriopatheia*)[123] [in grief] is not to be disapproved. 'Pray that we not become ill,' says the Academic Crantor, 'but if we be ill, pray that sensation may be left us, whether one of our members be cut off or torn out. For this insensibility to pain is attained by man only at a great price; for in that case, we may suppose, it is the body which has been brutalized into such insensibility, but in this present case the soul.'

It is plain, then, that Crantor comes out strongly on the side of what was at least later termed *metriopatheia,* moderation rather than extirpation of the passions. This as I have suggested, could be seen as a direct counterblast to an early version of Zenonian ethics, but it could also be a reflection of a difference in emphasis within the Academy itself, as between Polemo and Crantor. It is worth noting that, in his *History of Philosophy* (XVI), Philodemus records that, although a student of Polemo, Crantor differed significantly from him in his views,[124] and this could be one area in which they differed.

Another detail preserved by both Cicero (*Tusc.* I 115) and Ps.-Plutarch (*Cons.* 109B–C) is an *exemplum* of Crantor's concerning the Italian Euthynous, son of Elysius, of Terina,[125] who died suddenly

---

[122] This overtly refers to pseudo-Plutarch himself, but it can be seen from the parallel text in Cicero (see previous note) that he is borrowing even the first person singular from Crantor.

[123] The actual term *metriopatheia,* as opposed to *apatheia,* is not attested before Philo of Alexandria (whose reflections on Abraham's moderated grief at the loss of Sarah at *Abr.* 255–7 may well owe something to Crantor's work), but we cannot be sure that it does not go back to the earliest phase of Academic opposition to Stoic *apatheia.*

[124] The verb here is lost in the papyrus. Bücheler and Mekler proposed *egrapsen,* which makes good sense; Gaiser and Dorandi prefer *epaizen,* 'played', which makes little sense, though the traces on the papyrus seem to suggest *epa . . . n,* rather than *egra..n.* But the general sense should not be in doubt.

[125] A small town in Bruttium, in the toe of Italy. The story is told more circumstantially by Ps.-Plutarch, though without acknowledgement. Cicero, however, though briefer, identifies it as Crantor's.

227

when quite young. His father visited an oracle of the dead (*psykhoman-teion*), and during an incubation at the shrine received a vision of his own father, who introduced him to the shade of Euthynous, who hand-ed him a paper with three lines of elegiac verse on it, to the effect that Euthynous had died because it was better for him to be dead.

This is a fairly exotic tale, but Crantor also seems to have made use of the more famous story of Midas and Silenus, which he bor-rowed from Aristotle's *Eudemus* (Fr. 44 Rose), the punch-line of which is 'best for man never to be born at all, but second best, after being born, is to die as quickly as possible'.[126] This may lead us to the conclusion[127] that Crantor borrowed extensively, for his subject matter, not only from Plato's *Phaedo,* but also from the youthful Aristotle's essay in consolation, composed probably in the late 350s. The amount of originality, then, in Crantor's essay may not be high, but the evidence is that he presented his material succinctly and attractively, and that was the main reason for its high valuation in later times.

One thing we may conclude with probability, and that is that Crantor propounded the doctrine of the immortality of the soul. We find, in fact, in *Tusc.* I 26–81, an extended exposition of this doctrine which may well owe much to Crantor (it does not sound quite Stoic enough for Antiochus). Belief in the soul's immortality is accredited, first (27–8), to 'the ancients', by which is meant the beliefs presup-posed by the Greek myths,[128] and then to a sequence of inspired philosophers passing from Pherecydes, through Pythagoras, to Plato (38–41). Here, however, we find the interesting suggestion that the soul may be composed of air, or *pneuma,* or fire, or even of Aristotelian aether—the Xenocratean notion of it being a self-moving number

---

[126] Ps.-Plutarch presents this somewhat later than the previous anecdote (115B–E), but Cicero (*TD* I 114–15) mentions it briefly (though without acknowledgement) *just prior* to the tale of Elysius (for which he does acknowledge Crantor as his authority), so it seems that the two *exempla* were closely connected in the original. Cicero also includes a quotation from Euripides' *Cresphontes* (Fr. 452 N²), which he probably owes to Crantor.

[127] Advanced, very plausibly, by Gigon (1960: 31).

[128] This accords to some extent with Crantor's reference to 'ancient philosophy' at *Cons.* 104c, if I am right about the reference of that.

being dismissed with some irony (40–1). As we have seen, such a doctrine, far from being un-Academic, was championed by Heraclides and the youthful Aristotle, and possibly Polemo (above, p. 173), so that it would not be impossible for Crantor to have adopted it. It would be rash, however, to rank this as any more than a possibility.[129] All this, however, does not interfere with the author's assertion of the immortality of the soul, producing the argument from self-motion of *Phaedrus* 245C–E (53–4), and arguments from the *Meno* and *Phaedo* about recollection and memory (57–8). Certainly, Cicero is making use of a source which sounds more purely Old Academic on the subject of the soul's immortality and distinctness from the body than would seem likely for the rather Stoicized Antiochus.

Even more thoroughly Old Academic is an extract from Cicero's (self)-*Consolatio* for his daughter Tullia (a work deeply indebted to Crantor) which he produces in the midst of his exposition in *Tusc.* I (66):

No beginning of souls can be discovered on earth; for there is no trace of blending or combination in souls or any particle that could seem born or fashioned from earth, nothing even that partakes of either moisture or air or fire. For in these elements there is nothing to possess the power of memory, thought, reflection, nothing capable of retaining the past, or foreseeing the future and grasping the present, and these capacities are nothing but divine; and never will there be found any source from which they can come to men except from God. There is, then, a peculiar nature and power (*singularis natura atque vis*) of the soul, distinct from these common and well-known elements. Accordingly, whatever it is that is conscious, that is wise, that lives, that is active, must be heavenly and divine and for that reason eternal. And indeed, God himself, who is comprehended by us, can be comprehended in no other way but as a mind unfettered and free, severed from all perishable matter, conscious of all and moving all (*omnia sentiens et movens*), and self-endowed with perpetual motion. Of such sort and of the same nature is the human mind.

---

[129] An alternative is that Crantor supports a further possibility put forward by Cicero, or his source, that the soul has a substance all its own (*propria et sua*), though similar to aether or pure fire, and that this would be the same substance as that of the gods (Tusc. I 70).

If only one could claim the substance of this passage for Crantor (and I must say I am at a loss to see where else Cicero could have got it from), then one could, I think, lay to rest at a stroke the problem of the origin of the doctrine of the Forms as thoughts of God, since here we have a divinity which is a mind, but a mind not totally at rest and self-absorbed, like Aristotle's God, but 'conscious of all and moving all', and moreover itself engaged in eternal motion. This is precisely the sort of divinity that I have postulated for Xenocrates (cf. above, p. 107). It borrows something, certainly, from Aristotle's Unmoved Mover, but reconciles it with the providential aspect of the (demythologized) demiurgic figure of the *Timaeus*, of whose intellect the 'paradigm' becomes the contents. This would give Crantor a theology very much in line with at least the majority view of the Old Academy.

Speculation about the contents of the *On Grief* may be allowed to rest there. It was fairly plainly a document in the popular-philosophical mode, not penetrating very deeply into the mysteries of Platonist doctrine. The same may be said of the last nugget of Crantor that has been preserved for us, this time by Sextus Empiricus in his treatise *Against the Ethicists* (= *Adversus Mathematicos* XI), ss. 51–8. What we have here is an essay in the diatribe style,[130] owing something, no doubt, to such works as Prodicus' *Choice of Heracles*, dramatizing the Platonist scale of values, according to which such a 'good' as wealth is at the bottom of the scale, above that being pleasure, then health, and finally courage. Crantor imagines each of these entities coming forward, as it were, onto the stage in a theatre at a Panhellenic festival, and making their case, each of the later candidates dismissing its predecessor as inadequate, and winning the audience over to its side. That courage, rather than virtue in general, or wisdom, should appear as the culmination of this process, may seem very strange, but we may reflect that, not only in the *Laches*, but more significantly in *Laws* I (cf. esp. 630B–D), a 'higher' sort of courage, defined as 'stead-

---

[130] It is possible, but unlikely, that this somehow formed part of the essay *On Grief.* It is not easy to see how it would have fitted in. In any case, we know that Crantor composed many works, even if we do not have their titles.

fastness in face of what is truly to be feared', is presented as the highest virtue, at the fostering of which legislators should be aiming. Crantor might, therefore, be taking account of this in his presentation. The only problem with this suggestion, though, is that the courage which Crantor is commending is, on the face of it, very much of the conventional type (the argument goes (58) that, if you lack courage, your enemies will rejoice, and proceed to divest you of all your other goods), so that one would need to assume a hidden dimension here: Crantor would be overtly advocating 'vulgar' courage, while really commending a 'higher' courage. The alternative, however, is that this is just a work of popular philosophy, and it says no more than it means.[131]

Conclusion

This brings to an end our survey of those members of the Old Academy after Plato about whom we know anything of much significance. Of the last head of the Old Academy proper (apart from the very shadowy Socratides, who may not even have taken up office), Crates, we have some biographical details (from DL IV 21–3), but really no doctrinal information at all. He was an Athenian, son of Antigenes, of the deme of Thria, and so perhaps naturally gravitated to Polemo, whose intimate he is said to have been, since Polemo was an Athenian as well. Diogenes states that he left behind him works of philosophy, but also works on comedy, and a number of speeches delivered both to the assembly and when a delegate on embassies,[132] implying some degree of political activity, as well as an interest in literature. We may assume him to have hewed pretty closely to the doctrinal positions of Polemo, whom he succeeded for a few years as scholarch before dying himself.

---

[131] We may note, by the way, that, in this fairly short passage, Homer is quoted once, and Euripides twice, this being thoroughly in accord with Crantor's preferences.

[132] We know from Plutarch, *Vita Demetr.* 46, 30–4, that he went on an embassy to Demetrius Poliorcetes in 287.

Another very shadowy figure, probably from the first generation after Plato, is Hestiaeus of Perinthus. He is early enough, at any rate, to be mentioned in the same breath as Xenocrates by Theophrastus in his *Metaphysics* (6^{b}9–10), as having, like Xenocrates, and unlike most other Platonists, paid some attention to the whole range of reality. Apart from this mention of him, we have a number of scattered notices. We learn from Porphyry (Fr. 174 Smith) that he was one of those who produced an account of Plato's notorious lecture on the Good, and from the doxographer Aetius that he had views on the nature of time ('the motion of the stars—or planets—in relation to each other', *DG* 318, 15–16), and on the mechanism of vision (he is credited with coining a term for the mingled result of the visual ray and the sensible image: *aktineidōlon, DG* 403, 19–21).

Even these scraps, however, give some inkling of the range of interests being pursued in the generations after Plato's death. And there are others which we have hardly touched upon. To a certain degree the activities of mathematicians like Eudoxus' pupil Menaechmus, his brother Dinostratus, and Theudius of Magnesia will have continued into this period, in conjunction with those of Philippus of Opus, whose interests have already been noted. Proclus, in the brief history of mathematics incorporated into his *Commentary on the First Book of Euclid* (pp. 67–8 Friedlein),[133] gives honourable mention to all of these, and a few more of whom we know nothing else. Menaechmus seems to have discovered the conic sections; Dinostratus applied Hippias' quadratrix to the squaring of the circle; and Theudius, says Proclus, 'produced an admirable arrangement of the elements, and made many partial theorems more general'.

Lastly, we should not neglect to note how large a contribution seems to have been made by various of Plato's successors to the field of literary criticism—not hostile criticism, but literary *appreciation*. This is all the more remarkable in view of the Master's well-known views on the social role of poets and poetry. Neither Speusippus nor Xenocrates seem to have written on specifically literary subjects, but

---

[133] Drawing, in fact, on the history of mathematics by Aristotle's pupil, Eudemus.

Heraclides of Pontus certainly did—he was even alleged to have composed tragedies, which he fathered on Thespis! (DL V 92)[134]— and Polemo, Crantor, and Crates plainly continued these interests, Crantor, as we have seen, being himself a respected poet. The reconciliation with Greek literature was certainly firmly established in the Polemonian Academy—if there had ever really been a serious rift.

In both these areas, then, the interests of the Academy developed very much in parallel with those of the Lyceum, with, no doubt, some cross-over of pupils between the two institutions—Arcesilaus being a case in point (DL IV 29). It rather appears as if, in the second generation after Plato, the Academy had become a centre for the pursuit of practical ethics and general culture, rather than a powerhouse of metaphysical speculation. Indeed, it may well be that by the mid-270s there may have been a widespread perception that it was running out of steam, especially by comparison with the energy of the new dogmatic schools of Stoicism and Epicureanism, imbued as they were with evangelical zeal. It was time, many members must have thought, for a change of direction, a rediscovery of Socratic roots.

[134] We have evidence of works *On Poets and Poetry, On Homer, Solutions to Problems in Homer* (in two books), *On the Respective Ages of Homer and Hesiod* (two books), *On Archilochus and Homer* (two books), *On the Three Tragic Poets, On Questions in Euripides and Sophocles* (three books), and *On Music* (in two books, which probably concerned lyricists and dithyrambists, as well as pure musicians).

Epilogue: Arcesilaus and the Turn to Scepticism   6

It is no part of the concern of the present study to embark on a full-dress study of the 'sceptical' Academy.[1] However, some attention should be paid, at the conclusion of this work, to the remarkable change of direction initiated by Crates' successor as head of the school, Arcesilaus of Pitane, and the possible reasons behind this. As can be seen from the relatively copious biography in Diogenes Laertius (IV 28–45), Arcesilaus was no interloper on the Academic scene. He had joined the Academy back in the days of Crantor (probably in the mid-290s), after a short period with Theophrastus in the Lyceum,[2] and had pursued almost twenty years of study and discussion within the institution before taking over from Polemo's short-lived successor Crates in the mid-270s. And, of course, he was elected by his peers to the headship—the dim figure of Socratides, we are told (DL IV 32), standing down in his favour. So there is really no cause to regard Arcesilaus as having 'hijacked' the Academy, or having perverted the Platonic tradition against the will of its followers. Rather, if anything, he represents an attempt to reinvigorate a tradition that was running out of steam by turning it back to a recon-

---

[1] This has been well done in a series of works in recent years, of which we may mention Stough (1969: 35–66); Long (1974: 88–106); Schofield et al. (1980); Long and Sedley (1987); and now Algra et al. (1999), with full bibliography.

[2] DL IV 29–30. Theophrastus, it seems, ever afterwards lamented his loss.

sideration of its roots; and these lay, for Arcesilaus, in the methods and concerns of Plato's chief inspiration, Socrates.[3]

Before turning to consider what Arcesilaus did, however, we should briefly consider the philosophical context in which he did it.[4] When Arcesilaus took over the Academy, Zeno of Citium had been promulgating his distinctive philosophical doctrines for over twenty years, since about the turn of the century. He is said to have arrived in Athens in around 311 BC, at the age of twenty-two, and to have both attached himself to the Cynic Crates and studied with Polemo in the Academy, before setting up on his own. There is no reason for disbelieving either report, though whether he studied with Crates and Polemo simultaneously or consecutively, and if so, in what order, is not clarified. At any rate, he learned a good deal from both sources.

Both Zeno's physics and his ethics can be seen as developments and formalizations of contemporary Platonism, a reflection that cannot have been comfortable for a later head of the Academy. Stoic cosmology can, after all, be seen as little more than the pursuit of a non-literal interpretation of the *Timaeus* to its logical conclusions. We have seen, from our study of Xenocrates, Polemo, and Philippus of Opus, that, when the system of the *Timaeus* is demythologized, one is essentially left with an active principle, which may be regarded either as a cosmic intellect, or even as a rational World-Soul, imposing order upon a passive, material substratum, such an active principle not being regarded as transcendent, but rather as immanent in the cosmos, with its proper seat in the outer rim of the heavens. Whether or not this principle was ultimately viewed as immaterial is

---

[3] Significantly, Diogenes, later in his biography (IV 32), reports that 'he would seem to have held Plato in admiration, and he acquired copies of his works (*kai ta biblia ekektēto autou*)'—a rather curious thing to report about a head of the Platonic Academy, one would have thought. Such a report, though, may actually attest to a renewed interest in the dialogues, particularly the early ones, and such apparently aporetic works as the *Theaetetus*.

[4] I regard this context as comprising chiefly the Stoics and the Peripatetics, in that order. The Epicureans were, of course, a powerful force at this time also, but they were rather the Marxists of the Hellenistic era. One had to be absolutely with them or against them; they did not interact comfortably.

not quite clear, but it was not really a large step (especially in view of the speculations of such a figure as Heraclides of Pontus) to viewing it as composed of a special kind of pure fire.

In the sphere of ethics, in turn, while Zeno was plainly much influenced by the austerity, and even the antinomianism, of the Cynic Crates, he also seems to have adopted and developed the theories of Xenocrates and Polemo about 'the primary things of nature', and living in accordance with nature, though pressing such a doctrine to extreme and even paradoxical conclusions, by denying any role in human happiness for anything but the practice of virtue. Only in logic do the Stoics come across as substantially original, and their logical system does not seem to have been fully developed until the time of Chrysippus.

This development, then, can be seen as constituting a serious challenge for contemporary Platonism. Everything Polemonian Platonism could do, it would seem, Zeno could do better. For a Platonist, it was a case of either throwing in the towel, and admitting that Stoicism was the logical development and true intellectual heir of Platonism (a conclusion that commended itself to Antiochus of Ascalon two centuries later), or of going back to the drawing board, returning to the roots of one's tradition, and launching a radical attack on the whole concept of dogmatic certainty.

It was this course that Arcesilaus decided to take. As Diogenes Laertius says of him, disapprovingly (IV 28): 'He was the first to suspend judgement owing to the contradictions of opposing arguments. He was also the first to argue on both sides of a question, and the first to meddle with (*prōtos ekinēse*) the system handed down by Plato and, by means of question and answer, to make it more closely resemble eristic.' This evaluation, though it touches on the chief features of Arcesilaus' 'new departure', is tendentiously negative. What Arcesilaus would have seen himself as doing, on the contrary, was returning to the spirit of the early, 'Socratic' dialogues, and reviving the true spirit of dialectic, as practised in the Academy under Plato. He should not be taken as advocating scepticism in the modern sense. What he denied was that certainty in the Stoic sense (*katalēpsis*) was derivable from any sort of sense-perception, how-

236

ever persuasive; there may well be true states of affairs out there, but we can never be certain of having attained cognition of them, though it is legitimate to keep trying. That is the original sense of *skepsis*— 'enquiry'.

What Arcesilaus did about the considerable body of speculation which had grown up in the previous seventy years about the first principles and structure of reality we do not know. It would seem that he simply set it aside. The pious belief that grew up in the later period (possibly already promulgated by Philo of Larisa, but securely attested by Numenius, Fr. 25, ll. 75–83, and Sextus Empiricus, *PH* I 234), that Arcesilaus had only practised scepticism as a polemical tool against the Stoics, and to test the acumen of his students, but had dogmatized in private, is probably without foundation, a product of the desire to reassert the essential unity of the Academic tradition. Works like the *Timaeus,* in all probability, gathered dust on Arcesilaus' shelves, while such a work as the *Theaetetus* was well-thumbed.

In the establishment of a new philosophical position for the Academy not much help was to be derived from the other side of town, in the Lyceum. Under Theophrastus' successor, Strato of Lampsacus, who had succeeded to the headship in 286, the school of Aristotle seems to have taken a firmly 'scientific' turn. Although Strato is attested to have written a considerable number of works on a wide variety of topics, what he is particularly known for are his views on a number of purely physical questions. Strato in any case died in around 270–268, and for most of Arcesilaus' reign the Peripatos was presided over by the benign but undistinguished figure of Lyco. In the field of serious philosophy it was simply no longer in contention.

Arcesilaus thus may be seen as taking up the only philosophical position left open to him, consistent with the Socratic–Platonic heritage as he interpreted it, unless one is to follow lamely after Zeno. In reasserting the sceptical strand in Plato's thought, he is simply bearing witness to the impressive flexibility and openness of the Academic tradition, as I have tried to portray it. We must bear in mind that, although Xenocrates in fact succeeded to the headship in 339, Aristotle perfectly well could have, as could Heraclides of Pontus; it was not doctrinal unorthodoxy that excluded either of them. The accession of a figure like Arcesilaus two generations later becomes in this way a fitting conclusion to our story.

References

Note: This list of references does not aspire to completeness. It merely lists the works that I have found useful. For a more comprehensive list of all relevant works, see e.g. the bibliographies contained in Überweg–Praechter–Flashar, *Grundriss der Geschichte der Philosophie. Die Philosophie der Antike,* iii: *Ältere Akademie—Aristoteles—Peripatos* (Basle and Stuttgart ,1983).

ALGRA, K. et al. (1999), *The Cambridge History of Hellenistic Philosophy* (Cambridge).

ALLINE, H. (1915), *Histoire du texte de Platon* (Paris).

ANNAS, J. (1976), *Aristotle's* Metaphysics, *Books M and N,* trans. and comm. (Oxford).

BALTES, M. (1988), 'Zur Theologie des Xenokrates,' in R. van den Broek et al. (eds.), *Knowledge of God in the Graeco-Roman World* (Leiden). (Repr. in *Dianoemata: Kleine Schriften zu Platon und zum Platonismus* (Stuttgart and Leipzig).)

—— (1993), 'Plato's School, the Academy', *Hermathena,* 155: 5–26.

BALTES, M. and DÖRRIE, H. (1990–), *Der Platonismus in der Antike,* ii–vi (Stuttgart-Bad Cannstatt; two further volumes expected).

BARNES, J. (1971), 'Homonymy in Aristotle and Speusippus', *CQ* NS 21: 65–80.

—— (1975), *Aristotle's Posterior Analytics,* trans. and comm. (Oxford).

BICKERMANN, E. and SYKUTRIS, J. (1928), *Speusipps Brief an Könige Philipp,* Berichte Sächs. Akad. d. Wiss., Leipzig, Phil.-Hist. Kl., 80(3).

BOLTON, R. (1991), 'Aristotle's Method in Natural Science: Physics I 1, ', in L. Judson (ed.), *Aristotle's Physics: A Collection of Essays* (Oxford).

BOYANCÉ, P. (1934), 'Sur l'Abaris d'Héraclide le Pontique', *Revue des études anciennes* 36: 321–52.

239

References

BOYANCÉ, P. (1937), *Le Culte des Muses chez les philosophes grecs* (Paris).

—— (1948), 'Xénocrate et les Orphiques', *Revue des études anciennes*, 50: 218–31.

BRINK, C. O. (1955), '*Oikeiôsis* and *oikeiotês*: Theophrastus and Zeno on Nature in Moral Theory', *Phronesis*, 1: 123–45.

CHERNISS, H. (1944), *Aristotle's Criticism of Plato and the Academy*, i (Baltimore; repr. New York, 1964).

—— (1945), *The Riddle of the Early Academy* (Berkeley and Los Angeles; repr. New York, 1962).

CORNFORD, F. M. (1935), *Plato's Theory of Knowledge* (London).

—— (1937), *Plato's Cosmology* (London).

DETIENNE, M. (1958), 'Xénocrate et la démonologie pythagoricienne', *Revue des études anciennes*, 60: 271–9.

DIÈS, A. (1941), *Platon. Œuvres complètes, Tome IX: 2. Philèbe* (Paris).

DILLON, J.M. (1977), *The Middle Platonists* (London and Cornell; 2nd edn. 1996).

—— (1983), 'What Happened to Plato's Garden?', *Hermathena*, 133: 51–9 (repr. in Dillon 1990).

—— (1984), 'Speusippus in Iamblichus', *Phronesis*, 29: 325–32 (repr. in Dillon 1990).

—— (1986), 'Xenocrates' Metaphysics: Fr. 15 (Heinze) Re-examined', *Ancient Philosophy*, 5: 47–52 (repr. in Dillon 1990).

—— (1990), *The Golden Chain. Studies in the Development of Platonism and Christianity* (Aldershot).

—— (1994), 'A Platonist *Ars Amatoria*', *Classical Quarterly*, 44; 387–92 (repr. in Dillon 1997).

—— (1996), 'Speusippus on Pleasure', in K. A. Algra, P. W. van der Horst, and D. T. Runia (eds.), *Polyhistor: Studies in the History and Historiography of Ancient Philosophy presented to Jaap Mansfeld* (Leiden), 99–114 (repr. in Dillon 1997).

—— (1997), *The Great Tradition. Further Studies in the Development of Platonism and Early Christianity* (Aldershot).

DODDS, E.R. (1928), 'The *Parmenides* of Plato and the Origin of the Neoplatonic 'One', *Classical Quarterly*, 22:129–42.

DORANDI, T. (1991), *Filodemo, Storia dei filosofi: Platone e l'Academia* (Naples).

DÖRRIE, H. (1967), 'Xenokrates, 4', in *RE* IX A 2, 1512–1528.

DÖRRIE, H. and BALTES, M. (1987), *Der Platonismus in der Antike*, i (Stuttgart-Bad Cannstatt).

DÜRING, I. (1966), *Aristoteles. Darstellung und Interpretation seines Denkens* (Heidelberg).

References

FALCON, A. (2000), 'Aristotle, Speusippus, and the Method of Division', *Classical Quarterly*, 50: 402–14.

FESTA, N. (ed.) (1891), *Iamblichus. De Communi Mathematica Scientia Liber* (Leipzig: Teubner; repr. 1975).

FOUCART, P. (1873), *Des associations religieuses chez les Grecs, thiases, eranes, orgeons* (Paris).

FOWLER, D. H. (1987), *The Mathematics of Plato's Academy: A New Reconstruction* (Oxford).

GAISER, K. (1963), *Platons ungeschriebene Lehre*, Anhang: Testimonia Platonica: Quellentexte zur Schule und mündlichen Lehre Platons (Stuttgart).

GIGANTE, M. (1977), *Polemonis Academici Fragmenta* (Naples).

GIGON, O. (1960), 'Prolegomena to an Edition of the *Eudemus*', in I. Düring and G. E. L. Owen (eds.), *Aristotle and Plato in the Mid-Fourth Century* (Göteborg), 19–33.

GLUCKER, J. (1978), *Antiochus and the Late Academy*, Hypomnemata 56 (Göttingen).

GOSLING, J. C. B. (1975), *Plato, Philebus* (Oxford).

GOTTSCHALK, H.B. (1980), *Heraclides of Pontus* (Oxford).

GUTHRIE, W. K. C. (1975), *A History of Greek Philosophy*, iv (Cambridge).

——— (1978), *A History of Greek Philosophy*, v: *The Later Plato and the Academy* (Cambridge).

DE HAAS, F. (1997), *John Philoponus's New Definition of Prime Matter* (Leiden).

HACKFORTH, R. (1945), *Plato's Examination of Pleasure* (Cambridge).

HALFWASSEN, J. (1993), 'Speusipp und die metaphysische Deutung von Platons *Parmenides*', in L. Hagemann and R. Glei (eds.), *Hen kai Plēthos: Festschrift für Karl Bormann* (Würzburg), 339–73.

HAPP, H. (1971), *Hyle: Studien zum aristotelischen Materie-Begriff* (Berlin).

HEINZE, R. (1892), *Xenokrates. Darstellung der Lehre und Sammlung der Fragmente* (Leipzig; repr. Hildesheim, 1965).

HERCHER, R. (1871), *Epistolographi Graeci* (Paris).

HICKS, R.D. (1925), *Diogenes Laertius, Lives of Eminent Philosophers*, Loeb Classical Library (Cambridge, Mass. and London).

ISNARDI (PARENTE), M. (1956), 'Teoria e prassi nel pensiero dell'Accademia antica', *La Parola del Passato*, 11: 401–33.

——— (1969), 'Speusippo in Sesto Empirico, *Adv. Math. VII* 45–146', *La Parola del Passato*, 24: 203–14.

——— (1977), 'Dottrina delle idee e dottrina dei principi nell' Accademia antica', *Annali della Scuola Normale Superiore di Pisa*, Classe di Lettere e Filosofia, Serie III, Vol. VII, 3, 1017–1128.

241

References

—— (1979), *Studi sull'Accademia Platonica antica* (Florence).

—— (1980), *Speusippo, Frammenti* (Naples).

—— (1981), 'Per la biografia di Senocrate', *Rivista di Filologia e di Instruzione classica*, 109: 129–62.

—— (1982), *Senocrate—Ermodoro: Frammenti* (Naples).

JOHANN, H.-Th. (1968), *Trauer und Trost* (Munich).

KAYSER, F. (1841), *De Crantore Academico* (Heidelberg).

KLIBANSKY, R. (1929), *Ein Proklos-Fund und seine Bedeutung* (Heidelberg).

KRÄMER, H.-J. (1959), *Arete bei Platon und Aristoteles. Zum Wesen und zur Geschichte der platonischen Ontologie* (Heidelberg).

—— (1964), *Der Ursprung der Geistmetaphysik. Untersuchungen zur Geschichte des Platonismus zwischen Platon und Plotin* (Amsterdam).

—— (1971), *Platonismus und hellenistische Philosophie* (Berlin).

LANG, P. (1911), *De Speusippi Academici Scriptis: accedunt fragmenta* (Bonn; repr. Hildesheim, 1965).

LEO, F. (1901), *Die griechisch-römische Biographie nach ihrer literarischen Form* (Leipzig).

LONG, A. A. (1974), *Hellenistic Philosophy* (London and New York).

LONG, A. A. and SEDLEY, D. (1987), *The Hellenistic Philosophers*, 2 vols. (Cambridge).

LONG, H. S. (1964), *Diogenis Laertii Vitae Philosophorum*, Oxford Classical Texts (Oxford).

LOVEJOY, A. (1936), *The Great Chain of Being* (Cambridge, Mass.).

LYNCH, J. P. (1972), *Aristotle's School: A Study of a Greek Educational Institution* (Berkeley and Los Angeles).

MADDOLI, G. (1967), 'Senocrate nel clima politico del suo tempore', *Dialoghi di Archeologia*, i: 304–27.

MERLAN, P. (1960), *From Platonism to Neoplatonism*, 2nd edn. (The Hague).

METTE, H. J. (1984), 'Zwei Akademiker heute: Krantor von Soloi und Arkesilaos von Pitane', *Lustrum*, 26: 7–94.

MORROW, G. (1970), *Proclus, A Commentary on the First Book of Euclid's Elements* (Princeton).

MUGLER, C. (1948), *Platon et la recherche mathématique de son époque* (Strasbourg and Zurich).

MÜLLER, F. (1927), *Stilistische Untersuchungen der* Epinomis *des Philippus von Opus* (Berlin).

MÜLLER, G. (1951), *Studien zu den Platonischen* Nomoi (Munich).

PHILLIPPSON, R. (1925), 'Akademische Verhandlungen über die Lustlehre', *Hermes*, 60: 444–81.

References

PINES, S. (1961), 'A New Fragment of Xenocrates and its Implications', *Transactions of the American Philosophical Society*, 51: 3–33.

POHLENZ, M. (1900), *De Ciceronis Tusculanis Disputationibus* (Göttingen).

—— (1948–9), *Die Stoa: Geschichte einer geistigen Bewegung* (Göttingen; 3rd edn. 1967).

VAN RAALTE, M. (1993), *Theophrastus*, Metaphysics (Leiden).

RICH, A. N. M. (1954), 'The Platonic Ideas as Thoughts of God', *Mnemosyne*, 4.7: 123–33.

RIGINOS, A. S. (1976), *Platonica: The Anecdotes concerning the Life and Writings of Plato* (Leiden).

RIST, J. M. (1969), *Stoic Philosophy* (Cambridge).

ROBIN, L. (1908), *La Théorie platonicienne des idées et des nombres d'après Aristote* (Paris).

SCHNEIDER, J.P. (2000), 'Heraclide le Pontique', in R. Goulet (ed.), *Dictionnaire des philosophes antiques* iii (Paris), 565–7.

SCHOFIELD, M. (1971), 'Who were *hoi dyskhereis* in Plato, *Philebus* 44A ff.?', *Museum Helveticum*, 28: 2–20.

SCHOFIELD, M., BURNYEAT, M., and BARNES, J. (eds.) (1980), *Doubt and Dogmatism: Studies in Hellenistic Epistemology* (Oxford).

SEDLEY, D. (2002), 'The Origins of Stoic God', in M. Frede and A. Laks (eds.), *Traditions of Theology: Studies in Hellenistic Theology, its Background and Aftermath* (Leiden), 41–83.

STENZEL, J. (1929), 'Speusippos', in *RE* 6/III 2, 1636–69.

STOUGH, C. (1969), *Greek Scepticism* (Berkeley and Los Angeles).

TARÁN, L. (1975), *Academica: Plato, Philip of Opus and the Pseudo-Platonic Epinomis* (Philadelphia).

—— (1978), 'Speusippus and Aristotle on Homonymy and Synonymy', *Hermes*, 106: 73–99.

—— (1981), *Speusippus of Athens. A Critical Study with a Collection of the Related Texts and Commentary* (Leiden).

TARRANT, H. A. S. (1974), 'Speusippus' Ontological Classification', *Phronesis*, 19: 130–45.

TAYLOR, A. E. (1928), *A Commentary on Plato's Timaeus* (Oxford).

—— (1929), 'Plato and the Origins of the *Epinomis*', *Proceedings of the British Academy*, 15: 235–317.

—— (1937), *Plato, the Man and his Work*, 4th edn. (London).

THEILER. W. (1964), 'Einheit und unbegrenzte Zweiheit von Plato bis Plotin', in J. Mau and E. G. Schmidt (eds.), *Isonomia: Studien zur Gleichheitsvorstellung im griechischen Denken* (Berlin), 89–109.

243

References

TURNBULL, R. (1998), *The* Parmenides *and Plato's Late Philosophy* (Toronto).

WATERFIELD, R. (1988), *The Theology of Arithemetic* (Grand Rapids).

WEHRLI, F. (1953), *Herakleides Pontikos*, Die Schule des Aristoteles, Heft 7 (Basel: 2nd edn. 1969).

WILAMOWITZ-MÖLLENDORF, U. VON (1881), *Antigonos von Karystos* (Berlin).

—— (1919), *Platon*, 2 vols. (Berlin).

ZELLER, E. (1921–2), *Die Philosophie der Griechen in ihrer geschichtlichen Entwicklung*, II. i–ii (Leipzig).

General Index

This index is necessarily selective. I have tried to include all significant allusions to all important figures or concepts, though normally without duplicating information derivable from the Contents. In some cases, I give Greek versions of philosophical terms, but with cross-references to the English equivalents. In the case of Aristotle and Plato, I specify references to particular works (for actual quotations of passages, see Index of Passages Quoted).

General Index

Index of Modern Authorities Quoted

Index of Passages Quoted

I have included here all passages quoted verbatim or virtually verbatim in the text; mere references are excluded.

Index of Passages Quoted